French Colonial Archaeology in the Southeast and Caribbean

Florida Museum of Natural History: Ripley P. Bullen Series

UNIVERSITY PRESS OF FLORIDA

Florida A&M University, Tallahassee
Florida Atlantic University, Boca Raton
Florida Gulf Coast University, Ft. Myers
Florida International University, Miami
Florida State University, Tallahassee
New College of Florida, Sarasota
University of Central Florida, Orlando
University of Florida, Gainesville
University of North Florida, Jacksonville
University of South Florida, Tampa
University of West Florida, Pensacola

French Colonial Archaeology in the Southeast and Caribbean

———◆———

EDITED BY KENNETH G. KELLY
AND MEREDITH D. HARDY

University Press of Florida
Gainesville · Tallahassee · Tampa · Boca Raton
Pensacola · Orlando · Miami · Jacksonville · Ft. Myers · Sarasota

Copyright 2011 by Kenneth G. Kelly and Meredith D. Hardy
Printed in the United States of America on acid-free paper
All rights reserved

First cloth printing, 2011
First paperback printing, 2015

Library of Congress Cataloging-in-Publication Data
French colonial archaeology in the Southeast and Caribbean / edited by Kenneth G. Kelly and Meredith D. Hardy.
p. cm.—(Florida Museum of Natural History. Ripley P. Bullen series)
Includes bibliographical references and index.
ISBN 978-0-8130-3680-9 (cloth: alk. paper)
ISBN 978-0-8130-6145-0 (pbk.)
1. Archaeology and history—Southern States. 2. Archaeology and history—Caribbean Area. 3. French—Southern States—History. 4. French—Caribbean Area—History. 5. Excavations (Archaeology)—Southern States. 6. Excavations (Archaeology)—Caribbean Area. 7. France—Colonies—America—History. I. Kelly, Kenneth Goodley, 1962– II. Hardy, Meredith D. (Meredith Devereaux), 1972– III. Florida Museum of Natural History.
F212.F74   2011
975.'01—dc22   2011011172

The University Press of Florida is the scholarly publishing agency for the State University System of Florida, comprising Florida A&M University, Florida Atlantic University, Florida Gulf Coast University, Florida International University, Florida State University, New College of Florida, University of Central Florida, University of Florida, University of North Florida, University of South Florida, and University of West Florida.

University Press of Florida
15 Northwest 15th Street
Gainesville, FL 32611-2079
http://www.upf.com

Contents

List of Figures vii
List of Tables ix

1. Introduction 1
   Kenneth G. Kelly and Meredith D. Hardy

2. French Protestants in South Carolina: The Archaeology of a European Ethnic Minority 17
   Ellen Shlasko

3. French Refugees and Slave Abuse in Frederick County, Maryland: Jean Payen de Boisneuf and the Vincendière Family at L'Hermitage Plantation 29
   Sara Rivers-Cofield

4. Commoditization of Persons, Places, and Things during Biloxi's Second Tenure as Capital of French Colonial Louisiana 47
   Barbara Thedy Hester

5. The Moran Site (22HR511): An Early-Eighteenth-Century French Colonial Cemetery in Nouveau Biloxi, Mississippi 64
   Marie Elaine Danforth

6. The Greatest Gathering: The Second French-Chickasaw War in the Mississippi Valley and the Potential for Archaeology 81
   Ann M. Early

7. Colonial and Creole Diets in Eighteenth-Century New Orleans 97
   Elizabeth M. Scott and Shannon Lee Dawdy

8. Colonoware in Western Colonial Louisiana: Makers and Meaning   117
   David W. Morgan and Kevin C. MacDonald

9. Living on the Edge: Foodways and Early Expressions of Creole Culture on the French Colonial Gulf Coast Frontier   152
   Meredith D. Hardy

10. *La Vie Quotidienne*: Historical Archaeological Approaches to the Plantation Era in Guadeloupe, French West Indies   189
    Kenneth G. Kelly

11. Archaeological Research at Habitation Loyola, French Guiana   206
    Allison Bain, Réginald Auger, and Yannick Le Roux

12. Commentary   225
    John de Bry

List of Contributors   243
Index   245

Figures

1.1. Map of the southeastern United States, the Caribbean, and northern South America with locations of archaeological sites and places mentioned in the volume   7
2.1. Photograph of the Huger monument on the Santee River   18
2.2. James Cook map of South Carolina, 1773   19
2.3. Example of a cedar post located in a foundation trench (*poteaux-en-terre*)   24
2.4. Photograph of the excavation trench at Waterhorn Plantation   24
3.1. L'Hermitage Plantation, Monocacy National Battlefield, Frederick County, Maryland   30
3.2. The "stone house with upper storeys [sic] painted white"   41
4.1. *Carte de Partie de la Coste du Nouveau Biloxy, Avec Les Isles des Environs*, 1722   49
5.1. Map of burial locations at the Moran site   68
5.2. Crucifix recovered with Burial 14 before and after conservation   72
5.3. Carbon and nitrogen isotopes of collagen of the Moran cemetery   75
6.1. Map illustrating the locations of places mentioned in the text   86
7.1. Percentages of biomass of total domestic and wild species   102
7.2. Percentages of total biomass of beef versus pork remains   108
7.3. Percentages of total biomass of status-indicating cuts of beef   111
8.1. Map of Cane River plantations and Native American sites   127
8.2. Frequency of all colonowares described in text   130
8.3. Approximate chronological distribution of sites under comparison   131
8.4. Example of a Coincoin Plantation colonoware sherd, assignable to the type Natchitoches Engraved   138

9.1. Map of the Gulf Coast region showing the locations of archaeological sites   155
9.2. *The Kitchen Table*, by Jean Siméon Chardin, 1757   161
9.3. *Partie de la Coste de la Louisiane et de la Floride*, 1744   166
9.4. *Faience blanche*, Moustiers yellow on white   178
9.5. Albisola brown on black wares, ca. 1720–1740   178
9.6. *Faience blanche*, Seine polychrome   179
10.1. Map of Guadeloupe showing the locations of Habitations La Mahaudière and Grande Pointe   191
10.2. Photograph of a sign depicting cane field workers at the Damoiseau distillery, Guadeloupe   194
11.1. Map illustrating the layout of Habitation Loyola   208
11.2. *Cartouche extrait de la carte du gouvernement de l'isle et terre ferme et colonie de Cayenne*, 1730   213
11.3. Photograph of the brick-lined canal of the boiling house at Habitation Loyola   217

Tables

4.1. History of excavations at Vieux Biloxi 54
4.2. History of excavations at Nouveau Biloxi 56
4.3. History of excavations at Ship Island, Gulf Islands National Seashore 58
4.4. History of excavations at the African Habitation site 59
5.1. Demographic traits and mortuary indicators, the Moran site 71
7.1. Faunal remains, St. Augustine Plantation (16OR148), 1715–1775 103
7.2. Faunal remains, Madame John's Legacy (16OR51), de Lanzos occupation, 1788–1800 (fire and postfire) 104
7.3. Faunal remains, Madame John's Legacy (16OR51), Pascal-Marin occupation, 1730–1788 (prefire) 106
7.4. Meat cuts data, Madame John's Legacy (16OR51), de Lanzos occupation, 1788–1800 (fire and postfire) 110
7.5. Meat cuts data, St. Augustine Plantation (16OR148), 1715–1775 111
7.6. Meat cuts data, Madame John's Legacy (16OR51), 1730–1788 (prefire) 112
8.1. Low-fired earthenware attributes at the Lambre Point site (early 1700s) 137
8.2. Low-fired earthenware attributes at Coincoin Plantation (ca. 1788–1816) 137
9.1. Comparison of faunal remains (NISP) from various sites mentioned in the text 173
9.2. Unit and level summaries for butchering methods, Hermann-Grima House (16OR45) 175
9.3. Cut marks on faunal specimens, Hermann-Grima House (16OR45) 175
9.4. Comparisons of ceramic types from various sites mentioned in the text 177

1

Introduction

KENNETH G. KELLY AND MEREDITH D. HARDY

The voyages of exploration fielded by western European nations in the late fifteenth and early sixteenth centuries were the impetus that led to the creation of the Atlantic world, a network of interactions linking four continents across the Atlantic Ocean. Although sailors under the license of the Spanish nation were the first to successfully initiate regular crossings from Europe to the Americas, word of the vast wealth falling into the lap of Spain quickly spread, and mariners from other coastal nations of Europe joined in the search for plunder, power, and possessions. For readers in the United States and the United Kingdom, the role of English and later British explorers in the developing colonial world is familiar, and the importance of other nations is less known. However, this myopic perspective overlooks the important role the colonial ventures of other nations played in shaping the world we know today. While Spain played a relatively minor role in the Lesser Antilles and in North America north and east of the Rio Grande, with the exception of exploration *entradas* and the settlements of La Florida, the history of North America and the Caribbean was profoundly shaped by the colonial designs of France. From the earliest and short-lived sixteenth-century attempts to establish forts and permanent settlements along the eastern seaboard and along the waterways of the St. Lawrence River, to the later, more successful colonization efforts in various islands of the Caribbean, Canada, the Gulf Coast, and the Mississippi Valley, France rapidly rose to a position of wealth as a colonial power (Waselkov 1997). Yet as we well know, history tends to be written by the "winners" in order to construct national narratives that solidify their position. The same has held true, until that last couple of decades, for historical archaeologists who have tended to focus on the

British colonial sphere. Until relatively recently, the importance of the other contenders in the colonial struggle has tended to be overlooked.

Historical archaeology, which uses archaeological methods such as excavation, material culture studies, and spatial analysis in conjunction with historical sources such as letters, accounts, wills, and probate inventories, has contributed immeasurably to our understanding of the people not usually accorded importance in traditional history, such as poor people, workers, women, slaves, and children (Deetz 1996; Kelly 2005). Equally, historical archaeology can help to reintegrate complexity into national and international narratives by considering the nature and role of other colonial powers in the creation of the modern world (Orser 1996; Funari 1999). In this volume, we bring together researchers investigating a variety of French colonial ventures in the present-day United States, the Caribbean, and the northeastern coast of South America in an effort to explore the differences, similarities, and complexities of the French colonial experience in those regions outside the better known regions including Canada, the upper Mississippi Valley, and the Great Lakes. For those interested in the nature of French colonization and interaction in the northern portion of the continent, there is an extensive literature in French and English based upon a wide range of studies that have been carried out in Canada and, to a lesser extent, in the Great Lakes and upper Mississippi Valley regions of the United States (see the extensive bibliography in Waselkov 1997).

For 130 years, from the beginning of the second third of the seventeenth century to the end of the eighteenth century, the scope of the French colonial venture was truly outstanding (Boucher 1989; Eccles 1990). In North America, there was a permanent French presence that penetrated nearly halfway across the continent, spanning from Canada and the Great Lakes to the mouth of the Mississippi and spreading out along its tributaries. Additional French settlements extended both east and west from the Mississippi along the Gulf Coast, from the border of Texas to Florida. The nature of the settlements necessarily varied depending on their location and the resources and environments available for exploitation. In eastern Canada, there were farmers and fishers who had emigrated from France with the intent to settle, whereas in the Great Lakes region the French population was comparatively sparse and more itinerant, spread out among forts and trading establishments and geared toward taking advantage of the trade in fur. Farther south, along the middle Mississippi Valley, settled agricultural villages produced surplus grain for the Caribbean, and miners exploited lead deposits. New Orleans acted as the funnel or "node" for distribution to the Caribbean and beyond. In the subtropical climate, Louisiana agriculture was increasingly modeled on the plantation economies of the Caribbean and grew to rely to a greater extent on the labor of enslaved Africans. This pattern was evident along the Gulf Coast, though here the initial concerns of subsistence and survival tended to outweigh profit. By the middle of the eighteenth century, a nearly continuous belt of French settlement encircled the British colonies along the eastern coast of North America from Georgia to Maine. Yet even within the British colonies there were areas where the French presence was significant. For example, in South Carolina's Low Country, Protestant Huguenot refugees from France established plantations based on slave labor and grew rice and indigo among their British neighbors (Shlasko, this volume; Steen 1999). At the turn of the nineteenth century, a new wave of French immigrants would spread to Jamaica and the United States, especially to New Orleans, as refugees fleeing the turmoil of the Haitian Revolution settled and attempted to renew their lives (Geggus 2001; Rivers 2002; Rivers-Cofield, this volume).

The West Indies was another region where French and English endeavors got under way at an early date. During the 1620s and 1630s, French colonial ventures began to whittle away at the Caribbean possessions of the Spanish, first acquiring small toeholds on islands unoccupied by the Spanish such as St. Kitts, Nevis, Guadeloupe, Martinique, and St. Croix. Once it was clear that Spain was either unable or unwilling to contest these claims, English and French plantation economies became established, first producing tobacco and, in the second half of the seventeenth century, sugar. With sugar came slavery and profits heretofore undreamed of. By the end of the seventeenth century, nearly every habitable island of the Lesser Antilles had been claimed from the Spanish by either France or England, a few exceptions notwithstanding. The Greater Antilles were also claimed, with England seizing Jamaica from Spain by force in 1655, and France taking control of the western third of Hispaniola as the colony of Saint-Domingue at the close of the seventeenth century. In less than 100 years, Saint-Domingue would grow to be the richest and most populous (in both enslaved and free people) colony in the Caribbean, with nearly half a million enslaved Africans. Although Saint-Domingue overshadowed all other island colonies of any nation in virtually every way, during the eighteenth century the three principal French islands of Saint-Domingue, Guadeloupe, and Martinique, taken together, produced more sugar, rum, coffee, and indigo with more captive Africans than all the British Caribbean colonies combined (Blackburn 1997). To place the numbers of enslaved laborers in context, Martinique, an island "one fourth the size of Long Island . . . receiv[ed] roughly the same number of enslaved Africans as the whole of the United States" (Price 2001:58).

Yet a third arena in which French colonization occurred lay on the northeast coast of South America. There, between British and Dutch Guyana to the west and Portuguese Brazil to the east, the French colony of Guyane was established. This was the only mainland South American French colony, although in many ways it had more in common with its Caribbean cousins. Despite controlling a vast area of tropical forest, the relatively sparse settlement was focused on the coastal strip and a few rivers, where plantations producing tropical commodities could be established (Bain et al., this volume; Mam Lam Fouck 1997). The colonial population remained small; in 1759 the total population of Guyane was 5,847, of whom 5,571 were enslaved. After 1855, gold prospectors began to move into some of the interior regions, but to this day they remain largely the province of indigenous people (Mam Lam Fouck 1997).

Once the colonial chessboard was laid with pieces from Canada to Guyane, other historical developments played a role in the way the colonial world would be shaped. European conflicts between Britain and France repeatedly extended themselves to the Americas in a variety of ways. Some Caribbean islands changed hands as many as 17 times over 200 years. The Seven Years War of 1756–1763 was much more than the "French and Indian War" by which it is known from the U.S. perspective, and at its conclusion defeated France chose to surrender all of its Canadian territory to Britain rather than part with the small islands of Guadeloupe and Martinique. The aftermath of the Seven Years War also led to the arrival in Louisiana of the displaced French population of Acadia, who became known as les Acadiens (today's "Cajuns"), first in and around New Orleans and later moving to southwest Louisiana. The Gulf Coast east of New Orleans was ceded to the British, but over the following decades Spanish Louisiana (west of the Mississippi River) marched eastward and claimed the former French territories. Though the region was now Spanish, it was in name only. French colonial culture remained dominant until after the Louisiana Purchase in 1803 (Dawdy 2008).

Other historical developments continued to change the complexion of the French colonial experience, none more dramatically than the French Revolution and its aftermath. In the Caribbean, the debates surrounding the possibility of continued slavery in face of the universal rights of man led to civil upheaval between "free people of color" and white colonists. These, in turn, probably contributed to the slave uprisings in Saint-Domingue (1791), Guadeloupe (1790, 1791, 1793), Martinique (1789, 1791, 1793), and Guyane (1790) (Bénot 1997; Dubois 2004a, 2004b). In Martinique, rather than see their slaves turned into citizens, the planter class invited British occupation (Blackburn 1997). In contrast, in Guadeloupe and Guyane, slavery was officially abolished in 1794, only to be reinstituted eight years later by Napoleon (Bénot and Dorigny 2003).

As should be clear from this short review of the diverse range of French colonial economic and geographic experiences outside of Canada, the French colonial endeavor was no less varied or diverse than that of the English. It is worthwhile to investigate these settings for that reason alone. However, as the geography and economy of colonization varied between regions, so, too, did the worldview, or *mentalité*, of colonization vary between regions, and, more important, between colonizing nations.

In addition to the diversity of the French colonial experience, it has been suggested that the French worldview concerning colonization was just as distinct. Just as James Deetz (1996) and others have identified the development and spread of the "Georgian World View" and sought its origins in nascent capitalism (Leone 1988; Shackel 1994), so, too, have researchers posited that there were unique manifestations of French national and regional culture that placed their distinct imprint on French colonial endeavors. Aspects of French culture are proposed to have facilitated interaction with indigenous Native peoples through convergence (Moussette 2003), impacted the way slavery was conceived and implemented in the Gulf Coast and the Caribbean (Kelly 2002; Kelly, this volume; see also Rivers 2002; Rivers et al. 2003; Rivers-Cofield, this volume; Dawdy 2008), and resulted in unique attitudes toward the permeability of the "color barrier," as expressed in contemporary accounts and in the relatively large number of free people of color in French colonies. In addition to the ways French colonists interacted with others, were they Native peoples or enslaved Africans, French colonists also created new lives that were based upon deeply held cultural values that penetrated every aspect of colonial life. These include such mundane but fundamental notions as the ideas surrounding what foods are appropriate and how they should be prepared and consumed (Hardy, this volume; Scott and Dawdy, this volume), the correct ways to use architectural rules (Edwards and Kariouk 2004), and the notions governing the use and organization of space, whether domestic, urban, rural, or public.

Why this Volume?

With the recognition of the unique history and experience of French colonization, the researchers contributing to this book have taken it upon themselves to explore, through historical archaeology, the ways in which French colonists in a variety of settings created distinctive ways of life. Perhaps surprisingly, the chapters in this book signal a vanguard, because despite more than half a century of significant historical archaeological research on a range of sites relating to the colonial period of North America and the Caribbean, the French contribution to the history of North America and the circum-Caribbean region has often been relegated to the periphery of historical study. In spite of France's diverse colonial holdings, ranging from the fishery, farming, and trade settlements of Canada, to the farms and mines in the middle Mississippi Valley region, to the plantations and farms on the Gulf Coast, to the French refugee plantations in South Carolina, Maryland, and elsewhere, and to the vast colonial endeavors of the Caribbean, comparatively few historical archaeological studies have explored this history. In some of these regions, such as the circum-Caribbean, historical archaeological research of any kind on French sites is in its infancy, with very few published results and even fewer in English. In light of this situation, it is perhaps not surprising that there are no collections of French historical archaeological research that bring all this diversity together. The few that do exist, such as those edited by John A. Walthall (1991) for the Illinois Country, Kenneth G. Kelly (2004) for the French Caribbean, and Gregory A. Waselkov (1991; Waselkov and Gums 2000) for colonial-era Mobile Bay, deal with single regions within the broader French colonial venture (see Waselkov 1997 for an excellent overview and bibliography). This book brings together, in a single collection, historical archaeological research on the middle Mississippi Valley region, the Gulf Coast and Louisiana, the French Huguenot planters in British South Carolina, refugees from the Haitian Revolution in Maryland, and the Caribbean and Guyane (Figure 1.1).

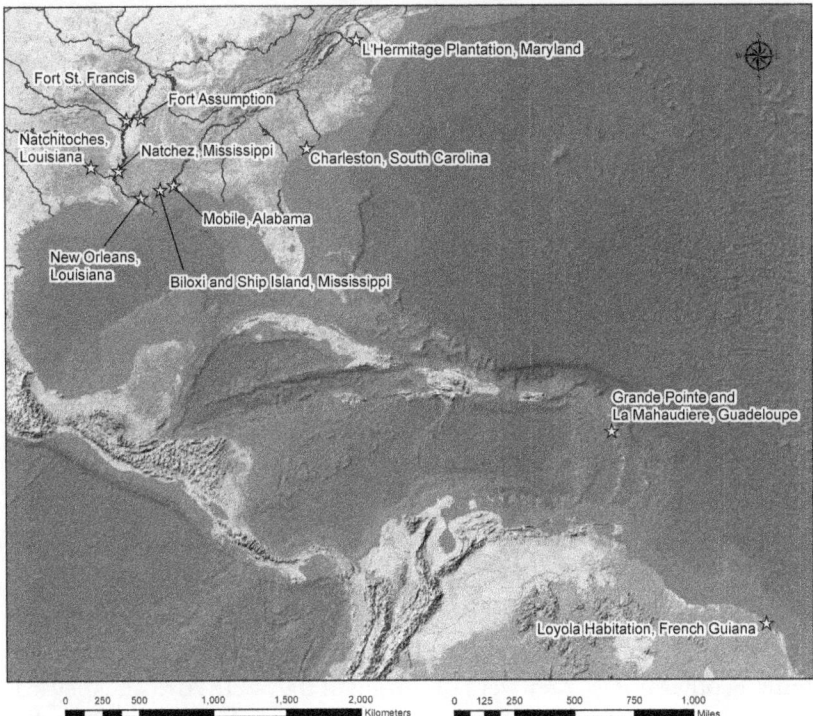

Figure 1.1. Map of the southeastern United States, the Caribbean, and northern South America with locations of archaeological sites and places mentioned in the volume.

Themes addressed by the chapters in this volume include the particular expressions of plantation slavery in French colonial settings, questions of French identity and how it was materialized and maintained in colonial settings, the relationships between identity and material culture, and the adaptation and manifestation of French cultural ideas to the new, exotic, and challenging environments of the Americas. Strategies of adaptation are explored through the material evidence of settlement patterning, architecture, foodways, colonoware pottery, artifact patterning, death, and cultural interaction and exchange with "others," be they Native peoples, Africans or those of African descent, or other European colonists.

The majority of the chapters that comprise this volume originated in a daylong session held at the 2004 Society for Historical Archaeology meetings in St. Louis, Missouri, which was organized and chaired by the editors. The contributions reflect a wide variety of research interests and cover a large geographic area that, to date, has not been well represented in the archaeological literature of the colonial and early antebellum eras.

Interestingly, several common themes thread throughout all of the contributions. These themes are centered on the concepts of dynamism and diversity, contact and change, hybridity, and adaptation. Regional and local variation and diversity within a macroregional system is emphasized again and again as an imperative and integral focus for the interpretation of systems of interaction and communication. However, rather than interpreting the "creolization" process as one of conformity to a singular set of developing cultural norms, we can begin to view this process as the melding of many historical trajectories at a node of contact and interaction, then continued divergence and development, within the parameters of a French colonial "rubric."

The first contribution to this volume is by Ellen Shlasko. Her chapter (Chapter 2) discusses historical archaeological research on an important but often overlooked group of early South Carolina settlers, the French Protestants known as the Huguenots. The diaspora of this group of colonists has had important ramifications in a number of parts of the world (among other things, they were the origin of the South African vineyards and wine industry in the Western Cape), and the role that they played in South Carolina was important in the formative years of the colony. These French refugees constituted an important minority in the colony and were founding members of a number of elite colonial lineages. Shlasko's chapter explores the implications of this founding group for the history of South Carolina, and particularly questions whether their "Frenchness" may have had a lasting, or even transitory, impact on the built environment of the colony, or whether, in contrast, their French identity was muted to rapidly assimilate into the dominant Anglo colonial society, as has been suggested (Butler 1983). By taking a more nuanced view of architecture, Shlasko argues that some of the distinctive archaeological traces of wall trench building techniques that diverged from what was expected from English colonists may be associated with French colonists, rather than with enslaved African builders. Whether these *poteaux-en-terre* structures were built by Africans or by French refugees, Shlasko suggests that as an architectural tradition, it may have signaled a different ideology of separation than that materialized by English building traditions. Although by no means conclusive, this reading of the archaeological record with greater attention to the multiethnic nature of the colonists suggests that there may be ways in which French Huguenots affirmed their French identity in a fashion that was otherwise overlooked by historians seeking to demonstrate assimilation. Indeed, in the setting of colonial South Carolina, where, as Shlasko points out, the distinct maintenance of a "French" identity was something that was apparently not seen as socially significant until the nineteenth century, when an association with French Huguenot heritage became desirable, as the monumental inscriptions she begins with note. We see this as a cautionary example that even in places where French colonists were present, multiple factors may have been in play that made "Frenchness" either something to be obscured through contemporary action or, conversely, something that is overlooked by present-day archaeologists who are focused on narrow associations of divergent patterns as an expression of African American presence.

Identity and assimilation (or lack thereof) among refugees is also a key theme of the third chapter in the volume. In her contribution, Sarah Rivers-Cofield uses an archaeological evaluation of L'Hermitage Plantation on Monocacy National Battlefield to explore issues of identity associated with a family of French planters who were refugees from the uprising of enslaved Africans on Saint-Domingue (the Haitian Revolution). In her study, Rivers-Cofield investigates the question: how would a French Caribbean planter (re-)create a plantation in the mid-Atlantic United States? Demonstrating that the context of this study is more complex than simply the arrival of planter elites fleeing the revolution, Rivers-Cofield shows that the Boisneuf and Vincendière families also brought with them a dozen enslaved individuals from Saint-Domingue, and attempted to re-create a plantation based upon the model of a Caribbean estate. Within a few years of their arrival, they had consolidated a large estate with a slave population of 90 individuals, three to six times the number of enslaved workers typically found on Maryland plantations of similar size. Although not necessarily a conscious expression of their French Caribbean identity, considerable cruelty toward their enslaved workers was recognized by passersby and neighbors of L'Hermitage Plantation. This evidence is one of the few examples that suggest that French Caribbean plantation owners may have behaved in ways distinct from other planters. Furthermore, Rivers-Cofield argues that, based upon the layout of the slave village, the refugee planters established a physical environment that reinforced their close control over a slave population that may have been "infected" by ideas of liberty. As this chapter discusses research associated with cultural resource management (CRM) work that was designed to identify and avoid archaeological resources, large-scale archaeological excavation was not conducted on the plantation settlement. However, given that virtually no research has been conducted on any sites associated with French refugees from Saint-Domingue, we find her chapter to be a compelling and significant contribution to understanding the ways in which specific national and historical contexts may manifest themselves archaeologically.

Chapters 4 and 5 present two studies that complement each other in developing an understanding of the early decades of the French colonial endeavor along the Gulf Coast of Mississippi. Barbara Hester's chapter (Chapter 4) sets the stage for an investigation of the ultimately unsuccessful efforts to establish the French capital of Louisiana in the environs of Biloxi Bay, Mississippi. She presents an inventory of sites identified or presumed to be associated with the short-lived proprietorship period in which the French colonial effort was effectively privatized in the hands of a monopolistic arrangement directed by Scottish financier John Law. Although this period, from 1720 to 1722, was brief, the archaeological data from a series of sites associated with the second capital at Biloxi demonstrates that the colonists who were thrown into a precarious situation developed strategies of resistance to the commoditization of people, places, and things.

Marie Danforth, in her contribution in Chapter 5, presents bioarchaeological data from the Moran site, a colonial-era cemetery that is probably associated with the failed second colonization efforts at Biloxi. The cemetery at the Moran site is likely the second oldest French colonial cemetery in the United States to be archaeologically investigated, predating the St. Peter's Cemetery in New Orleans. As the bioarchaeological analyses of the human remains at the Moran site reveal a demographically skewed population overwhelmingly male and young that was hastily buried, they provide an excellent view of the physical conditions of life "enjoyed" by prospective colonists who were probably from the lower socioeconomic strata of France and Europe and who met their demise shortly after arriving in Louisiana.

Ann Early's contribution (Chapter 6) is a call for future archaeological research focused on a fascinating episode in the history of the Mississippi Valley during the second quarter of the eighteenth century. By using historical documentation and observations and eyewitness accounts, Early provides insight into the social relations (and their potential material correlates) between French colonials, their multicultural allies, and the Chickasaw peoples during the period commonly referred to as the first and second French-Chickasaw Wars (1736–1740). The Chickasaw, allied with the English since the seventeenth century, had established control over lines of communication and circulation, both overland and water routes, that were vital for the establishment and success of French settlement ventures in the Mississippi Valley. These efforts resulted in the "bringing together" of many Native American groups from across the Francophone region of North America (namely, the Great Lakes region), freed and enslaved Africans and African Americans, and French settlers and military from Canada, south Louisiana, and the homeland to establish a garrison near St. Francis, Arkansas. The archaeology of the region has the potential to provide insight into conceptions of ethnicity and social identity, processes of site settlement, resource acquisition, and urban development surrounding military-based endeavors of expansion and territoriality.

Elizabeth Scott and Shannon Dawdy (Chapter 7) present another example of multicultural contact—the development of creolized societies—in the developing urban environment of New Orleans. Through a comparison of faunal remains from two archaeological sites representing both the French (1718–1763) and Spanish (1763–1801) colonial periods, Scott and Dawdy examine processes of creolization as evidenced in subtle changes in food selection and preference over time. The complexities of studying a developing, dynamic creole society are many, especially when identifying differences in ethnicity and socioeconomic status. Scott and Dawdy present alternative ways of interpreting status and potentially ethnicity via food remains that are dependent on context—namely, urban versus rural environments, resource availability, and the cultural backgrounds of the actors being investigated. For example, while differences in proportions of beef versus pork remains were observed between the French and Spanish occupational periods, associations between particular cuts of meat and socioeconomic status cannot be so easily discerned because of differences in ethnicity and market availability.

David Morgan and Kevin MacDonald (Chapter 8) discuss the ongoing debate on colonoware production in the colonial southeastern United States, namely in French colonial Louisiana. Colonowares, low-fired coarse earthenwares of coiled manufacture that resemble European ceramic forms, are regarded as yet another material example of the confluence of various cultural traditions during early colonial and settlement efforts in the Natchitoches frontier region of north-central to northwest Louisiana. In this case, they are the traditions of low-fired coiled pottery created and used for utilitarian purposes by slaves and low-status individuals prior to the establishment of reliable lines of trade related to European settlement. Morgan and MacDonald call into question old assumptions regarding the identities of makers of colonowares by focusing their study on French colonial contexts instead of the English colonial world of the Atlantic Southeast Coast and Tidewater regions. The authors propose that colonoware production was largely the result of local interactions between Native American groups and African and African American slaves. The potential for future studies in this region is great, as colonowares can be viewed as a nexus of communication and interaction in frontier settings.

Meredith Hardy (Chapter 9) continues the examination of creolization processes in developing French colonial and creolized societies through a discussion of foodway systems, a holistic approach that incorporates food production, acquisition, preparation, service, and consumption. Using a regional approach, Hardy compares archaeologically defined patterns of food remains (consumption) and ceramics (preparation and service) with the culinary traditions of seventeenth- and eighteenth-century France. These traditions were brought to the Gulf Coast and New Orleans area, where they came into contact with a multiplicity of other culinary traditions—namely, those of Spanish, West African, and Native American groups. These traditions were then combined with new foods that were adopted when the traditional ingredients of the homeland cuisine were not available. Social identity can be inferred from the kinds of foods that were prepared as a result of the histories and places of origin. For example, cuisines of southern France differed from those of northern France, evident in the foods selected (seafood versus wild game), the tools used in their preparation, and preferences for particular wares for their service (that is, ceramics). The continued presence of French ceramics, representative of particular regional styles, is also evidence for the maintenance of social identity even during the Spanish colonial period, while simultaneously the methods and ingredients of French cuisine were already becoming "creolized" traditions.

In his contribution in Chapter 10, Kenneth Kelly discusses the application of historical archaeological methods to the investigation of daily life of enslaved workers on sugar plantations in Guadeloupe, one of the principal French sugar colonies of the Caribbean. Despite 30 or more years of historical archaeology investigating the African Diaspora in the English-speaking Caribbean, the work reported here is the first historical archaeological research conducted on French Caribbean plantations. Kelly argues that the distinct histories of the French Caribbean colonies, particularly those relating to the transformations arising from the French Revolution, had important and unique manifestations in each colony. He particularly focuses on the divergent impact of the revolutionary abolition of slavery that occurred in Guadeloupe from 1794 to 1802 as a key moment in precipitating transformations in slavery from a more materially impoverished, ancien régime version toward a more typically nineteenth-century expression that was due in part to the violent reimposition of slavery in 1802, and some of the "negotiations" that were a part of that process. Furthermore, he sees the eight-year period of revolutionary abolition as a key factor in the relative invisibility of the material traces of plantation slavery on the built landscape of Guadeloupe.

Moving to the former French South American colony of Guyane, or French Guiana, Allison Bain, Reginald Auger, and Yannick Le Roux (Chapter 11) report on a multiyear archaeological investigation of the ruins of Habitation Loyola, a Jesuit-run sugar plantation founded in 1668 and abandoned in 1768 after the dissolution of the Jesuit order. Their study investigates a range of plantation contexts, from the industrial buildings and the ancillary activities to the residence of the Jesuit planters. This study is a significant contribution to plantation studies as it investigates an important, yet frequently overlooked, aspect of the sugar economy in the French colonies, the plantations run by religious orders. Studies of other religious plantations (such as Habitation Perrinelle and Fonds St. Jacques) in Martinique have not been as comprehensive, nor were the Martinican plantations as important in the overall wealth and development of the colony. In contrast, in Guyane, the Jesuits operated an unusual expression of a successful plantation in an otherwise marginal colonial possession. Furthermore, Bain, Auger, and Le Roux's chapter provides data on an early exploitation of a mainland colony, using a Caribbean model.

The final chapter of the book, the "Commentary" by John de Bry, originated in his role as a discussant in the original Society for Historical Archaeology session. Here, he has expanded his thoughts considerably, drawing upon his extensive knowledge of the holdings of French archival repositories. His commentary expands upon many of the chapters by pointing out parallels in other geographical and temporal settings of the French colonial world. In addition to his identification of links that crosscut the research presented in the other chapters, de Bry also eloquently makes the case that archival research is too important to archaeological work to be left only to the historians—by the very nature of the two disciplines, we are looking for different clues and insights from the views recorded by people in the past.

The fragile nature of much of this region was regrettably made evident with the landing of Hurricane Katrina on August 28, 2005, on the Mississippi and Louisiana coasts. Just as the region's residents during past centuries had done following similar storms, today's residents have begun the rebuilding process, once again pulling together the historical past and the experienced present to plan for the future. What remains of the past should be studied, documented, preserved, and presented to the public. This disaster makes the presentation of the French colonial past even more pressing.

References Cited

Bénot, Yves
1997   *La Guyane sous la Révolution: ou l'impasse de la Révolution pacifique.* Ibis Rouge Editions, Kourou, Guyane.
2003   The Chain of Slave Insurrections in the Caribbean, 1789–1791. In *The Abolitions of Slavery: From L. F. Sonthonax to Victor Schoelcher, 1793, 1794, 1848*, edited by Marcel Dorigny, 147–154. Berghan Books, New York.

Bénot, Yves, and Marcel Dorigny, editors
2003   *Rétablissement de l'esclavage dans les colonies françaises.* Maisonneuve et Larose, Paris.

Blackburn, Robin
1997   *The Making of New World Slavery: From the Baroque to the Modern, 1492–1800.* Verso, London.

Boucher, Philip P.
1989   *Les Nouvelles Frances: France in America, 1500–1815. An Imperial Perspective.* John Carter Brown Library, Providence, R.I.

Butler, Jon
1983 *The Huguenots in America: A Refugee People in New World Society*. Harvard Historical Monographs 72. Harvard University Press, Cambridge, Mass.
Dawdy, Shannon L.
2008 *Building the Devil's Empire: French Colonial New Orleans*. University of Chicago Press, Chicago.
Deetz, James
1996 *In Small Things Forgotten: An Archaeology of Early American Life*. Anchor Books, New York.
Dubois, Laurent
2004a *A Colony of Citizens: Revolution and Slave Emancipation in the French Caribbean, 1789–1802*. University of North Carolina Press, Chapel Hill.
2004b *Avengers of the New World: The Story of the Haitian Revolution*. Harvard University Press, Cambridge, Mass.
Eccles, W. J.
1990 *France in America*. Michigan State University Press, East Lansing.
Edwards, Jay D., and Nicolas Kariouk Pecquet du Bellay de Verton
2004 *A Creole Lexicon: Architecture, Landscape, People*. Louisiana State University Press, Baton Rouge.
Funari, Pedro Paulo A.
1999 Historical Archaeology from a World Perspective. In *Historical Archaeology: Back from the Edge*, edited by Pedro Paulo A. Funari, Martin Hall, and Sian Jones, 37–66. Routledge, London.
Geggus, David P., editor
2001 *The Impact of the Haitian Revolution in the Atlantic World*. University of South Carolina Press, Columbia.
Kelly, Kenneth G.
2002 African Diaspora Archaeology in Guadeloupe, French West Indies. *Antiquity* 76:333–334.
2004 Historical Archaeology in the French Caribbean: An Introduction to a Special Volume of the *Journal of Caribbean Archaeology*. *Journal of Caribbean Archaeology* Special Issue No. 1: 1–10.
2005 Historical Archaeology. In *Handbook of Archaeological Methods*, edited by Herbert D. G. Maschner and Christopher Chippendale, 2:1108–1137. Altamira, Lanham, Md.
Leone, Mark P.
1988 The Georgian Order as the Order of Merchant Capitalism in Annapolis, Maryland. In *The Recovery of Meaning: Historical Archaeology in the Eastern United States*, edited by Mark P. Leone and Parker B. Potter, Jr., 235–261. Smithsonian Institution Press, Washington, D.C.
Mam Lam Fouck, Serge
1997 La France en Guyane: Conquête et mode d'occupation de l'espace. In *L'Archéologie en Guyane*, edited by Guy Mazière, 143–159. Association pour la Protection du Patrimoine Archéologique en Architectural de la Guyane, Cayenne.

Moussette, Marcel
2003   An Encounter with the Baroque Age: French and Amerindians in North America. *Historical Archaeology* 37(4): 29–39.

Orser, Charles E., Jr.
1996   *A Historical Archaeology of the Modern World*. Plenum, New York.

Price, Richard
2001   The Miracle of Creolization: A Retrospective. *New West Indian Guide / Nieuwe West-Indische Gids* 75(1&2): 35–64.

Rivers, Sara J.
2002   *Contextualizing the Hermitage: A Maryland Plantation with French Caribbean Ties*. Report submitted to the National Park Service and the University of Maryland.

Rivers, Sara J., Joy Beasley, and S. Jordan
2003   L'Hermitage: Interpreting a French-Caribbean Plantation in Western Maryland. Paper presented at the Society for Historical Archaeology Conference.

Shackel, Paul A.
1994   Town Plans and Everyday Material Culture: An Archaeology of Social Relations in Colonial Maryland's Capital Cities. In *Historical Archaeology of the Chesapeake*, edited by Paul A. Shackel and Barbara J. Little, 85–96. Smithsonian Institution Press, Washington, D.C.

Steen, Carl
1999   Stirring the Ethnic Stew in the South Carolina Backcountry: John de la Howe and Lethe Farm. In *Historical Archaeology, Identity Formation, and the Interpretation of Ethnicity*, edited by M. Franklin and G. Fesler, 93–120. Colonial Williamsburg Research Publications, Williamsburg, Va.

Walthall, John A., editor
1991   *French Colonial Archaeology: The Illinois Country and the Western Great Lakes*. University of Illinois Press, Urbana.

Waselkov, Gregory A.
1991   *Archaeology at the French Colonial Site of Old Mobile (Phase I: 1989–1991)*. Anthropological Monographs No. 1. University of South Alabama, Mobile.
1997   *The Archaeology of French Colonial North America: English-French Edition*. Guides to Historical Archaeological Literature 5. Society for Historical Archaeology, Tucson, Az.

Waselkov, Gregory A., and Bonnie L. Gums
2000   *Plantation Archaeology at Rivière aux Chiens, ca. 1725–1848*. University of South Alabama Center for Archaeological Studies, Mobile.

2

French Protestants in South Carolina

The Archaeology of a European Ethnic Minority

ELLEN SHLASKO

Remembering Huguenot Heritage

In 1829, Elias Horry IV, former mayor of Charleston, South Carolina; president of the South Carolina Railroad Company; trustee of the College of Charleston; and president of the Charleston Orphan's Home, erected a monument on a small plantation on the south bank of the Santee River in the South Carolina Low Country (Figure 2.1). The monument, an obelisk of dark stone, bore a lengthy inscription:

> Near this Spot rest the Remains of the Venerable Daniel Huger, one of the earliest Settlers on Santee. He was the son of John Huger, a royal Notary of the Town of Loudon in France, and was born at Turrence April 1st 1651. To avoid the persecution of the Huguenots which Followed the Revocation of the Edict of Nantz [sic] by Louis XIV in 1685 he fled from France and emigrated to South Carolina with many other French refugees. He died December 24th 1711 in his 61st year and was buried at this, his plantation, then called Wambaw. He had married in May 1677, Margaret Perdriau of Rochelle, who died in 1717, and by whom he had twelve children. Two only of them survived him; Margaret, who was born at Rochelle, February 21st 1679, and Daniel Huger, who was born in St. James, Santee, March 16th 1688.
>
> On the 17th of Aug. 1704 Margaret Huger married Elias Horry. He was also a French Refugee and had fled from Paris where he was

born in the year 1664. He survived his wife. Died in Charleston in 1736 in his 72nd year and was buried in the French Church yard. Their children were four sons, Daniel, Elias, John and Peter Horry and two daughters, Henrietta who married Anthony Bonneau and Magdalen who married Paul Trapier. Elias Horry, the present owner of this plantation, has caused this Stone to be erected in the memory of his G.G. Grandfather, Daniel Huger. 1829.

This monument, and others like it, bears witness to the pride many members of the antebellum Charleston elite took in their Huguenot ancestors. Huguenots, or French Protestants, made up a sizable minority

Figure 2.1. Photograph of the Huger monument on the Santee River.

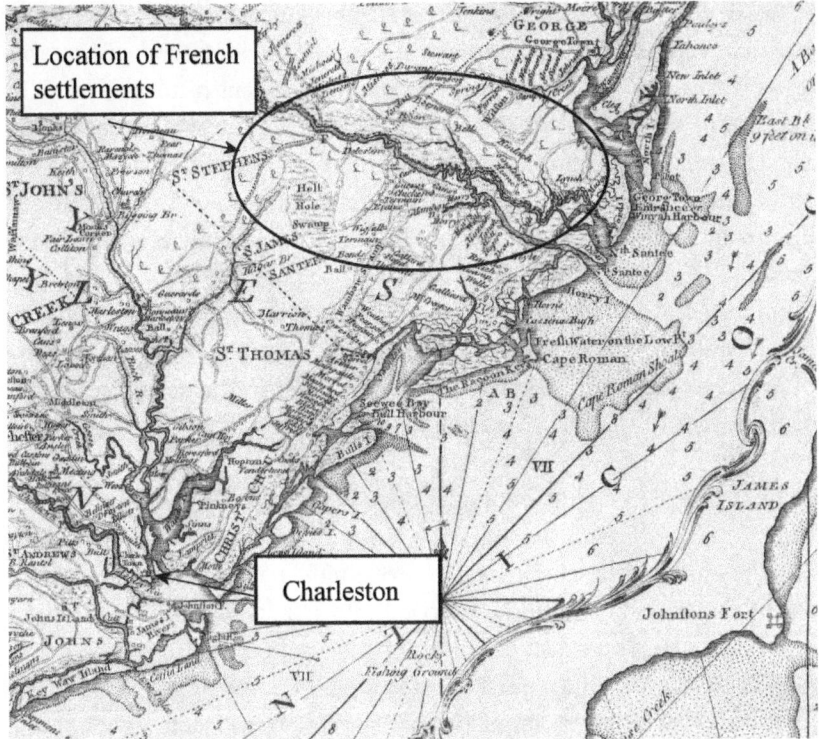

Figure 2.2. James Cook map (1773) illustrating the locations of French Huguenot settlements north of Charleston, South Carolina. Courtesy of the David Rumsey Map Collection, www.davidrumsey.com.

of the early settlers of colonial South Carolina (Figure 2.2). French immigrants began arriving in Charles Towne in 1680, just 10 years after the first English settlers founded the colony in 1670 (Hirsch 1928). As mentioned in the inscription on the Huger obelisk, they were refugees escaping religious persecution in France. This persecution had been increasing throughout the seventeenth century, and it reached a climax with the revocation of the Edict of Nantes in 1685, which stripped French Protestants of their rights. Following the revocation, the pace of Huguenot emigration increased, and by the end of the seventeenth century Huguenots made up 10 to 15 percent of South Carolina's white population (Butler 1983:102). Because of the pattern of land distribution in the colony, they wielded a surprising amount of political power, even triggering an anti-French backlash among some of their Anglo-American neighbors (Butler 1983:103–106).

Yet despite the importance people such as Elias Horry placed on their Huguenot ancestry, historians have questioned the long-term impact this group made on South Carolina. The most significant history of the Huguenots in the American colonies, Jon Butler's 1983 work, *The Huguenots in America: A Refugee People in New World Society*, emphasized the speed and success with which Huguenot immigrants assimilated into the dominant Anglo-American culture. In Butler's view, Huguenots willingly shed their French and Calvinist identity in exchange for social and economic success in the New World. High rates of intermarriage between French and English settlers, movement away from the traditional centers of French settlement, and ongoing conversion from Calvinism to Anglicanism were all signs of Huguenot integration into Anglo society (Butler 1983).

Elias Horry IV's Huguenot ancestors followed this model. In the first generation, his French-born great-grandmother, Margaret Huger, married the immigrant Elias Horry. However, in the next generation, only two out of the six Horry children married into Huguenot families (Shlasko 1997). Elias Horry IV had far more English than French ancestors, and neither he nor his children showed any preference for Huguenot spouses. Very little that is known about Horry suggests a special connection to the Huguenot community. In fact, when faced with falling rice prices in the early 1800s, he directed his Charleston business managers to sell his pew in the French church as a cost-cutting measure (Horry 1807–1808).

However, in the 1820s Elias Horry IV purchased not only the elaborate grave monument in honor of his great-great-grandfather, he also erected a large marble plaque for the French church in Charleston to celebrate the memory of Elias Horry I, the Huguenot refugee. Horry did not purchase monuments to honor any of his many English ancestors, even his grandfather Branford, from whom he inherited his mansion in Charleston and a substantial fortune. It is also significant that Horry was not alone in these rituals of remembrance. In the early nineteenth century, other Huguenot descendents were looking back with pride at their refugee ancestors. For instance, the stone marking the grave of Samuel Prioleau, while extolling his patriotism during the Revolutionary War, as well as his noble character, begins by invoking his connection to the Huguenot past, stating that "he was a descendant in the 3d. Degree of the Rev.d Elias Prioleau who accompanied by several French Protestants fled from Persecution after the Revocation of the Edict of Nantes in 1685."

The inscription on the Huger monument follows a distinct pattern. It contains two main elements. First is the description of persecution in France, the mention of the revocation of the Edict of Nantes, and the subsequent flight to South Carolina. This recital of the origin myth of the Huguenots often follows a generic formula: persecution, revocation, flight. This formula is followed despite variations in actual Huguenot experience. Although the Huger obelisk states that he left "to avoid the persecution of the Huguenots which Followed the Revocation," in fact Daniel Huger and his family left France in 1683, two years before the revocation.

The second element found on the Huguenot memorial is the tracing of family lineage and ancestral ties. While he erected the obelisk "in memory of his G.G. Grandfather," Elias Horry devotes two-thirds of his text to genealogical information covering four generations. The inscription also clearly identifies Horry's own family connection to the venerable ancestor.

> To the Memory of ELIAS HORRY the venerable Ancestor of the Horrys of South Carolina. He was born in France in the year 1664, and was the son of an Elder of a Church in Paris, who died a Martyr, for the Protestant Faith, when the Edict of Nantes was revoked by Lewis XIV, in 1685. Escaping the persecution, He fled to Holland, thence to England, and came to South Carolina, about the year 1690, and Settled near the Santee, in the Parish of Prince George Winyaw, where he resided 46 years. He died in Charleston, on the 25th of September 1736, aged 72 years, and was buried in the Cemetery of the French Church. "The South Carolina Gazette," which records his death, states that he was "One of the eldest Settlers in the province, and who by his merits and Services to the Country, had left behind him a very good Character." ELIAS, the Son of THOMAS and Grandson of Col: ELIAS HORRY, erects this Monument to the Memory of the Great Grand Father. 1825.

This same pattern appears on Prioleau's gravestone, which recites persecution, revocation, and flight, and describes ancestral connections; Prioleau is "a descendant in the 3d. Degree" of the Huguenot refugee. The recital of family connections goes even farther back, as there is also mention in the inscription that Elias Prioleau (the Huguenot refugee) was "himself descended of a Venetian Ancestry his Grandfather having been elected in 1618 Doge of Venice." Once again, the subject of the inscription (Samuel

Prioleau) is situated in a context that emphasizes both the Huguenot myth and ancestral connections over several generations.

> Sacred to the memory of Samuel Prioleau Esqr of Charleston who departed this life on the 23rd Feb a.D. 1813 in the 71st year of his age. He was a descendant in the 3d. Degree of the Rev.d Elias Prioleau who accompanied by several French Protestants fled from the Persecution after the Revocation of the Edict of Nantes in 1685. Being himself descended of a Venetian Ancestry his Grandfather having been elected in 1618 Doge of Venice. He who is entombed beneath this marble exhibited through a long Life a pattern of Industry, Integrity, firmness of character, Patriotism and the domestic virtues. In the American Revolution "which tried Mens Souls" He early devoted himself and his all, to the liberties of his Country. And in the darkest hour of that Conflict neither wavered nor compromised with the Enemy whose Persecutions, in Confiscation, Imprisonment, Contumely and Exile, He bore with unshaken Firmness even when at St. Augustine as a Victim with his Compatriots, He could not know where or to what state of suffering His Family still retained in the Power of an implacable Enemy might be destined That Family consisting of his bereaved Widow and Eight children rescued by his care and endowed by his tenderness, as a Memorial of their Love Consecrate this Monument to his Memory. In the spot where he directed his Earthly Remains to be Deposited.

It would be easy to dismiss these monuments as meaningless memorials to the past, but as more are identified and as a pattern of monument placement and language becomes apparent, they can be seen as clues that point to a new interpretation of the Huguenot past. They are significant indicators that despite the high rates of intermarriage and the mass conversion to Anglicanism, people with strong Huguenot identity remained an important element of South Carolina society well into the nineteenth century.

While historians agree that Butler's description of the assimilation and success of the Huguenots in America is essentially correct, there is increasing interest in how these successful immigrants contributed to South Carolina's development. Various researchers have begun to examine what the Huguenots of South Carolina and elsewhere retained of their ethnic identity (Shlasko 1997; Nash 2003; Van Ruymbeke 2003) and how that identity influenced their lives and the lives of their English neighbors. Butler himself has recently discussed contributions Huguenots made to American religious and cultural pluralism (Butler 2003:201).

French Architecture and Identity

If Huguenot identity survived as a powerful undercurrent in South Carolina, did it manifest itself in more significant ways than the creation of gravestones and memorials? Recent work looking at architecture (Steen 1999; Shlasko 2002) and economics (Nash 2003) suggests that Huguenot culture was an important ingredient in the success and shaping of South Carolina society.

For historical archaeologists, architectural remains provide a range of information, including clues about social status, group dynamics, and cultural background. In analyzing one such group of architectural remains, the "post-in-trench" structures found on plantation sites in the South Carolina Low Country, both Steen and Shlasko examine the possible French antecedents of what is widely regarded as an African style of architecture.

Poteaux-en-terre, or post-in-trench, is a construction technique often found on French colonial sites, particularly in the Mississippi Valley. The building method begins with the excavation of foundation trenches that outline the exterior walls of the structure (Figure 2.3). Into this trench are placed upright posts that form the walls and roof support of the building. The spaces between the posts are filled with *bouzillage*, a variety of materials such as straw, twigs, stone, or animal hair, mixed with clay (Franzwa 1973:28), or *pierrotage*, a stone and mortar chinking (Gums et al. 1991:115). A few *poteaux-en-terre* structures still survive in North America, notably in Ste. Genevieve, Missouri (Franzwa 1973), and several have been excavated in the Mississippi Valley—for instance, at Fort Massac in Illinois (Walthall 1991:52).

This construction technique leaves a distinctive architectural signature—namely, defined wall trenches with regularly spaced posts. Structures showing this pattern of features have been identified on several archaeological sites in the South Carolina Low Country, including Yaughan and Curriboo plantations (Wheaton and Garrow 1985), Daniel Island (Zierden et al. 1986), Lethe Farm (Steen 1999), and Waterhorn Plantation (Figure 2.04) (Shlasko 1997).

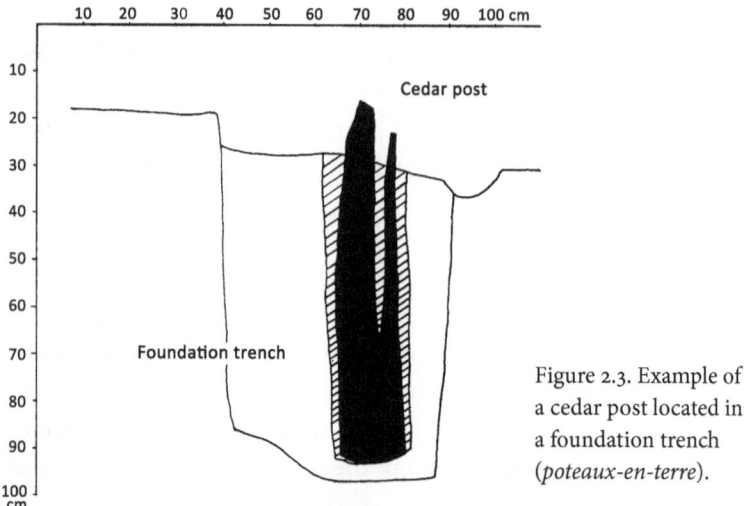

Figure 2.3. Example of a cedar post located in a foundation trench (*poteaux-en-terre*).

Figure 2.4. Photograph of the excavation trench at Waterhorn Plantation.

Waterhorn Plantation was originally settled by Daniel Huger in the seventeenth century and was subsequently purchased by his great-great-grandson Elias Horry. Excavations there uncovered a *poteaux-en-terre* structure dating to the end of the eighteenth century. The remains of this structure consisted of a 50-cm-wide trench that traced the outline of a rectangular building that was 10 m long by 5 m wide. A series of 30-cm-diameter postholes were spaced approximately 1 m apart in the center of the trench. Nearby was a second structure constructed using a series of smaller trenches that each held two posts. Like the post-in-trench structures from Yaughan and Curriboo plantations, the trenches at Waterhorn were deep (approximately 1 m below modern ground surface) with vertical sides and flat bottoms (Shlasko 1997; Wheaton and Garrow 1985:244). Two of the corner posts remained in situ and were identified as cedar (Shlasko 1997:56).

All of the South Carolina examples follow the pattern described in the 1800s by a resident of Cahokia, who wrote that the *poteaux-en-terre* structures were "formed of large posts or timbers: the posts being three or four feet apart in many of them" (Reynolds, as cited in Gums 1988:87).

The precise origin of South Carolina post-in-trench architecture remains a subject of debate. When these structures were originally identified in the 1980s, *poteaux-en-terre* architecture was recognized as being distinct from the well-known Anglo architectural traditions. Because this unique architectural signature deviated from the expected, researchers suggested that it was associated with another overlooked demographic, African Americans. As a result, making note of the unique architecture, the researchers suggested an African antecedent for the building technique (Wheaton and Garrow 1985). This interpretation changed the way archaeologists looked at plantation architecture in South Carolina as the potential of additional non-Anglo influences or expressions were sought and seen as hallmarks of African-ness. However, the discovery of additional post-in-trench buildings at other sites raised questions regarding the hypothesized African origin of the post-in-trench building technique. Specifically, Steen argues that post-in-trench architecture found at a site such as John de la Howe's Lethe Farm is a direct reflection of the owner's French heritage (Steen 1999). Shlasko suggests that the French background of Low Country planters at sites such as Waterhorn (Shlasko 1997), Yaughan and Curriboo (Wheaton and Garrow 1985), and Daniel's

Island (Zierden et al. 1986) led to a distinct pattern of interaction between the plantation owners and their enslaved workers (Shlasko 2002).

The crux of that argument is that South Carolina post-in-trench architecture is neither purely French nor purely African in origin. The use of earthen architecture is prevalent in Africa (Ferguson 1992:63–82), and, as the examples from the Mississippi Valley attest, post-in-trench architecture was widely used in French colonial settlements in North America. Additionally, the use of trench foundations is quite distinct from the traditional English earthfast building tradition seen in Virginia and in other English settlements, which used individual excavated postholes rather than continuous trenches.

Does this mean that South Carolina's post-in-trench architecture is a French tradition or an African tradition? The answer is probably neither. It is a distinct product of a social and economic situation found only in the South Carolina Low Country, where enslaved Africans and French Huguenot refugees, working together, produced structures familiar to both groups. African workers recognized the technique of building earthen-walled structures, while Huguenot landowners accepted or demanded the construction of French-style *poteaux-en-terre* homes in the South Carolina wilderness. The unique character of these houses was recognized as early as 1700, when the surveyor John Lawson remarked that John Gaillard's house on the Santee River was "a very curious contriv'd House, built of Brick and Stone" (Lawson 1718:20–22, cited in Bridges and Williams 1997:17).

Outside the field of historical archaeology, Nash's (2003:208–240) study of colonial South Carolina trade and the rise of the merchant class examines the ways in which a Huguenot tradition of family ties and a strong sense of community gave French refugees in South Carolina a significant role in the development of the Charleston merchant class. Nash finds that about 30 percent of the merchants operating in Charleston during the first generation of settlement (approximately 1680–1720) were Huguenots (Nash 2003:210–211). For the next two generations (through 1767), over 20 percent of the Charleston merchant class was of direct Huguenot descent (Nash 2003:211). The tendency of Huguenot merchants to support and work closely with other Charlestonians of Huguenot descent created a cohesive community and helped to foster economic and social ties (Nash 2003:221–229).

The traits that Nash singles out as significant contributors to the Huguenot success as merchants include the reliance on family connections in business and the sense of shared history that bound the Huguenot community (Nash 2003:225–229). These are exactly the same traits emphasized in the memorial inscriptions described at the beginning of this essay. When Elias Horry IV dedicated a memorial in the French church to "the memory of Elias Horry the venerable ancestor of the Horrys of South Carolina," he was indicating his membership in an exclusive group that strengthened both his individual role in society and helped to create the success of that society. It can be argued that as the Huguenot community of South Carolina moved farther in time from the original settlers and their children, monuments such as Elias Horry IV's served as reminders of the commonalities that bound the community and helped foster the success of French refugees in the colony.

References Cited

Bridges, Anne Baker Leland, and Roy Williams III
1997   *St. James Santee, Plantation Parish: History and Records, 1685–1925.* Reprint Company, Spartanburg, S.C.

Butler, Jon
1983   *The Huguenots in America: A Refugee People in New World Society.* Harvard Historical Monographs 72. Harvard University Press, Cambridge, Mass.
2003   The Huguenots and the American Immigrant Experience. In *Memory and Identity: The Huguenots in France and the Atlantic Diaspora*, edited by Bertrand Van Ruymbeke and Randy J. Sparks, 194–207. University of South Carolina Press, Columbia.

Ferguson, Leland
1992   *Uncommon Ground: Archaeology and Early African America, 1650–1800.* Smithsonian Institution, Washington, D.C.

Franzwa, Gregory M.
1973 [1967]   *The Story of Old Ste. Genevieve.* Patrice Press, Gerald, Mo.

Gums, Bonnie L.
1988   *Archaeology at French Colonial Cahokia.* Studies in Illinois Archaeology No. 3. Illinois Historic Preservation Agency, Springfield.

Gums, Bonnie L., William R. Iseminger, Molly E. McKenzie, and Dennis Nichols
1991   The French Colonial Villages of Cahokia and Prairie du Pont, Illinois. In *French Colonial Architecture: The Illinois Country and the Western Great Lakes*, edited by John A. Walthall, 85–122. University of Illinois Press, Urbana.

Hirsch, A. H.
1928 *The Huguenots of Colonial South Carolina*. Duke University Press, Durham, N.C.

Horry, Elias
1807–1808 Letters to Thomas Horry, 1807–1808. (43/810) Manuscript. South Carolina Historical Society, Charleston.

Nash, R. C.
2003 Huguenot Merchants and the Development of South Carolina's Slave-Plantation and Atlantic Trading Economy, 1680–1775. In *Memory and Identity: The Huguenots in France and the Atlantic Diaspora*, edited by Bertrand Van Ruymbeke and Randy J. Sparks, 209–240. University of South Carolina Press, Columbia.

Shlasko, Ellen
1997 *Carolina Gold: Economic and Social Change on a South Carolina Rice Plantation*. Ph.D. diss., Yale University. University Microfilms, Ann Arbor, Mich.
2002 Frenchmen and Africans in South Carolina: Cultural Interaction on the Eighteenth Century Frontier. In *Another's Country: Archaeological and Historical Perspectives on Cultural Interactions in the Southern Colonies*, edited by J. W. Joseph and Martha Zierden, 133–144. University of Alabama Press, Tuscaloosa.

Steen, Carl
1999 Stirring the Ethnic Stew in the South Carolina Backcountry: John de la Howe and Lethe Farm. In *Historical Archaeology, Identity Formation, and the Interpretation of Ethnicity*, edited by Maria Franklin and Garrett Fesler, 93–120. Colonial Williamsburg Foundation, Williamsburg, Va.

Van Ruymbeke, Bertrand
2003 Minority Survival: The Huguenot Paradigm in France and the Diaspora. In *Memory and Identity: The Huguenots in France and the Atlantic Diaspora*, edited by Bertrand Van Ruymbeke and Randy J. Sparks, 1–25. University of South Carolina Press, Columbia.

Walthall, John A.
1991 French Colonial Fort Massac: Architecture and Ceramic Patterning. In *French Colonial Architecture: The Illinois Country and the Western Great Lakes*, edited by John A. Walthall, 42–64. University of Illinois Press, Urbana.

Wheaton, Thomas R., and Patrick H. Garrow
1985 Acculturation and the Archaeological Record in the Carolina Lowcountry. In *The Archaeology of Slavery and Plantation Life*, edited by Theresa A. Singleton, 239–259. Academic Press, New York.

Zierden, Martha A., L. M. Drucker, and J. Calhoun
1986 *Home Upriver: Rural Life on Daniel's Island, Berkeley County, South Carolina*. Carolina Archaeological Services / Charleston Museum, Charleston, S.C.

3

French Refugees and Slave Abuse in Frederick County, Maryland

Jean Payen de Boisneuf and the Vincendière Family
at L'Hermitage Plantation

SARA RIVERS-COFIELD

Among the properties owned by Monocacy National Battlefield in Frederick County, Maryland, is a 274-acre tract known as the Best Farm. In the 1790s, a family of French refugees, fleeing the Reign of Terror in France and the subsequent slave uprising in Saint-Domingue (now Haiti), established a plantation at the site that they called L'Hermitage.

In 2000, Monocacy National Battlefield launched an Archaeological Identification and Evaluation Study of the Best Farm, which was being considered as a possible location for a new visitor's center (Figure 3.1). In an effort to inform the project about the French refugee occupation of the site, the Maryland Historical Trust sponsored a graduate internship designed to draw together archaeological studies of plantation sites in Maryland and Virginia as well as the Caribbean, and combine this context with primary historical research on the family that occupied the site. This study was designed to identify practices that the family may have carried with them from France and the Caribbean, and consider how this imported vision may have manifested itself on the landscape. What would a French-Caribbean plantation owner build if the plantation were removed to northern Maryland? Was the family heavily influenced by the local cultural and physical landscape? And how did the trauma of the French and Saint-Domingue revolutions affect the life that this specific family established in Frederick County?

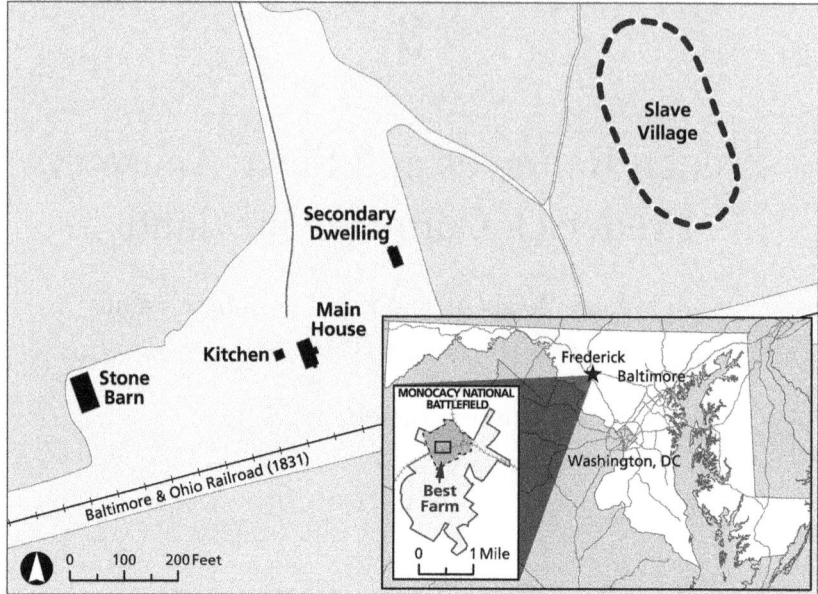

Figure 3.1. L'Hermitage Plantation, Monocacy National Battlefield, Frederick County, Maryland. The parcel of land is now popularly known as the Best Farm because the Best family lived there during the Civil War. In the plan view of the site, the stone house with the white upper story is labeled the "Secondary Dwelling" because of the presence of a larger extant house at the site today. Courtesy of Monocacy National Battlefield, National Park Service.

The subsequent research performed by the author revealed a story of a refugee family that established a lifestyle centered on large-scale ownership of slaves, including blatantly inhumane treatment of slaves that contributed to an antagonistic relationship between L'Hermitage residents and the surrounding community. These details, in combination with contextual data compiled from plantation archaeology in Maryland and the Caribbean, have helped to shape the direction of the excavations conducted at the Best Farm and interpretations of the resources unearthed there so far.

Becoming Refugees

L'Hermitage Plantation was founded when its inhabitants, the Vincendière family and Jean Payen de Boisneuf, were forced out of Saint-Domingue and France by the French Revolution and subsequent slave uprising in

Saint-Domingue. In 1780, Saint-Domingue was the richest French colony, with exports from the relatively small island outpacing those of the United States (Babb 1954:13–14). The wealth of the nation came from the utilization of enslaved labor to produce high-demand crops such as sugar and indigo. By 1789, the colony's population was comprised of about 54,000 white planters, 36,000 free mulattos, and over 675,000 enslaved individuals (Blackburn 1997:440). The cruel regime of enslaved human labor that created the island's riches also created an imbalanced population with the majority forced into such harsh working conditions that suicide and infanticide were not uncommon, and thousands of new slaves were imported each year to keep up populations (Geggus 1982:25; Rivers 2002:28–29).

When the French Revolution broke out, Jean Payen de Boisneuf was associated with a crowd of French politicians who supported the revolution in France as long as the situation in Saint-Domingue remained status quo (Childs 1940). As the proprietor of three large sugar plantations in central Saint-Domingue, Boisneuf was active in the colony's trade and politics, and he used what political clout he had to maintain the system of slavery upon which his livelihood depended (Mastromarino 2000:77–78, 385–386; Ministère des Finances 1832).

Slavery and the subjugation of free mulattos were not politically supportable when the ideas of *"Liberté, Egalité, Fraternité"* swept in with the French Revolution, however. Educated Saint-Domingue mulattos in Paris demanded equal rights when the French Revolution broke out. Their movement fueled the abolition movement in France, which quickly spread to Saint-Domingue, and by August 1791 Saint-Domingue was experiencing a revolution of its own (Reinhardt 2000:19).

In his capacity as a member of the Estates General of France and the Colonial Assembly of Saint-Domingue, Boisneuf and a colleague traveled to Philadelphia in November 1791 to appeal for U.S. military aid in halting the uprising. The two deputies met with Secretary of State Thomas Jefferson, who delivered their letter of appeal to Congress, but the United States took no action, and Boisneuf returned to France (Mastromarino 2000:77–78).

In 1793, Boisneuf attempted to return to Saint-Domingue by way of the United States, but word of the deteriorating situation in Saint-Domingue prevented him from completing his trip (Catterall 1968:56). In the summer of 1793, the white population of the colony lost all control as Saint-Domingue revolutionaries burned the capital, Cap Français, and massacred many of the white residents. Saint-Domingue's white, mulatto, and enslaved residents fled the island to Cuba, Louisiana, South Carolina, Maryland, and other U.S. states (Babb 1954; Fiehrer 1992:26).

Boisneuf decided to remain in the United States until the situation calmed down, for the political atmosphere in France may have been just as dangerous for him as it was in the colony. By 1793, Boisneuf was socializing with a group of Frenchmen in Philadelphia that one Republican sympathizer described as "the most gangrenous aristocrats," indicating that Boisneuf was out of favor with the Jacobins leading the Reign of Terror (Childs 1940:109, 163). Unable to return to the colony, and apparently unwilling to return to revolutionary France, Boisneuf took up residence in Maryland with his cousin's wife, Madame Marguerite Magnan de la Vincendière, and her children (Catterall 1968:55–56).

Saint-Domingue Refugees in Maryland

Maryland was an attractive location for refugees fleeing Saint-Domingue thanks to strong trade ties that connected Saint-Domingue and Maryland ports. Hundreds of refugees fleeing by sea stepped onto ships already destined for Baltimore (Babb 1954:63; Morrow 2000:123). Many Marylanders were sympathetic to the refugees, who arrived with horrific depictions of the rebellion led by the "cannibal insurgent bondsmen" (Fiehrer 1992:28). Reports of the massacre filled the Baltimore newspapers, prompting residents to open their homes to refugees in need and launch benefits to raise money for them. The 1793 wave brought 53 ships with approximately 1,000 white and 500 enslaved refugees to Baltimore (Rivers 2002:34–36). By 1794, there were more refugees needing aid in Maryland than in any other U.S. state (Babb 1954:86).

As refugees flooded the country, fear spread that slaveholders in the United States might suffer a similar uprising if they did not keep the slaves arriving from Saint-Domingue under tight control. White Virginians referred to the enslaved refugees as "infected with the contagion of liberty," and Louisiana prohibited importation of Saint-Dominguan slaves altogether (Debien and Le Gardeur 1992:146; Egerton 2000:96). These fears were not entirely unfounded. In the decade of the 1790s, slave uprisings in the United States increased by 150 percent, and many Americans blamed the refugees (Babb 1954:242–243). In order to maintain control, various states with a high number of refugees passed laws to regulate them.

Maryland's response was to limit the number of slaves that the refugees could import. In 1792, the legislature adopted "An act respecting the slaves of certain French subjects," which allowed the refugees to retain five household servants for a head of household and three domestic servants for a single man, as long as they registered these individuals in their county of residence (Maryland 1792). This law compelled Boisneuf and the Vincendières to register their imported slaves when they arrived in Frederick County, Maryland, marking the first documentary evidence of their intent to settle there.

The Founding of L'Hermitage

On December 28, 1793, Boisneuf and the Vincendières registered 12 enslaved individuals in Frederick County. As head of household, Marguerite Magnan de la Vincendière registered five servants: Janvier, age 24; François Arajou, age 20; Jean Sans-nom, age 16; Véronique, also 16; and Maurice, age 15. Her sons also registered slaves, presumably within their rights as single men, though the youngest son, Henry, was only 11 years old at the time (Russell 2001:230). Étienne Paul Mario de la Vincendière registered three servants: Marianne, age 40; Cécile, age 18; and Souris, age 15. Henry de la Vincendière registered Saint-Louis, age 14. Finally, Boisneuf registered a man and two children: Pierre Louis, age 35; Lambert, age 5; and Fillete, age 8 (Rivers 2002).

Along with Madame Vincendière's daughters, this group presumably comprised the founding settlers at L'Hermitage Plantation, though it is unclear how the group could afford the undertaking. It is possible that an inheritance from another refugee, Pierre Laberon, who arrived with the family just before dying in 1794, may have supported the plantation, but the amount of money he bequeathed to Boisneuf and the Vincendières is unknown (Rivers 2005). Marguerite and her husband, Étienne Bellumeau de la Vincendière, were estranged at the time of the revolutions—she in France and he in Saint-Domingue. Étienne had been a planter in Saint-Domingue, but he fled in December 1792 "to avoid being murdered by the assassins armed by the Civil Commissioners Polverel and Sonthonax against all the planters of . . . St. Domingo" (South Carolina Will Book

D 1800–1807). He lived out his life in Charleston, South Carolina, as a destitute refugee who relied heavily on charity (Rivers 2005).

Boisneuf was in debt when he arrived in the United States and remained an insolvent debtor until his death, so he could not have backed the venture unless his assets were hidden in the Vincendières' name (Rivers 2005). He did play an important founding role at the plantation, however, as he negotiated the purchase of the first 451 acres that would comprise L'Hermitage on behalf of Victoire Vincendière, Marguerite's oldest daughter. It is unclear how or why, but Victoire Vincendière, who was 17 years old in 1794, legally owned all of the family's assets from the time they arrived in Maryland, including all of the land and slaves that many observers of the plantation attributed to Boisneuf. Despite Victoire's legal status as owner, evidence suggests that no one resident of the plantation completely controlled its formation, but rather the Vincendières, Boisneuf, and other refugees that they took in worked and lived there together for the benefit of the whole group (Rivers 2005).

By 1798, the plantation had grown to 748 acres, including the land now owned by Monocacy National Battlefield (Rivers 2002). Large plantations were still common in Frederick County, but L'Hermitage was unusual in that it was populated with a very high number of enslaved laborers for its size and location. Cereal crops such as grain, wheat, and clover dominated the area, and fewer laborers were necessary for growing these crops than the tobacco that dominated southern Maryland. Typical cereal plantations of 700–1,000 acres had 12–25 slaves (Rivers 2002:53).

L'Hermitage broke with local trends. With a population of 90 enslaved individuals in the 1800 census, Victoire was one of the largest slaveholders in Frederick County. There were iron furnaces in the area that might have created opportunities to rent slaves out and draw income for the family, but the Caribbean background of the refugees may have been a greater motivator in the acquisition of such a large number of individuals. Prior to the revolution, Marguerite's husband had been a planter, her parents had owned an indigo plantation, and Boisneuf had owned three large sugar plantations. Any attempt to re-create what they lost would have compelled them to own a large population of slaves, and they may have done so whether they truly needed them to work the land or not.

Slave Abuse at L'Hermitage

Evidence that the refugees attempted to perpetuate their Saint-Domingue lifestyle is found in their treatment of the slaves at L'Hermitage. Disciplinary practices varied from plantation to plantation, but mutilation, whipping, and other violence has been recorded throughout the Caribbean and plantation-holding areas of North America (Blackburn 1997). Since the proprietors at L'Hermitage had derived their livelihood from a regime of forced human labor, they probably arrived in Maryland accustomed to using such violence to maintain control. Atrocities committed against slaves were by no means limited to French colonials, nor is it supportable based on this author's research to conclude that the French in general were more cruel than slaveholders from other countries, but the losses that the proprietors of L'Hermitage suffered upon their unwilling expulsion from Saint-Domingue may well have escalated the violence they employed in Maryland.

Not only did the family lose their land and livelihood, but they also lost relatives. One of Victoire's uncles was reputedly shot by a slave while seated at his dinner table (Lowe 1913:17). From the perspective of Boisneuf and the Vincendières, these were crimes perpetrated by individuals whom they had been conditioned to see as highly inferior beings—mere chattel to be exploited as a means to a profit. The revolution created a situation ripe for a volatile emotional response from the refugees. While the proprietors of L'Hermitage may have employed the exact same methods in Maryland as they had in Saint-Domingue, it is also possible that the uprising that attained freedom for thousands of enslaved laborers in Saint-Domingue led to an increase in violence visited upon the slaves at L'Hermitage. Either way, historical documents show that the practices they employed were considered extreme and illegal in Frederick County, despite that fact that it was not against the law to beat a slave in Maryland (Rivers 2005).

The most potent account of slave abuse at L'Hermitage was recorded by the Polish writer and politician Julian Niemcewicz, who saw the plantation as he traveled from Georgetown to Frederick in June 1798 (Niemcewicz 1965:111–112). The following is an excerpt from his journal:

> June 15. After dozing till four in the morning, I set out the next day for Frederik Town. . . . I took up my favorite place, that is, on the

driver's seat next to the citizen driver. The reasons for my predilection to this place are, coolness, the fresh and open air, a view on all sides, and finally a pleasant, interesting and intimate conversation with the citizen coachman. My friend the coachman was a third-generation German settled in America.... The driver not only told me about everything I asked, but even things I did not ask; and we were yet 40 miles from Frideriks [sic] Town when I already knew the whole history of the town and its environs.... Four miles from the town we forded the river [blank: Monocacy]. On its banks one can see a row of wooden houses and one stone house with the upper storeys [sic] painted white. This is the residence of a Frenchman called Payant [sic: Boisneuf], who left San Domingo with a substantial sum and with it bought two or three thousand acres of land and a few hundred negroes whom he treats with the greatest tyranny. One can see on the home farm instruments of torture, stocks, wooden horses, whips, etc. Two or three negroes crippled with torture have brought legal action against him, but the matter has not yet been settled. This man is 60 years old, without children or relatives; he keeps an old French woman with two daughters; she, in sweetness of humour, even surpasses him. This charming group has caused about 50 legal actions to be brought. They foam with rage, beat the negroes, complain and fight with each other. In these ways does this man use his wealth, and comforts his life in its descent toward the grave. (Niemcewicz 1965:111–112)

In order to fully explore the implications of the Niemcewicz account, it is necessary to point out that it expresses a bias common among the residents of Frederick at the time. An abundance of available land attracted French refugees to Frederick in the late eighteenth century, but the demographics of the area were primarily dominated by settlers of German Protestant descent who migrated south to Maryland from Pennsylvania as land there became increasingly scarce (Rivers 2002:38). These German residents, including the coachman relating the story of the plantation to Niemcewicz, were inclined to dislike all of the Frenchmen in the area. Aside from the usual French/German ethnic tension, resentment grew when the French Revolution disrupted the grain trade upon which area farmers relied (Niemcewicz 1965:111–119). Frederick was a border county between tobacco-growing regions to the south and Pennsylvania to the north, where slavery was an unpopular and marginal practice (Blackburn 1997:359, 476–477). By 1850, Frederick was one of the counties of northern Maryland that had developed industries and a free labor system (Fields 1985).

The Neimcewicz account depends upon a storyteller who may have had these "northern" sympathies and who clearly disliked the proprietors of L'Hermitage, but the distaste he expressed for the family's actions is an important part of the story. Without individuals like him, the cruelty at L'Hermitage may never have been recorded. Instead, travelers along the road saw acts of torture, and several witnesses were offended enough to testify in court. While the coachman's tale included some exaggerations, his description of a stone house with the upper story painted white matches a structure at L'Hermitage that still stands in 2009, and archival records indicate that the lawsuits he mentioned did exist.

Most of the family's appearances in court relate to debts that Boisneuf acquired in town and Victoire's participation in bailing him out (Frederick County Court Docket 1797). Just as Niemcewicz indicated, however, Victoire and Boisneuf were also charged with abusing their slaves. In 1797, the state of Maryland brought Victoire up on charges for assaulting a slave named Rosina Cécille, and also for "Especially cruelly and immercifully beating her slave Jenny" (Frederick County Court Docket 1797). Jenny's case was dismissed by a grand jury, and Rosina Cécille's case was also struck off, but Victoire did have to pay at least $272 in court fees (Frederick County Court Docket 1797; Frederick County Court Minutes, March 1797:65; Reed 2004:99). Similarly, the 1797 Criminal Dockets charged Boisneuf on six separate counts for "Cruelly and immercifully beating and whipping his slave[s]" Harry, Jerry, Abraham, Stephen, Soll, and George. Nine witnesses testified against him, but these cases were also dismissed, possibly because it was not illegal to beat a slave in Maryland (Frederick County Court Docket 1797; Rivers 2005).

Boisneuf was not acquitted of all cruelty charges, however. Another long list of witnesses came forward in a case brought on behalf of the slave Shadrack Hinton, and this time a jury found Boisneuf guilty of "Excessively, cruelly, and unmercifully beating, etc. of his slave Negro Shadrack" (Frederick County Court Minutes, March 1797:91; Reed 2004:99). Boisneuf also was convicted for "not sufficiently clothing and feeding his negroes etc." (Frederick County Court Minutes, March 1797:97; Reed 2004). It was perhaps their failure to feed their slaves that landed Boisneuf and

Victoire in court again in 1799 when Rebecca Dulany, owner of neighboring land, sued them for "trespass by slaves." The term "trespass" has several legal meanings, including "unlawfully striking, chasing, if alive, and carrying away to the damage of the plaintiff, a personal chattel" ('Lectric Law Library 2010). The case may be evidence that hungry slaves from L'Hermitage were stealing food from the neighbors. Victoire paid damages in the amount of $251 after the case went to trial (Frederick County Court Dockets 1799).

A final case involving a slave at L'Hermitage demonstrates that members of the community did more than testify about slave cruelty; they must have intervened and done some research in order to help the slaves. In 1797, Pierre Louis, one of the slaves registered by Boisneuf in 1793, filed a petition for freedom on the grounds that Maryland law prohibited his importation. As previously stated, single male refugees were permitted by Maryland law to import three of their domestic slaves. Pierre Louis had been the domestic servant of Boisneuf's deceased brother prior to his importation to Maryland. Representatives on his behalf argued that because Louis had belonged to Boisneuf's brother, not Boisneuf himself, Boisneuf had no right to register him in the first place (Catterall 1968:55–56). Frederick County Court minutes indicate that Boisneuf and Victoire tried unsuccessfully to keep Pierre Louis from attending the trial. The court issued a "summons on complaint for ill usage contrary to their recognizance entered into to permit the complainant to attend the court to present his petition for freedom" (Frederick County Court Minutes 1797). Thanks to the court's intervention, their efforts failed. Three years after his arrival in Maryland, a jury of 12 granted Pierre Louis his freedom, and though Boisneuf and Victoire appealed, the ruling was upheld (Catterall 1968:55–56). This case serves as evidence of outside intervention because somebody identified the legal loophole that would grant Louis's freedom and made sure that he could appear in court, despite Boisneuf and Victoire's attempts to stop him.

Their numerous appearances in court evidently weighed on the proprietors of L'Hermitage. On January 16, 1806, the following announcement appeared in the *Frederick-Town Herald*:

> TAKE NOTICE: I do hereby forewarn all persons whomsoever from dealing with my slaves from this date, without their having leave in writing from me. If any person or persons should hereafter disregard

this notice, I will put the law in force against them. V. Vincendière January 11 (*Frederick-Town Herald* 1806)

The Decline of L'Hermitage

The settlements that the family had to pay with regard to their many lawsuits were a draw on their resources and may have contributed to the downfall of the plantation. Over half of L'Hermitage Plantation was advertised for sale in January 1816 and again in 1819 (Rivers 2002:39). Unless the family rented laborers to nearby farms or industries, owning so many enslaved individuals for a wheat- and grain-producing plantation such as theirs may have been a failing venture anyway.

Financial hardship may not have been the only motivation for selling L'Hermitage, however. The advertisements to sell land correspond closely with the deaths of the elder generation of the family. Boisneuf died in October 1816, and Marguerite Vincendière followed in 1819 (Russell 2001). Given the timing of the advertisements, it is possible that Boisneuf's health was failing, and Victoire, whose roots in Saint-Domingue slavery did not run as deep, decided to abandon the plantation.

Victoire started selling off L'Hermitage slaves in 1822. By the time she succeeded in selling L'Hermitage in 1828, she had sold at least 25 individuals, including 17 slaves whom she sold to a dealer from Louisiana. One of the slaves sold south was Fillelle, who had been eight years old when Boisneuf imported her to Maryland from Saint-Domingue. As the years passed following the sale of L'Hermitage, Victoire sold or manumitted all but a very few of her slaves, and her will manumitted the three slaves remaining in her possession when she died in 1852 (Rivers 2002:57–58).

Instead of clinging to a proprietary lifestyle, it seems that Victoire and her sister Adelaide preferred to express their cultural affiliation through the Catholic Church. In 1913, Victoire's niece, Esther Lowe, gave an account of the sisters' Catholicism:

> They were strictly religious Catholics and at that period there were few of such—of their social standing—in Frederick. The population was mostly German, and . . . the teachings of Calvin and Luther, bitterly antagonistic to Catholicism, had taken so strong a hold on their prejudices as to control neighborly feelings. . . . I remember how systematically once a year [Adelaide Vincendière] called

formally upon certain persons of her acquaintance—how formal her demeanor, and a remark I once heard her make speaking of Mrs. T. "She is very sweet, but we are like two lambs upon the brink of a precipice—a gulf between; we look across the gulf and smile at each other; but that impassable gulf is there." She seemed never able to throw off that feeling. (Lowe 1913:12)

An examination of the Vincendière sisters' finances demonstrates their support of St. John's Catholic Church in Frederick. After they sold L'Hermitage, Victoire and Adelaide provided a $10,000 cash mortgage to the St. John's reverends to keep up Catholic assets in the town. They then built a home less than a block from the church and engaged in a number of Catholic charities (Lowe 1913; Rivers 2002:54–56). Of their charitable work, Victoire's niece claimed that "self-sacrifice was their rule of life. They were most generous and appeal from any charity was never unheeded, unless it savored of Protestant progress, and in that they were as stern as rocks. No compromise was the watchword and to give to the rearing of Protestant churches was considered by them as such" (Lowe 1913:10). Not surprisingly, their charitable efforts and devout faith, rather than the cruel enslavement practices at L'Hermitage, were most prominent in Esther's recollections of the family.

Locating L'Hermitage Slave Village

The background research conducted on the refugee family has helped to guide archaeological research and place its findings in context. With the aid of the Niemcewicz travel account, archaeologists learned that the "row of wooden houses" that most likely comprised the plantation's slave village was located in view of the main road and a "stone house with the upper storeys [sic] painted white." One extant structure fits the description of the house, and this structure stands atop a slope that looks down on the Georgetown Pike (Route 355) (Figure 3.2). The Georgetown Pike has shifted slightly, but is essentially the same route taken by Niemcewicz in 1798. Between the road and the house is a 20.14-acre field (Bies and Gallagher 2003).

For purposes of surveying the field between the house and the road, five metal detector transects were laid out at regular intervals on an east–west axis. These transects covered 2.24 acres, or 11.2 percent of the field.

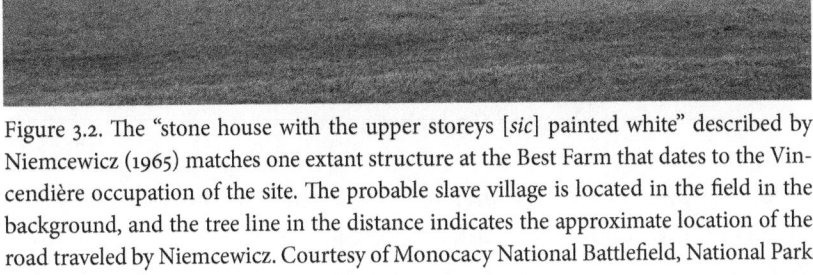

Figure 3.2. The "stone house with the upper storeys [sic] painted white" described by Niemcewicz (1965) matches one extant structure at the Best Farm that dates to the Vincendière occupation of the site. The probable slave village is located in the field in the background, and the tree line in the distance indicates the approximate location of the road traveled by Niemcewicz. Courtesy of Monocacy National Battlefield, National Park Service.

Experienced metal detectors swept each transect twice, and all targets were flagged and excavated by staff archaeologists. Artifacts received unique numbers and were mapped with an electronic total station. Data was then downloaded and incorporated into GIS so that distributions could be mapped on the landscape (Bies and Gallagher 2003).

As with most of the areas surveyed at the Best Farm, Civil War–related artifacts such as military buttons and accoutrements were recovered, but the survey also identified a dense concentration of domestic artifacts in the western portion of the field near the stone and wood house. This domestic scatter ran 400 feet north–south and 100 feet east–west, with the long axis paralleling the Georgetown Pike. Buttons, eating utensils, nails, coins, tools, and padlocks were among the metal finds, and in the course of excavating these targets nonmetal items including bricks, ceramics, glass, and pipes were also recovered. Diagnostic artifacts such as 71 buttons, eight pearlware sherds, and three coins with the dates 1808, 1809, and 1811, respectively, indicate an occupation from the late-eighteenth to the mid-nineteenth centuries (Bies and Gallagher 2003). The assemblage is comparable to those found on slave village sites at Poplar Forest and Yaughan and Curriboo plantations (Beasley 2003:37).

More excavation is certainly needed to define the slave village, but the design of the metal-detector survey leaves little doubt as to its identification. The Archaeological Identification and Evaluation Study of the Best Farm was a comprehensive survey of the 274-acre property. Each field was either surface collected, shovel tested, or surveyed with metal-detector transects (Beasley 2005). Several nail concentrations were identified, as were Civil War encampments, but the site between the stone and wood house and Route 355 was the only one containing the density of domestic debris that would be expected of a slave settlement. Given the time period, location, historical documents, and absence of any other comparable artifact concentrations on the property, Monocacy archaeologists are confident that this is the location of the main slave quarters (Baker 2004; Beasley 2003; Bies and Gallagher 2003).

By the time archaeologists located the slave village, park officials had decided to place the new visitor's center elsewhere, so the site is not slated for development, and no further excavations are planned at this time. When a more in-depth research excavation does take place, however, the background research conducted by the author may serve as a quick reference that archaeologists can utilize to understand the plantation. Although too lengthy to include here, the background study not only compiled research on the family, but it also summarized previous research on slave cemeteries, African-derived spiritual practices, overall plantation layouts, and layouts and yard usage within slave villages that can aid archaeologists seeking to understand the physical and cultural landscape at L'Hermitage (Rivers 2002, 2005).

As an example of the usefulness of this context, the placement of the village at L'Hermitage has already supported one of the predictions derived from the compilation of archaeological work in the Caribbean. After synthesizing information on Caribbean plantation layouts, in particular Higman's (1987) study of plantation layouts and Armstrong and Kelly's (2000) analysis of the Seville plantation, the author hypothesized that

> if [the refugees] reacted to the revolt by trying to exert more control over the slaves, then it is likely that the slave dwellings would have been organized in efficient rows or barracks within the view of the main house. Alternatively, if the Vincendières decided to try to grant their slaves increased autonomy to try to prevent them from wanting to rebel, there might have been greater freedom allowed to the enslaved to arrange their houses based upon topography, desired yard arrangements, and social and family groupings. (Rivers 2002:26)

The placement of the slave houses in a row directly in front and downhill of the proprietor's house at L'Hermitage is consistent with the archaeological footprint of a plantation practicing tight control over enslaved people, and this in turn is consistent with historical data on the French refugees who inhabited the site.

Conclusion

Thanks to its discovery as part of the Archaeological Identification and Evaluation Study at the Best Farm, Monocacy National Battlefield now knows that it has stewardship of a unique slave village site with enormous research potential. L'Hermitage represents an experiment where large-scale sugar and indigo planters of the Caribbean tried to remake themselves in a region of Maryland that was steadily moving away from dependence upon slave labor.

Primary historical research revealed a painful story of a family clinging to a lifestyle that clashed with their community, but little is known about the enslaved individuals at L'Hermitage aside from the evidence that they suffered torture and intolerable conditions. Archaeologists for the National Park Service have already been thinking about the insights that excavations might provide into the lives of these individuals (Baker 2004). For example, will they find differences between quarters belonging to Saint-Domingue slaves versus their American- or African-born counterparts? And if so, can archaeology tell us about how they interacted?

Armed with a detailed context for the site, archaeologists are well positioned to plan a research excavation that may fill in the stories that have not yet surfaced. In the meantime, Monocacy National Battlefield can continue to protect the site and decide how best to incorporate the story of Maryland's own French-Caribbean plantation into its public interpretation programs.

References Cited

Armstrong, Douglas, and Kenneth G. Kelly
2000 Settlement Patterns and the Origins of African Jamaican Society: Seville Plantation, St. Ann's Bay, Jamaica. *Ethnohistory* 47(2): 369–397.

Babb, Winston C.
1954 French Refugees from Saint-Domingue to the Southern United States: 1791–1810. Ph. D. diss., University of Virginia, Charlottesville.

Baker, Joe
2004 L'Hermitage Plantation: Investigating a Landscape of Pain at Monocacy National Battlefield. *Common Ground* (Winter): 14–25.

Beasley, Joy
2003 The Occupational History of the Best Farm: Research and Excavation Results. *Maryland Archeology* 39(1&2): 31–48.

Beasley, Joy, editor
2005 *Archaeological Overview and Assessment and Identification and Evaluation Study of the Best Farm: Monocacy National Battlefield, Frederick, Maryland.* Occasional Report No. 18 of the Regional Archaeology Program, National Capital Region of the National Park Service. U.S. Department of the Interior, Washington, D.C.

Bies, Brandon S., and Mark Gallagher
2003 The Use of Systematic Metal-Detector Surveys as a Site Identification Method in Historic Landscapes. *Maryland Archeology* 39(1&2): 61–73.

Blackburn, Robin
1997 *The Making of New World Slavery: From the Baroque to the Modern, 1492–1800.* Verso, New York.

Catterall, Helen Turncliff
1968 *Judicial Cases Concerning American Slavery and the Negro.* Octagon Books, New York.

Childs, Francis Sergeant
1940 *French Refugee Life in the United States 1790–1800.* Johns Hopkins University Press, Baltimore.

Debien, Gabriel, and René Le Gardeur
1992 The Saint-Domingue Refugees in Louisiana, 1792–1804. In *The Road to Louisiana: The Saint-Domingue Refugees 1792–1809*, edited by Carl A. Brasseaux and Glenn R. Conrad, 113–243. Center for Louisiana Studies, Lafayette.

Egerton, Douglas R.
2000 The Tricolor in Black and White: The French Revolution in Gabriel's Virginia. In *Slavery in the Caribbean Francophone World: Distant Voices, Forgotten Acts,*

     Forged Identities, edited by Doris Y. Kadish, 91–105. University of Georgia Press, Athens.

Fiehrer, Thomas
1992   From *La Tortue* to *La Louisiane*: An Unfathomed Legacy. In *The Road to Louisiana: The Saint-Domingue Refugees 1792–1809*, edited by Carl A. Brasseaux and Glen R. Conrad, 1–30. Center for Louisiana Studies, Lafayette.

Fields, Barbara Jeanne
1985   *Slavery and Freedom on the Middle Ground: Maryland during the 19th Century.* Yale University Press, New Haven, Conn.

Frederick County Court Dockets
1797   MSA S498-3. Maryland State Archives, Annapolis.
1799   MSA S498-4. Maryland State Archives, Annapolis.

Frederick County Court Minutes
1797   Maryland State Archives, Annapolis.

Frederick-Town Herald
1806   Ad placed by Victoire Vincendière about her slaves. 16 January.

Geggus, David P.
1982   *Slavery, War, and Revolution: The British Occupation of Saint Domingue, 1793–1798.* Oxford University Press, New York.

Higman, Barry W.
1987   The Spatial Economy of Jamaican Sugar Plantations: Cartographic Evidence from the Eighteenth and Nineteenth Centuries. *Journal of Historical Geography* 13(1): 17–39.

'Lectric Law Library
2010   The 'Lectric Law Library's Lexicon on Trespass. www.lectlaw.com/def2/t049.htm. Accessed June 2, 2010.

Lowe, Esther Winder Polk
1913   *Memories*. Tms (Photocopy). Enoch Louis Lowe Papers, Maryland Historical Society, Baltimore.

Maryland
1792   *Laws of Maryland, Chapter LVI: An Act respecting the slaves of certain French subjects.* Archives of Maryland, Vol. 3181, 688–689. Maryland State Archives, Annapolis.

Mastromarino, Mark, editor
2000   *The George Washington Papers, Presidential Series 9, September 1791–February 1792.* University Press of Virginia, Charlottesville.

Ministère des Finances
1832   *État Détaille des Liquidations: Opérées Á l'Époque du I.er Janvier 1832.* Vols. 1–4. De l'Imprimerie Royale, Paris.

Morrow, Diane Batts
2000   Francophone Residents of Antebellum Baltimore and the Origins of the Oblate Sisters of Providence. In *Slavery in the Caribbean Francophone World: Distant Voices, Forgotten Acts, Forged Identities*, edited by Doris Y. Kadish, 129–139. University of Georgia Press, Athens.

Niemcewicz, Julian Ursyn
1965   *Under Their Vine and Fig Tree: Travels through America in 1797–1799, 1805 with some further account of life in New Jersey.* Translated and edited by Metchie J. E. Budka. Collections of the New Jersey Historical Society, Vol. 14. Grassman Publishing, Elizabeth, N.J.

Reed, Paula Stoner, with Edith B. Wallace
2004 [1999]   Cultural Resources, Monocacy National Battlefield. Manuscript on file, Monocacy National Battlefield. Paula S. Reed and Associates, Hagerstown, Md.

Reinhardt, Catherine
2000   French Caribbean Slaves Forge Their Own Ideal of Liberty in 1789. In *Slavery in the Caribbean Francophone World: Distant Voices, Forgotten Acts, Forged Identities*, edited by Doris Y. Kadish, 19–38. University of Georgia Press, Athens.

Rivers, Sara
2002   Contextualizing the Hermitage: A Maryland Plantation with French Caribbean Ties. Manuscript on file, University of Maryland, College Park.
2005   A French Caribbean Plantation in Maryland: Understanding the Regional and Global Context of L'Hermitage. In *Archeological Overview and Assessment and Identification and Evaluation Study of the Best Farm, Monocacy National Battlefield, Frederick, Maryland*, edited by Joy Beasley, 5.1–5.32. Occasional Report No. 18 of the Regional Archaeology Program, National Capital Region of the National Park Service. U.S. Department of the Interior, Washington D.C.

Russell, George Ely
2001   Frenchmen in Early Frederick County, Maryland. *Genealogist* 15(2): 225–255.

South Carolina Will Book D
1800–1807   Book D, Vol. 28, 323–326. South Carolina Department of Archives and History, Columbia.

4

Commoditization of Persons, Places, and Things during Biloxi's Second Tenure as Capital of French Colonial Louisiana

BARBARA THEDY HESTER

While archaeologists of eighteenth-century French colonial settlements may expect to find landscape configurations and artifact forms reflective of an ancien règime preoccupation with social and economic order, archaeological investigation may also reveal expressions of local resistance much akin to those mobilized in the contemporary era of globalization (Appadurai 2001; Dawdy 2008). Our ongoing research on and in the environs of the Biloxi peninsula, a region that served as administrative seat of French Louisiana on two separate occasions, is providing archival and archaeological evidence of these phenomena. Anomalous artifact forms excavated at Vieux Biloxi and Ship Island suggest the possibility of expedient designs, cultural contact modifications, and illicit interregional trade networks. While testing is still in the early stages and excavation continues at the Moran site in Nouveau Biloxi, osteometric and dental traits suggest the possibility of prohibited interethnic border crossings. Persistent transference of settlement location and redefinition of land tracts evidence deference to intransigent natural disorder.

The early eighteenth century saw a continuation of the ancien règime preoccupation with order and the centralization of power, influence, and economic gain, particularly as it began with Jean-Baptiste Colbert, *contrôleur général* during the reign of Louis XIV (King 1972). The order of the day *was* order, from the king at the pinnacle of power, authority, science, and reason, and his ministers, secretaries, and regional intendants, to the *États-Généraux* (three estates system) of clergy, nobility, and commoners. The masses at the lowest end of the social hierarchy were identified, assessed, managed, and classified via official reports, rolls, and censuses in the French *métropole*, an enumeration effort that reverberated to the colonies (King 1972:147–191; Dawdy 2008:153–158). At the edges of the colonial empire, cartographers prepared territories for ownership by appropriating and redefining already inhabited places, by crosscutting land expanses with rows of latitude and columns of longitude, and by apportioning territory by borders, town grids, and lot lines (Wood 2004:516; Dawdy 2008:158–162). A mercantile system of exchange orchestrated the distribution of goods and the apportionment of wealth (Thackeray and Findling 1998:49). *Captifs* and *forçats*—captive Africans, American Indians, and European social outcasts—were transformed into chattels and assessed according to their skill levels and capacities for work (Thackeray and Findling 1998:50; Hall 1992:67–68; Dawdy 2008:150–152, 296n.29).

This attempted imposition of order from the top encountered local resistance on the ground, just as in today's world the forces of "globalization from the top" meet with processes of "globalization from below" (Appadurai 2001:3). Therefore, archaeologists might do well to look to the ethnographic literature on "grassroots globalization" (Appadurai 2001:3) for an understanding of local resistance and improvisation and insights into artifact forms that may present themselves in archaeological contexts. Was the French government's scheme of wholesale commoditization from the top successful in the colonies, or was it met with resistance from the folk on the ground? Did Europeans, Africans, and American Indians carve their own version of social order from a unique encounter of persons, places, and things? This essay attempts to answer these questions within the context of the brief occupation of Biloxi from 1720 to 1722, a period of time that witnessed the demise of the proprietorship of John Law. My exploration of this period is guided by the settlement layout depicted on Le Blond de la Tour's 1722 map entitled *Carte de Partie de la Coste du Nouveau Biloxy, Avec Les Isles des Environs*, and this essay will address those sites on and in the environs of the Biloxi peninsula (Figure 4.1).

First, I provide a bit of historical background, following which I address the main topic of this essay, that is, the process of commoditization as conceptualized from above and archaeological evidence suggesting

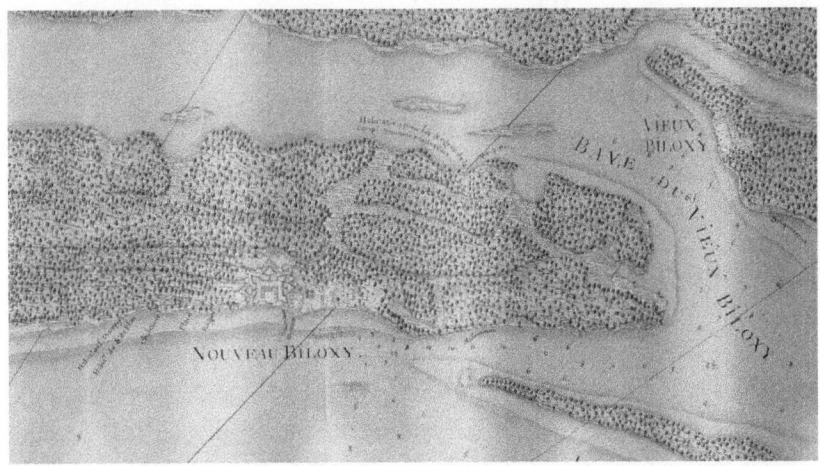

Figure 4.1. *Carte de Partie de la Coste du Nouveau Biloxy, Avec Les Isles des Environs*, by La Blond de la Tour, 1722. Courtesy of the Bibliothèque Nationale de France, Paris.

unique configurations of commoditization mobilized from below. At the conclusion of the essay, I offer tables of (known) surveys and excavations accomplished to date at the four sites discussed herein—Vieux Biloxi, Nouveau Biloxi, Ship Island, and the African Habitation site—located on and in the environs of the Biloxi peninsula during Biloxi's second tenure as colonial capital of French Louisiana.

Historical Background

In the late seventeenth century, France sought to strengthen its position in its "New World" colony by settling along the northern shores of the Gulf of Mexico and taking control of the mouth of the Mississippi River, and thereby securing its point of greatest vulnerability, the southernmost riverine access to the Mississippi Valley, Illinois Country, and Canada. Also, control of the area from the Mississippi Delta to the St. Lawrence River would thwart the western expansion of the British colonies that lined the eastern Atlantic seaboard (Giraud 1974a:11, 14). To accomplish these ends, France called upon the Canadian brothers Pierre Le Moyne, Sieur d'Iberville, and Jean-Baptiste Le Moyne, Sieur de Bienville, to reconnoiter the area and choose a suitable site to establish a colony. Finding the river's mouth log-jammed and unnavigable, the explorers looked to the east and chose a site on Biloxi Bay, where they began settlement of their Louisiana colony (Giraud 1974a:32–33).

Biloxi served as the administrative seat of French Louisiana over two separate periods of time; however, physically wedged between Mobile and New Orleans, it is oftentimes overlooked or forgotten in historical accounts of the colony. This is probably attributable to the fact that Mobile and New Orleans experienced longer spans of occupation and more established settlements during their administrative terms. While Biloxi served as capital for much shorter spans of time, these two periods may have been the most challenging and tumultuous periods of French colonial history, which may account for their brevity. First, Iberville faced the challenges of initial settlement in an alien environment and oppressive climate, instituted contact with the indigenous inhabitants of the area, and erected a fort in 1699. After two years of struggling to cultivate the colony and enduring untold hardship, he moved the capital to Mobile in 1702 (Giraud 1974a:44–45).

In the second and third decades of the eighteenth century, the French treasury faced impending bankruptcy due to the burdensome expense of war, particularly the War of the Spanish Succession. Unable to support his colonies, King Louis XIV looked to an infusion of funds and provisions from the private sector. In 1712, he granted Antoine Crozat monopolistic control of the colony of Louisiana, whose capital at this time was located in Mobile (Giraud 1974a:249). When the Crozat enterprise failed, the Duke of Orleans, regent for young Louis XV, conferred proprietary control to John Law in 1717, authorizing him to implement his scheme for financial recovery by replacing gold and silver specie with bank notes, credit, and stock and by sending thousands of Europeans and slaves to the colony (Giraud 1966:6–7). Mobile's tenure as administrative seat lasted until 1719 when Bienville, who assumed command after the death of his older brother, and the Council of Commerce of Louisiana decided to relocate the capital back to or near the site of original settlement due to heightened French-Spanish hostilities and a fierce hurricane that split Dauphin Island in two and created immense sand deposits that rendered the roadstead unnavigable (Rowland and Sanders 1932:281–283; Giraud 1966:311; Sullivan 1985:17). Biloxi's second tenure as capital of French Louisiana lasted until 1722, when the capital was finally transferred to New Orleans (Rowland and Sanders 1932:342–344; Giraud 1966:311–312, 314–315).

During the three years that followed the move from Mobile back to Biloxi, the capital was situated in two locales. In 1719, it was reestablished on the site of, or in the vicinity of, Iberville's first settlement on the eastern shore of Biloxi Bay, and it came to be known as Vieux Biloxi. From 1720 to 1722, it was located in Nouveau Biloxi, a site situated on the southern Gulf shore of the Biloxi peninsula on the western side of the bay. While living conditions were expected to improve with the relocation of the settlement to Nouveau Biloxi near a freshwater source and away from the mosquito-infested marshes of Vieux Biloxi, the dire circumstances in the Louisiana colony were only intensified by the sheer numbers of immigrants who were deposited on the shores of the Mississippi Sound. The massive immigration effort set into motion by the forces from above—namely, John Law and the French government—placed formidable stressors on incoming and local populations, creating a set of circumstances ripe for a response fashioned from below and a context begging for the mobilization of change.

Commoditization from Above

Crisis oftentimes engenders change in unconventional ways. With the postwar economy of France nearly bankrupt, the French government looked to the private sector for funds, and in exchange, it transferred proprietary control over its Louisiana colony, first to Antoine Crozat (from 1712 to 1717) and then to John Law (from 1717 to 1720) (Giraud 1966:6–7, 1974a:249), despite the fact that such monopolistic endowments during the Colbert administration proved to be failures (King 1972:233–236; Allain 1995:11). John Law was in control during Biloxi's second tenure as capital; however, his enterprise met its demise only a year after relocation from Mobile (Garber 2000:95–103).

During the "proprietorship period" (Dawdy 2008), profit was the immediate goal of the bureaucrats, while survival was the main goal, and possibly the only goal, of the immigrants and settlers. In a massive effort to sow colonial success and reap concomitant economic gains, colonial proprietors, sanctioned by the French government, attempted the mobilization of people, as well as places and things, into a commodity context (Appadurai 1986:15). First, in the age of colonization, maps were tools in the production of empire (Wood 2004), and the Louisiana colony itself was commoditized through initial claim and subsequent settlement, followed by trade, distribution, and consumption of territory through the segmentation of the colony into concessions (land grants) (Giraud 1966:154–220) and the apportionment of profits through John Law's massive stock offering designed to generate wealth and restore the financial solvency of the Crown (Garber 2000).

Second, things were commoditized according to the dictates of mercantilism (King 1972:232), and mercantilists of the seventeenth and eighteenth centuries recognized the economic advantages that lay in the far-flung reaches of the colonial empire. Colonial markets supplied products and raw materials that were not readily available in the mother country, such as peltry, lumber, pitch, tar, tobacco, and rice produced in colonial French Louisiana (Miller Surrey 2000:161). Also, the colonies provided a fresh supply of consumers awaiting the exportation of the finished products from the *métropole*. To ensure the order and functionality of the mercantile market, regulations allowed only trade between the colonies and the mother country (Thackeray and Findling 1998:49). The principles of mercantilism directed the commoditization of things, and Colbert, in effect, wrote the rule book for his administration and for those that followed him. He considered work "the divine source of the welfare of the state and, correlatively, of laziness as its greatest scourge" (King 1972:203). Dismayed by what he perceived as the increasing apathy, self-interest, and reluctance of wealthy Frenchmen to associate themselves with commerce (King 1972:204), in the mid-seventeenth century Colbert set out to establish general regulations that would assure the perfection and desirability of the product in an international marketplace (King 1972:207). These industrial regulations "were aimed at creating a uniformity and order of operation and production which would not only assure high quality but transform industry and commerce into calculable units in the sphere of law and public finance" (King 1972:207). Colbert's initial intense regulatory oversight was a trifle in comparison to that of the eighteenth century. Between 1683 and 1753, Jean François Boissonade "counted no less than a thousand regulations issued by the central government" (King 1972:209n.31).

Finally, the success of the Louisiana colony depended on an expanded workforce, and settlers in the colonies were begging for laborers (Rowland and Sanders 1929:23, 28). Since word spread about the hardships endured in colonial Louisiana, the French citizenry were not eager to board the vessels headed for the colonies. Some Europeans, many of them Germans, were lured by propaganda schemes (Rowland and Sanders 1929:219–220) portraying the Louisiana colony as the land of milk and honey. Others, deemed socially undesirable, were plucked out of French prisons and hospitals and off the streets of France (Hardy 1966:210). American Indians and Africans were forcibly taken or procured through trade (Hall 1992; Usner 1992:56–59). Most, if not all, were directed down a path to servitude.

The forces that drove commoditization devised well-marked paths from production, through exchange/distribution, to depletion/consumption; however, locally crafted diversions based on New World realities were engineered from below (Appadurai 1986:16–29; Dawdy 2008). The process of commoditization engineered from above motivated change on the northern shores of the Gulf of Mexico. Resistance from the ground effectuated it.

Commoditization on the Ground

In 1722, Le Blond de la Tour, chief engineer of the Louisiana colony, drew a map entitled *Carte de Partie de la Coste du Nouveau Biloxy, Avec Les Isles des Environs*, which laid out the settlement configuration on and in the environs of the Biloxi peninsula. Four sites are depicted on the map, and they are addressed in this essay in this order: Vieux Biloxi on the eastern bank of Biloxi Bay; Nouveau Biloxi on the southern shore of the Biloxi peninsula, which included the proposed site of Fort Louis and surrounding concessions; Ship Island, located south of Nouveau Biloxi across the Mississippi Sound; and the African Habitation site and adjacent brickworks on the northern shore of the Biloxi peninsula.

As stated earlier, Vieux Biloxi may have been situated at or near the supposed site of Fort Maurepas (22JA534), the fort constructed by Iberville and his crew in 1699 that served as the first site of Biloxi's second term as capital of Louisiana after its relocation from Mobile in 1719. While the location of Fort Maurepas has not been conclusively determined, La Tour's map clearly places Vieux Biloxi on what is now called Fort Point peninsula in the area of Lover's Lane, Ocean Springs, Mississippi. A number of archaeological excavations had taken place at the site between 1972 and 1998, but the extent of the excavations was severely limited due to the unwillingness of a few of the landowners to allow access to their property (Table 4.1). The most significant artifact assemblage to date to come from the site is the Poitevent collection.

Table 4.1. History of excavations at Vieux Biloxi

State Site Number	Site Name	Director(s)/Recorder(s) (Source)	Survey/Excavation Date
22JA534	Old Ft. Maurepas I	Dale Greenwell (letter to Elbert Hilliard dated Mar. 12, 1972)	Mar. 1972
	Old Ft. Maurepas I	Sam McGahey (MDAH 1973)	May 1973
	Old Ft. Maurepas I	Dale Greenwell (Jack Elliott, personal communication 2009)	1985
	Old Ft. Maurepas I	John Blitz / Baxter Mann (limited surface collection)(Blitz et al. 1995:42)	1992
	Old Ft. Maurepas I	Douglas C. Sims (survey during sewer trenching) (Jack Elliott, personal communication 2009; Oct. 13, 1997 memorandum filed with MDAH)	1997
	Old Ft. Maurepas I	Jack Elliott (personal communication 2009)	Nov. 1998
22JA538	Old Ft. Maurepas IB	Dale Greenwell (letter to Elbert Hilliard dated Mar. 12, 1972)	Mar. 1972
22JA539	Old Ft. Maurepas II	Dale Greenwell (letter to Elbert Hilliard dated Mar. 12, 1972)	Mar. 1972
22JA542	Biloxi Bay Shipwreck	Eugene Tiblier Jr. (*Daily Picayune* 1892, per Blitz et al. 1995:28)	1892
	Biloxi Bay Shipwreck	Jack Hudson (Hudson 1973)	Nov. 1997
	Biloxi Bay Shipwreck	Panamerican Maritime (Panamerican Maritime 1998)	Jun. 1998

Shuyler Poitevent owned property on Lover's Lane that fronted Biloxi Bay. From the late 1880s until his death in 1936, he amassed an extensive collection of artifacts that he found on his property (Blitz et al. 1995:29), and he recorded his finds in what he called his "relic lists," catalogs that number the artifacts and give their locations. Included in his collection were artifacts typical of early-eighteenth-century French colonial sites: tin-enameled earthenware, green lead-glazed earthenware (Saintonge), cannonball fragments, ax heads, musketballs, thin brick slabs, and olive green glass fragments, among others (Waselkov 1999; Olin et al. 2002; Waselkov and Walthall 2002). One of the olive green glass shards had been reworked by what appears to be an aboriginal flintknapping technique to create a borer, an indication of modification as a result of cultural contact and expedient design. These items, as well as others found on recent excavations of nearby sites, evidence a French colonial presence in the area and possibly the location of Vieux Biloxi.

As explained in the minutes of the Council of Commerce held at Biloxi, dated November 25, 1720, unhealthy conditions, lack of a freshwater source, distance from the Ship Island roadstead, and little room for settlement growth demanded the relocation of the settlement (Rowland and Sanders 1932:299). After its brief one-year tenure, the capital was moved from Vieux Biloxi to Nouveau Biloxi, the second site depicted on La Tour's map, where the proprietorship period collapsed in 1720, an event that has been dubbed by historians as the bursting of the "Mississippi Bubble" (Garber 2000). During the proprietorship period, Ship Island served as the port of entry for Law's massive immigration effort, and Nouveau Biloxi was the temporary stopover for an unprecedented influx of European immigrants—some willing, some forced—and African captives. These newcomers arrived first at Ship Island, many of whom were ferried across the Mississippi Sound to the mainland Biloxi peninsula, and then were either placed in the employ of Law's Company of the West or as transportation became available were dispersed to concessions along the shores of the northern Gulf of Mexico and along the course of the Mississippi River (Giraud 1974b:168–195; Usner 1992:32–33). An anonymous memoir of the period entitled *Memoir on the Situation in Louisiana and What Is to Be Hoped For* reported that during the month of January 1721, 1,249 persons awaited transportation to their appointed concessions, with another 880 more arriving soon thereafter (Conrad 1970:43). Due to a chronic insufficiency of flatboats, the new arrivals from Europe and Africa were sometimes stranded for up to a year on the Biloxi peninsula under the most adverse conditions while awaiting transportation to their final destination (Conrad 1970:43). They were inadequately supplied—especially after the collapse of the Law enterprise—disillusioned, malnourished, and ill from diseases carried over from the port of embarkation, exacerbated by the long, arduous voyage from the mother country, or contracted after debarkation. Many perished (Giraud 1974a:135).

The Moran site (22HR511) is a French colonial cemetery situated in the area depicted on La Tour's map as Nouveau Biloxi, an area where bioarchaeologist Marie Danforth and historical archaeologist Amy Young are conducting an ongoing excavation (see Danforth, this volume) (Table 4.2). To date, the skeletal remains of 30 individuals have been uncovered

Table 4.2. History of excavations at Nouveau Biloxi

State Site Number	Site Name	Director(s)/Recorder(s) (Source)	Survey/ Excavation Date
22HR511	Moran	Dale Greenwell (Greenwell 2008)	Nov. 1969
	Moran	Marie Danforth / Amy Young (forthcoming)	Ongoing
22HR513	Old. Ft. Louis	Dale Greenwell (Greenwell 1969)	1969
	Old. Ft. Louis	French ax reported / no excavation (Edmond Boudreaux, personal communication Feb. 2009)	None
22HR998	Chamber	Jack Elliott (notes on file at Cobb Institute, Mississippi State University)	Nov. 1997
	Chamber	Jack Elliott (Edmond Boudreaux, personal communication Feb. 2009)	Nov. 2000
	Chamber	Amy Young (forthcoming)	May–Jun. 2008

at the site. While most observations of both cranial morphology and metrics suggest Europeans, a few of the individuals do have traits possibly indicative of a Native American and African presence, which might be suggestive of multiethnic burials in a single mortuary context—in other words, interethnic marriage alliances (Rowland and Sanders 1929:58) and cross-cultural liaisons (Usner 1992:59). While it is too soon to make any definitive comments, the possibilities are recognizable.

The processes of commoditization in all culture groups on the Biloxi peninsula during the early eighteenth century created common spaces where alliances were fashioned. As early as the first decade of the eighteenth century, American Indians were captured and traded by enemy aboriginal groups, as well as by Europeans, and placed into servitude; however, this practice abated with the trafficking of African captives to, and within, the colonies (Usner 1992:25n.22). The importation of slaves from the West Coast of Africa to the Louisiana colony officially began during the proprietorship period and accelerated during the administration of John Law (Hall 1992:58–60; Usner 1992:32). Bounty hunters, called "*bandouliers du Mississippi,*" scoured the streets of Paris, arresting people they considered to be "vagabonds, petty criminals, loose women, and blasphemous youth and loaded them onto boats for exile to the colonies"

(Dawdy 2007:137). Army deserters were included in the ranks of these *forçats*, people forced into exile (Conrad 1995:131). In the "frontier economy" (Usner 1992) of colonial French Louisiana, these victims of enslavement and forced immigration constructed their own versions of personal and economic alliances in the struggle for survival in the Louisiana colony (Usner 1992:108; Dawdy 2008:116–117). Such alliances continued through the proprietorship period, albeit on a more clandestine basis once they were decreed illegal (Usner 1992:27–28; Dawdy 2008:116–117).

Two additional sites situated in Nouveau Biloxi, one to the east of the Moran site and one to the west, yielded a few French colonial artifacts. Excavations of the Chamber site (22HR998), the property adjacent to the Moran site on the east, in 1997 and 2000 produced a clay pipe and hand-wrought nails and in 2008 a cloudy, transparent wineglass stem. To the west, a French ax was discovered by a local resident at a site thought to be the location of the proposed Fort Louis (22HR513) (Edmond Boudreaux, personal communication 2009). The fort is depicted on La Tour's map but was never constructed, beyond perhaps preparing the initial earthworks before the capital was relocated to New Orleans.

All told, the artifacts from Vieux Biloxi and Nouveau Biloxi are typical finds in a French colonial context, but venturing south across the Mississippi Sound produces some anomalous artifact forms that indicate establishment of prohibited interregional trade networks. When Iberville decided to locate the capital of his colony in Biloxi in 1699, he ordered not only a fort to be built on the eastern shore of Biloxi Bay, but he also ordered the construction of a warehouse on Ship Island (Hammersten 1990:3), the third site depicted on La Tour's map. While the primary documents attest to the existence of a French warehouse on the site, the archaeological remains were never officially recorded until 1973, when Louis D. Tesar of Florida State University was contracted to do an archaeological survey of portions of the Gulf Islands National Seashore (Table 4.3). He reported the existence of a surface scatter of historic artifacts approximately 60 feet in diameter in the general vicinity of the purported French warehouse site. Dating of the artifacts found—brick, tabby, iron fragments, glass, and ceramics—placed the site in the early eighteenth century (Tesar 1973:60).

No further work was done at Ship Island until 1986, when Robert C. Wilson and Allen Cooper, archaeologists from the Southeast Archaeological Center in Tallahassee, Florida, conducted shovel tests and unit excavations at the site and found artifacts such as "white kaolin pipe fragments,

Table 4.3. History of excavations at Ship Island, Gulf Islands National Seashore

State Site Number	Site Name	Director(s)/Recorder(s) (Source)	Survey/Excavation Date
22HR638	Warehouse	Louis Tesar (Tesar 1973)	Apr.–Dec. 1973
	Warehouse	Robert Wilson (Hammersten 1990)	Mar. 1986
	Warehouse	Robert Wilson (Hammersten 1990)	Aug.–Sept. 1988

brick, mortar, aboriginal pottery, tin-enameled earthenware, lead-glazed earthenware, salt-glazed stoneware and metal fragments" (Hammersten 1990:7). In addition to these typically French colonial artifacts, they also found a ring-footed, tin-enameled coarse earthenware sherd with a blue stripe at the base suggestive, perhaps, of a British origin, red lead-glazed coarse earthenwares with a brownish red paste typical of the El Morro type such as found in Spanish colonial archeological contexts (Gregory Waselkov, personal communication 2009), and a number of aboriginal coarse earthenwares with anomalous designs (H. Edwin Jackson, personal communication 2009). Although still in the early stages of analysis, these artifact types seem to suggest the possibility of illicit trade activities during the proprietorship period (Usner 1992:27–28), albeit on a much smaller scale than that which occurred later in colonial French New Orleans (Dawdy 2008).

The fourth site depicted on La Tour's map is situated on the northern shore of the Biloxi peninsula in the region of Keegan's Bayou. It incorporates a broad swath of land that extends from Keegan's Bayou east to Rhode's Point, and it is labeled "*Habitation pour les Negres de la Camp Nommée Rendezvous.*" At its easternmost extremity and adjacent to it is a brickworks. Were the Africans engaged in brickmaking, perhaps actually producing the materials to construct Fort Louis, the central structure in the urban grid? In September and October 2008, the city of Biloxi afforded Barbara Hester and Bonnie Gums access to the Old Brick House property, a site listed on the National Register of Historic Places, for site survey and shovel testing (Table 4.4). The house was badly gutted by Hurricane Katrina's tidal surge in August 2005, and the city was soon to begin restoration. To date, this has been the only (known) investigation

Table 4.4. History of excavations at the African Habitation site

State Site Number	Site Name	Director(s)/Recorder(s) (Source)	Survey/Excavation Date
22HR1010	Old Brick House	Barbara Hester / Bonnie Gums (Hester 2009)	Sept.–Oct. 2008

of this area for evidence of an early-eighteenth-century presence, and unfortunately the site was found to be overlain with landfill that at some points exceeded a meter in depth. The use of heavy equipment, possibly a backhoe, will be necessary to get beneath the fill. Plans for future excavations in the area are currently underway.

As stated earlier, La Tour's map guided this study and the selection of sites. This in no way denies the existence of other French colonial sites on the Mississippi Gulf Coast. For example, two other sites of French colonial significance where eighteenth-century artifacts have been found are Deer Island in Harrison County and the Krebs House in Jackson County. However, discussion of these will have to be reserved for another occasion.

Conclusion

In summary, in its efforts to establish an orderly system, the French government attempted to centralize political control by classifying, enumerating, and assessing populations; apportioning land; and regulating the distribution of things. However, ongoing archival and archaeological investigation of the settlement landscape and material culture of the Biloxi peninsula and its environs suggests signs of resistance amid configurations of hegemonic order. Anomalous artifact forms and osteological data suggest possible interregional trade networks and interethnic border crossings despite imposed ancien régime prohibitions. On the verge of bankruptcy and in desperate need to swell the coffers of the state and of its noble citizenry, the French government and its colonial proprietors mobilized all available forces—persons, places, and things—into a commodity context to be marketed for the benefit of the colony, the *métropole*, and ultimately the Crown. Consequently, it seems that archaeology of the early-eighteenth-century Biloxi peninsula and its environs may be producing evidence of processes much akin to those of globalization in the twentieth and twenty-first centuries (Appadurai 1986, 2001).

Acknowledgments

Along with the theoretical and editorial assistance of Marie Danforth, Bridget Hayden, and Ed Jackson of the University of Southern Mississippi, I would like to thank Greg Waselkov and Bonnie Gums of the University of South Alabama for their tutelage and advice on the interpretation of French colonial sites. I would also like to thank David Abbott with the Mississippi Department of Archives and History, who was a great help in the assembly of the table of excavations.

References Cited

Allain, Mathé
1995 [1988]   Colbert and the Colonies. In *The Louisiana Purchase Bicentennial Series in Louisiana History*. Vol. 1, *The French Experience in Louisiana*, edited by Glenn R. Conrad, 5–30. Center for Louisiana Studies, University of Southwestern Louisiana, Lafayette.

Appadurai, Arjun
1986   Introduction: Commodities and the Politics of Value. In *The Social Life of Things*, edited by Arjun Appadurai, 3–63. Cambridge University Press, Cambridge.
2001   Grassroots Globalization and the Research Imagination. In *Globalization*, edited by Arjun Appadurai, 1–21. Duke University Press, Durham, N.C.

Blitz, John H., C. Baxter Mann, and Ray L. Bellande
1995   Fort Maurepas and Vieux Biloxi: Search and Research. *Mississippi Archaeology* 30(1): 23–58.

Conrad, Glenn R.
1995   *Emigration Forcée*: A French Attempt to Populate Louisiana, 1716–1720. In *The Louisiana Purchase Bicentennial Series in Louisiana History*. Vol. 1, *The French Experience in Louisiana*, edited by Glenn R. Conrad, 125–135. Center for Louisiana Studies, University of Southwestern Louisiana, Lafayette. Originally published 1979, *Proceedings of the Fourth Meeting of the French Colonial Historical Society*, University Press of America, Washington, D.C.

Conrad, Glenn R., translator
1970   *Immigration and War, Louisiana: 1718–1721 from Memoir of Charles Le Gac*. University of Southwestern Louisiana, Lafayette.

Daily Picayune [New Orleans]
1892   A Mysterious Find. September 18.

Dawdy, Shannon L.
2007   Scoundrels, Whores, and Gentlemen: Defamation and Society in French Colonial Louisiana. In *Coastal Encounters: The Transformation of the Gulf South in the Eighteenth Century*, edited by Richmond F. Brown, 132–150. University of Nebraska Press, Lincoln.

2008   *Building the Devil's Empire: French Colonial New Orleans*. University of Chicago Press, Chicago.

Garber, Peter M.
2000   *Famous First Bubbles: The Fundamentals of Early Manias*. MIT Press, Cambridge, Mass.

Giraud, Marcel
1966   *Histoire de la Louisiane Française, Tome III, L'Époque de John Law (1717–1720)*. Presses Universitaires de France, Paris.
1974a   *A History of French Louisiana. Vol. 1, The Reign of Louis XIV, 1698–1715*, translated by Joseph C. Lambert. Louisiana State University Press, Baton Rouge.
1974b   *Histoire de la Louisiane Française, Tome IV, La Louisiane Après le Système de Law (1721–1723)*. Presses Universitaires de France, Paris.

Greenwell, Dale
1969   Report on Indian Archaeological Studies. *Mississippi Coast Historical & Genealogical Society* 2:8.
1972   Letter to Elbert Hilliard. Mississippi Department of Archives and History, Jackson.
2008   *Moran Burial Site (22HR511): Archaeological Project of 1969 (Post Hurricane Camille)*. D'Iberville Historical Society, D'Iberville, Miss.

Hall, Gwendolyn Midlo
1992   *Africans in Colonial Louisiana: The Development of Afro-Creole Culture in the Eighteenth Century*. Louisiana State University Press, Baton Rouge.

Hammersten, Susan
1990   *Archeological Investigations at the French Warehouse Site, East Ship Island, Mississippi, Gulf Islands National Seashore*. Southeast Archeological Center, National Park Service, Tallahassee, Fla.

Hardy, James D., Jr.
1966   The Transportation of Convicts to Colonial Louisiana. *Louisiana History: The Journal of the Louisiana Historical Association* 7(3): 207–220.

Hester, Barbara T.
2009   *Archaeological Investigation of the Old Brick House Property (22HR1010)*. Report No. 09-1524, prepared for the Mississippi Department of Archives and History, Jackson.

Hudson, Jack C.
1973   *Field Report and Magnetometer Survey Analysis: Biloxi Bay, Mississippi*. Report prepared for the Mississippi Department of Archives and History by Gulf South Research Institute, Baton Rouge, La.

King, James E.
1972   *Science and Rationalism in the Government of Louis XIV, 1661–1683*. Octagon Books, New York.

La Tour, Le Blond de
1721   *Carte de Partie de la Coste du Nouveau Biloxy, avec les isles des environs*. Original at Bibliotèque Nationale de France, Division of Cartes et Plans, Cote du document GE SH 18E PF 138BIS DIV 2 P 6, Coste IFN-8022332.

McGahey, Sam
1973   *Account of the Attempted Location of Fort Maurepas.* Report prepared for the Mississippi Department of Archives and History, Jackson.

Miller Surrey, Nancy M.
2000 [1916]   *The Commerce of Louisiana during the French Régime, 1699–1763. A facsimile of the first edition with an introduction by Gregory A. Waselkov and new index.* University of Alabama Press, Tuscaloosa.

Mississippi Department of Archives and History (MDAH)
1973   *The Establishment of the Fort Maurepas Historical Site.* Official Records Collection, Record Group 31, MDAH, Jackson.

Olin, Jacqueline S., M. J. Blackman, Jared E. Mitchem, and Gregory A. Waselkov.
2002   Compositional Analysis of Glazed Earthenwares from Eighteenth-Century Sites on the Northern Gulf Coast. In *French Colonial Archaeology at Old Mobile: Selected Studies. Society for Historical Archaeology* 36(1): 62–78.

Owsley, Douglas W., and Charles E. Orser Jr.
1985   An Archaeological and Physical Anthropological Study of the First Cemetery in New Orleans, Louisiana. Manuscript on file, Division of Archaeology, Louisiana Department of Culture, Recreation, and Tourism, Baton Rouge.

Panamerican Maritime, L.L.C.
1998   *Relocation and Evaluation of the Back Bay Biloxi Shipwreck Site 22JA542, Jackson County, Biloxi Bay, Mississippi.* Report prepared for the Mississippi Department of Archives and History, Jackson.

Rowland, Dunbar, and Albert Godfrey Sanders, editors and translators
1929   *Mississippi Provincial Archives: 1704–1743, Vol. 2.* Mississippi Department of Archives and History, Jackson.
1932   *Mississippi Provincial Archives: 1704–1743, Vol. 3.* Mississippi Department of Archives and History, Jackson.

Sullivan, Charles L.
1985   *The Mississippi Gulf Coast: Portrait of a People.* Windsor Publications, Northridge, Calif.

Tesar, Louis D.
1973   Archeological Survey and Testing of Gulf Islands National Seashore, Part II: Mississippi. Manuscript on file, National Park Service, Southeast Archeological Center, Tallahassee, Fla.

Thackeray, Frank W., and John E. Findling, editors
1998   *Events That Changed the World in the Eighteenth Century.* Greenwood, Westport, Conn.

Usner, Daniel H., Jr.
1992   *Indians, Settlers, and Slaves in a Frontier Exchange Economy: The Lower Mississippi Valley before 1783.* University of North Carolina Press, Chapel Hill.

Waselkov, Gregory A.
1999   *Old Mobile Archeology.* University of Alabama Press, Tuscaloosa.

Waselkov, Gregory A., and John A. Walthall
2002   Faience Styles in French Colonial North America: A Revised Classification. In *French Colonial Archaeology at Old Mobile: Selected Studies. Society for Historical Archaeology* 36(1): 62–78.

Wood, William R.
2004   (Virtual) Myths. *Critical Sociology* 30(2): 513–548.

5

The Moran Site (22HR511)

An Early-Eighteenth-Century French Colonial Cemetery in Nouveau Biloxi, Mississippi

MARIE ELAINE DANFORTH

Although New Orleans is the area most widely associated with the French presence in the southeastern United States, the earliest colonization efforts of the Louisiana colony actually took place in Mississippi and Alabama. In 1699, on the eastern shores of Biloxi Bay, Pierre Le Moyne, Sieur d'Iberville, constructed Fort Maurepas, the site of the first capital of French Louisiana (Giraud 1966). Three years later, however, Iberville moved the capital 30 miles east to Mobile because of its advantageous location at the mouth of a large river with a more navigable bay. During this same time, France was incurring severe financial troubles after decades of wars, causing the Crown in 1717 to transfer its proprietary control over the colony to Scottish financier John Law. He was given the mandate to colonize the territory as the French government. By maintaining a foothold on the lower Mississippi River valley, it was hoped to protect the Mississippi River and the valuable trade route it provided from encroachment by the British and Spanish (Giraud 1966). In 1720, the capital of the Louisiana colony was returned to Mississippi once again, but this time to the western shores of Biloxi Bay. New Biloxi then became the staging area for this settlement effort, which ultimately collapsed in failure a few years later (Conrad 1970). Under dire circumstances, the capital of the colony was moved to its final location at New Orleans (Giraud 1974).

Between 1720 and 1722, New Biloxi was the temporary stopover for masses of people awaiting transportation to land grants, or concessions, located along the course of the Mississippi River and its tributaries. Ship manifests reveal some details about the backgrounds of the colonists (Roland and Sanders 1927–1984). Most came from France, but several other European nations, most notably Switzerland and Germany, were represented. A number of immigrants were reported to be soldiers, convicts, or tradesmen. Still others who arrived in New Biloxi had been branded social outcasts in their homelands and were forced to emigrate. The relatively few women on the lists were described primarily as wives or daughters of male colonists, although a few may have been nuns. There were also Africans and American Indians, virtually all of whom were captives destined for enslavement (Conrad 1970). Unfortunately for the immigrants, supplies from the financially ailing mother country were sparse. Law furthermore oversold shares in his Company of the Indies, causing a major financial implosion known as the Mississippi Bubble that was felt throughout much of Europe (Garber 2000). Thus, instead of the promised wealth and prosperity, the new arrivals in Mississippi met with hunger, disease, and frequently death.

Accumulating archaeological and historical evidence strongly suggests that the Moran site (22HR511), located on the beach near the famous Biloxi Lighthouse (see Hester, this volume), is an early French colonial cemetery containing the remains of those who were victims of the Law debacle. If this is the case, it then represents the oldest known French colonial cemetery in the South, predating St. Peter's Cemetery in New Orleans by a few years (Owsley et al. 1987). The only older cemetery with French affiliation in the United States is located at St. Croix Island, Maine, and dates to 1604–1605 (Crist n.d.). Thus far, some 30 burials have been excavated at Moran, and those interred may have been residents of the LeBlanc concession, which was located in the area of the site according to a local map from the period (French 1853:19–20). Although much is not recorded in the historical records about individual experiences of those who participated in the Mississippi Bubble, bioarchaeological and archaeological analysis of their remains will shed greater light on their brief, unfortunate lives in the New World.

The Archaeology of the Moran Site

The Moran site is located on the Biloxi peninsula in the Mississippi Sound about two miles from the western edge of the bay and within 300 feet of the original shoreline. The first indication that a cemetery was present there is found in a newspaper account dated May 1, 1914, which reported that four skulls and a "number" of postcranial bones were discovered on the property during ground-leveling activities in preparation for construction. At the time, one supposition was that the remains "evidently were those of Indians who were buried there at some time in the remote past in one of the old burial mounds. That they were very old was evident from the fact that the skulls were broken and none of the bones were intact" (Anonymous 1914a). Another newspaper account suggested the possibility that the individuals were four slaves who were aboard a Spanish pirate ship laden with gold (Anonymous 1914b). With such diverse and fanciful theories flying about, the remains were reburied in the area where they were found.

Over 50 years later, in the aftermath of Hurricane Camille, workers encountered skeletal material while repairing the foundations of the home and adjacent art studio, which now belonged to the Moran family. The burials were located in an open area under the house with the floor above being supported on piers. Anthropologists Richard Marshall and Charles Pine of Mississippi State University, Dale Greenwell of Biloxi, and local volunteers began an excavation of the site, and they discovered the skeletal remains of 12 individuals (Greenwell 2008), although at least one newspaper article reported 13 (MacIntire 1970). The only artifact recovered was a two-inch metal pin, perhaps a shroud pin, found beneath the wrist of one individual. The pin was sent to Stanley South at the University of South Carolina for analysis, where it was determined to be of European origin (MacIntire 1970). Based on the artifacts, some limited osteological analysis, and historical reconstruction, it was determined that the remains likely represented early-eighteenth-century French colonists (Greenwell 2008).

The discovery of the cemetery created a media stir that is still recalled by local residents, with newspapers across the state following the progress of the excavation (e.g., Anonymous 1970; Greenwell 1970; MacIntire 1970). Eventually, the bones of a number of the individuals were covered with shellac and displayed beneath Plexiglas panels in the floor of the art studio for public viewing. Pottery and assorted cultural materials not recovered during the excavation were added to the exhibit to suggest that the remains were Native American.

In 2003, anthropologists at the University of Southern Mississippi (USM) were given permission by the Moran family to analyze the remains of several of the burials that were on display or could be easily disinterred. Eight individuals (Burials 1–8) were identified, and Figure 5.1 illustrates where the bones were found in 2003. Their partial disarticulation and missing elements, however, suggest that at least some of the skeletons had been disturbed over the years, possibly to facilitate display and/or to allow for other work to be done under the house. It was assumed that the remaining 4 of the 12 burials discovered in 1969 were simply inaccessible, but eventually it was learned that they had disappeared years earlier during the construction of a chain wall on the south side of the property (Greenwell 2008). Osteological analysis of the 8 burials was unfortunately limited by a number of factors, including the very cramped working conditions and the shellac coating on the skeletal material, which caused the bone and surrounding sand to form a solid block. However, permission was given for several of the crania and some of the postcranial remains from two individuals to be removed for laboratory evaluation, which did allow for more careful observation. Bone isotope chemistry was evaluated for two individuals, and a carbon-14 test using bone collagen was also conducted. Results of all the analyses largely supported those of the 1969 investigation (Carter et al. 2004). The skeletal material was then placed back as it had been found.

On August 29, 2005, Hurricane Katrina tragically washed away the Moran family home, leaving only a slab and highly disturbed, debris-laden exposed ground where the raised art studio once stood. In early October, human bone was reported to have been found strewn about the site. Fearing looting, anthropologists from USM were called in by the Mississippi Department of Archives and History for consultation. For the next 18 months, excavation took place in an effort to protect the site since it was exposed to the public and the presence of a cemetery was well known, but efforts were sporadic due to logistical and funding constraints. The remains of several of those previously identified in 2003 were recovered, although the bone was badly fragmented and found in highly disturbed contexts. As work progressed, two new burials were revealed, including a young adult male with a crucifix.

After support from the National Endowment for the Humanities was obtained, the first large-scale excavation session took place for two weeks in May 2007 under the direction of bioarchaeologist Marie Danforth and historical archaeologist Amy Young. Since part of the site was still largely covered by a foundation slab, work began in "the pit," as the open area

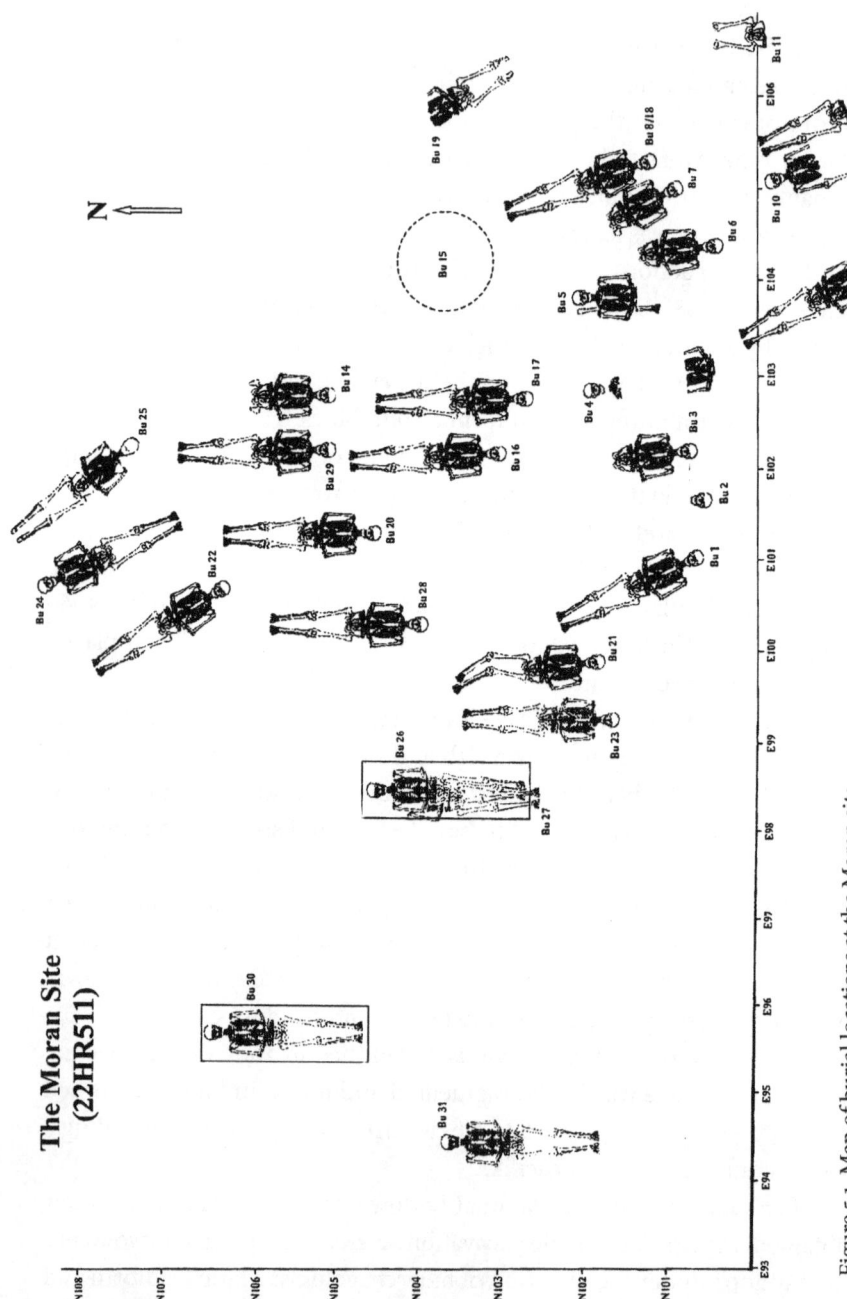

Figure 5.1. Map of burial locations at the Moran site.

previously under the house had become known. The 11 burials found in the pit were generally several centimeters below the surface, and, as is typical of beach sites, skeletal material was located only by moving the sand. No evidence of grave shafts was present. Only a few burials had any sort of associated staining, and usually it became visible only immediately before encountering bone. Bone preservation is poor to fair, and graves are at times intruded upon by modern construction features.

The removal of the slab in December 2007 finally opened the entire property for excavation. Excavation units were opened to the north and west of the pit, essentially extending in the directions where burials had been previously uncovered. Ground-penetrating radar was considered in order to aid in grave location, but was rejected for several reasons: the top 20 to 40 cm of soil were heavily intermixed with remnants of construction debris; there were virtually no grave artifacts; and the bone texture was only somewhat denser than the sand. Two additional field sessions, including a summer field school, have been completed thus far. Although it is impossible to determine how much of the cemetery remains unexcavated, it likely is not extensive. Situated immediately to the west of the property lot on which the site lays was a small bayou, which was filled in during the early twentieth century to create Porter Avenue. The land to the south was graded down several feet over 50 years ago during construction of a gas station, so any burials present were likely lost. Sporadic archaeological excavation on land to the east has not revealed any burials thus far (Boudreaux 1997a, 1997b; Young n.d.). Unfortunately, the highly variable spacing of the burials limits the efficacy of shovel testing to determine the northern limits of the Moran site. The following discussion concerning the cemetery and the associated skeletal remains is based primarily upon the work conducted since 2006, but it also incorporates some information from the 2003 analysis (Carter et al. 2004).

Mortuary Analysis

The typical configuration of interments in European Christian cemeteries, including those of French Catholics, consists of rows of burials placed side by side, and the bodies laid out with heads to the west and hands crossed (Thurston 1908). There are no apparent rows or consistent spacing evident (see Figure 5.1), and burial depth below the current ground surface ranges between 40 and 85 cm, although it should be remembered that the property likely has been graded and filled numerous times during construction activity over the last three centuries. The general arrangement of the graves is heads to the south, although some are to the north and a few lie slightly off of true north–south (Table 5.1). Nearly all were extended supine with hands/lower arms placed over the midsection of the body, but one individual did have arms at the side. Burial 25 is especially noteworthy since he was interred facedown.

In French colonial tradition, most bodies were covered with a shroud and placed directly in the grave (G. Waselkov, personal communication 2007). Two individuals, Burials 26 and 30, however, were interred in coffins as indicated by the presence of iron nails around the skeleton. Burial 26 was also unusual in that it was located directly over another burial, one that was not in a coffin. The torso area of the individual underneath was almost entirely missing, leading to speculation that the remains may have been disturbed during the subsequent coffin burial, such as by ropes or straps that were used in the middle of the casket to lower it. Such an arrangement might suggest that the coffin burials date to a later time, but with only two, there is no other evidence in support of this hypothesis.

Despite idealized regularity in European burials, the high variability in mortuary practices seen at the Moran cemetery is not unexpected. In their excavation of the roughly contemporary St. Peter's Cemetery in New Orleans, Owsley and Orser (1985–1986:95) reported that although the burials were placed in coffins, they were oriented parallel to the streets of St. Peter and Toulouse, with some heads to the northwest, some to the north, and some to the southeast. A suggestion proffered to explain the variation from European Christian norms at the Moran site is lack of concern for custom and tradition due to haste because of increased mortality rates due to malnutrition and disease. Although it is tempting to suggest that the prone male burial may have been a social outcast or a heretic of some sort, his interment otherwise conformed to the rest of the burials; thus his unusual positioning may have been the result of hasty burial. It is entirely possible, however, that variability itself may be the norm.

Only a very limited number of artifacts have been found to date among the burials, which contrasts with interments at St. Peter's Cemetery (Owsley et al. 1987). Grave accompaniments at Moran include two shroud pins, the previously mentioned one from the 1969 excavation and another found in 2007. It has been conjectured that the paucity of burial accoutrement may be due to the impoverished condition of the settlement at

Table 5.1. Demographic traits and mortuary indicators, the Moran site

Burial Number	Sex	Age (yrs)	Orientation	Position	Hand Placement	Grave Goods
1	M	30–40	SE–NW	supine, ext.		
2	M	20–30	S–N	supine		
3	M?	adult	S–N	supine, ext.?		
4	M	25–35	N–S	supine, ext.?		
5	M	35–50	N–S	supine, ext.?		
6	F	25–40	S–N	supine, ext.?		
7	M	30–40	SSE–NNW	supine, ext.?		
8	F	20–30	S–N	supine, ext.?		
9–13[a]						
14	M	18–25	S–N	supine	not recorded	crucifix, 3 beads
15	U	6 m	isolated teeth scattered in fill			none
16	M	15–20	SSE–NNW	supine, ext.	over abdomen	none
17	M	20–25	SSE–NNW	supine, ext.	over abdomen	none
18	U	20–30	SSE–NNW	supine, ext.	undetermined	none
19	M	>30	NW–SE	supine, ext.	over pelvis	none
20	F	15–20	S–N	supine, ext.	over pelvis	none
21	U	adult	S–N	supine, ext.	L over chest, R over pelvis	none
22	M	20–30	S–N	supine, ext.	over pelvis	shroud pin
23	M	>30	S–N	supine, ext.	over pelvis	none
24	M	20–30	NNW–SSE	supine, ext.	L over abdomen, R arm missing	none
25	M	20–30	SSE–NNW	supine, prone	over abdomen	none
26	M	20–25	N–S	supine, ext.	at sides	coffin nails
27	M	adult	S–N	supine, ext.	on chest	none
28	M	20–30	S–N	supine, ext.	L on chest, R on pelvis	none
29	M	20–30	S–N	supine, ext.	on pelvis	none
30	M	adult	N–S	supine, ext.	undetermined	none

Note: a. Burials indentified in 1969 but lost during subsequent building construction.

Figure 5.2. Crucifix recovered with Burial 14 before and after conservation.

Nouveau Biloxi and the need to retain items such as buttons and buckles; however, it reportedly was typical European custom during this period to bury the naked or nearly naked body in a shroud (G. Waselkov, personal communication 2007). Clothing would have been considered part of the estate and thus left to the family. This does not preclude the fact, however, that the family may have found value in their inheritance as trade items in the trying circumstances of the early colonization efforts.

The remains of a rosary, consisting of a crucifix and several beads, in the lower lumbar region of Burial 14, a young adult male, are the most impressive artifact find to date. The crucifix measures 4.5 cm from top to bottom and approximately 3.0 cm on its horizontal member. It was badly corroded when found and along with the three wooden beads was sent to Texas A&M University for restoration and conservation (Figure 5.2). The presence of a crucifix and beads provides strong support for European origins, and a cross-match with a crucifix excavated at Fort Michilimackinac, a French fur trading center and military post in the Upper Great Lakes region constructed in 1715, aligns it with the French colonial period (Rinehart 1990) as well as with a crucifix found in a Native American contact period site in Louisiana (Brain 1979). The crucifix is an indicator of French colonial temporality because the dominant and state-sanctioned religion in France in the early eighteenth century was Roman Catholic (O'Neill 1966). The several wooden rosary beads recovered likely owed their survival to their proximity to the preservative quality of the copper in the crucifix (McIntyre and Freeman 2008). They measured approximately 6 mm in length and 3 mm in width. Analysis of the wood from one of the broken beads indicates that it appears to be from the pear or apple family, possibly from the spindlewood tree (M. Alford, personal communication 2007; L. Newsom, personal communication 2007).

Bioarchaeological Analysis

Osteological analysis of the human remains recovered at the Moran site is still in its preliminary stages. The demographic findings are summarized in Table 5.1. Sex was determined using standard cranial and pelvic markers as outlined in Buikstra and Ubelaker (1994). Aging was accomplished primarily through tooth development and eruption, cranial suture closure, and auricular area morphology. Most individuals are young adult males, with several individuals in the subadult age category. In contrast to the St. Peter's Cemetery sample in New Orleans, in which over one-quarter of the individuals (n=29) were juveniles (Owsley et al. 1987), there was but one child found at Moran. The evidence for Burial 15 consists only of several deciduous molar crowns in the same general area of fill in the eastern side of the pit, all consistent with a six-month-old, and there was considerable debate over whether even to label it a separate burial. Also in contrast to what was seen at the Moran site, those interred in New Orleans had a larger range of age at death, with half of the males surviving past 40 years, as well as a more even sex distribution (Owsley et al. 1987). These differences suggest that St. Peter's Cemetery in New Orleans was somewhat more representative of a typical population, but the obviously biased Moran sample is reflective of what might be expected of a staging community.

Ancestry is a more difficult determination in the skeleton, even when skeletal material is well preserved (Novotny et al. 1993). In the Moran series, most facial bones crumbled away upon removal. However, field observations of the facial region have thus far indicated European features in most individuals, as was generally anticipated. However, the presence of different ancestries (African, European, and Native American) at St.

Peter's Cemetery does present the possibility of a similar finding at Moran (Owsley et al. 1987). Indeed, three individuals (Burials 14, 20, and 23) have slight shoveling of the incisors, and at least three of the crania (Burials 20, 24, and 28) are very brachycephalic. Although these traits are typically considered more characteristic of Asians and Native Americans, they do occur in Caucasian and African populations at times (Novotny et al. 1993). These individuals may also be of mixed ancestry as well.

One line of evidence supporting a predominantly European cultural affiliation can be found in the dietary analysis of those buried in the cemetery. Page (2007) evaluated stable isotope composition of nitrogen and carbon in bone collagen and carbon in apatite carbonate within both bone and teeth for Burials 1–14 as well as for several unassigned femoral fragments. As Figure 5.3 demonstrates, the $\delta^{13}C$ values of collagen range from -7.8 to -19.77 percent, with a mean of -18.48 percent. All individuals display $\delta^{13}C$ values congruent with a diet consisting of almost exclusively C_3 foods such as wheat and other Old World grains, or, more accurately, terrestrial animals such as pigs and chickens that consumed C_3 foods since these values are from the collagen, which preferentially derives its carbon from protein sources. These findings were confirmed through evaluation of tooth and bone apatite carbon isotopes, which were also considered since they display $\delta^{13}C$ values from the entire diet rather than just from one macronutrient. One sample, labeled #23, taken from a bone fragment found on the surface after Hurricane Katrina, did have an isotope value of -7.84 percent, which is congruent with a diet largely consisting of C_4 foods such as maize. This could indicate a Native American, but it could also be a European or African who was raised in the New World; for example, some of those who came to New Biloxi were Canadian (Conrad 1970) and thus may have consumed maize for many years. The $\delta^{15}N$ values for the entire set of samples ranged from 7.19 to 13.44 percent, with a mean of 10.20 percent. The range of $\delta^{15}N$ values indicates a mixture of marine and terrestrial protein components to the diets.

If the individuals are indeed European, preliminary analysis of health indicators seen in the skeletal remains of those interred at Moran also supports expectations from the historical record, which suggest that most of the individuals came from the lower socioeconomic strata of French society (Conrad 1970). Bioarchaeological evidence of their status may be seen in their generally short stature and high frequencies of enamel hypoplasias. Height is generally regarded as a cumulative indicator of childhood

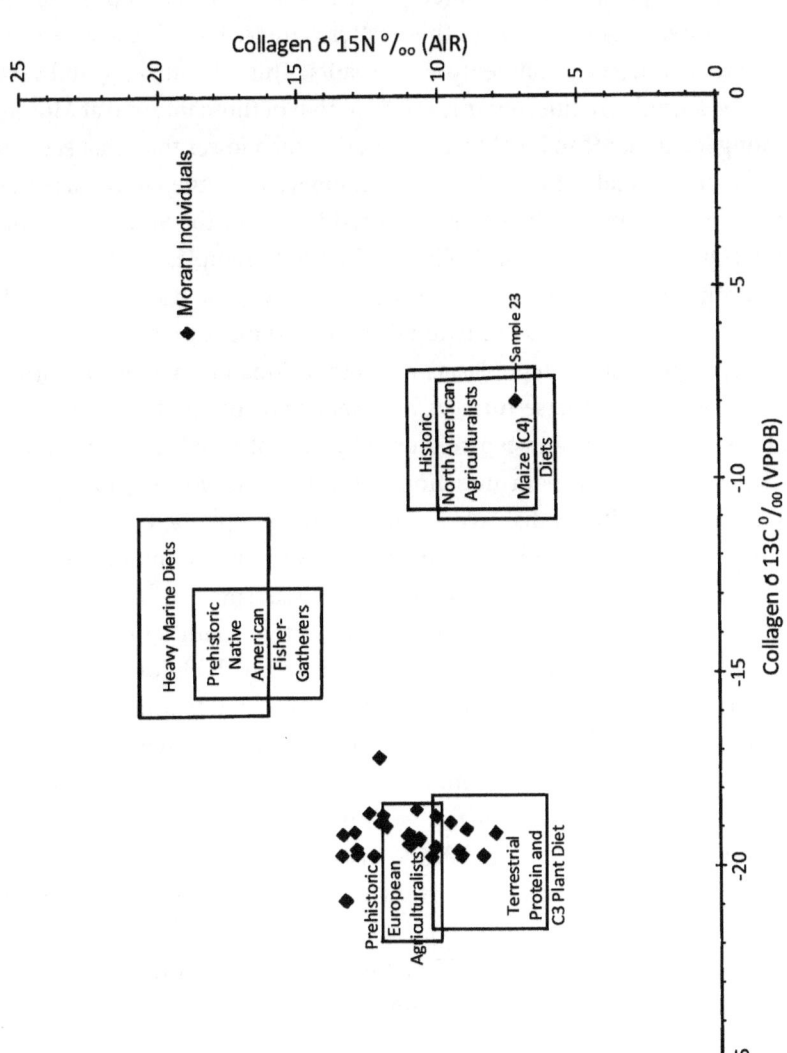

Figure 5.3. Carbon and nitrogen isotopes of collagen of the Moran cemetery (adapted from Page 2007:66).

health experiences (Bogin 1999). Although there is a genetic component, final stature is most substantially affected by environmental factors. Chief among these is nutrition, with protein levels being especially critical. At Moran, male height (n=10) ranged from 157.7 to 175.1 cm with a mean of 167.1 cm, whereas female height (n=2) ranged from 149.0 to 154.9 cm with a mean of 151.5 cm. All statures were estimated using the Trotter and Gleser (1958) formulae for whites. Among males, this is substantially shorter than average stature among U.S. colonial males (Angel 1976) but very comparable with other contemporaneous European groups (Kolmos and Cinnirella 2005), although these latter samples included a large proportion of convicts and indentured servants. This, of course, would very likely be a similar socioeconomic group to that of those interred at Moran. Among females, mean height was similarly much lower than that seen in U.S. colonial females, but it must be remembered that the sample size was only two. No stature values were reported for either the St. Peter's Cemetery (Owsley et al. 1987) or St. Croix (Crist n.d.) samples.

Another marker that speaks to the generally poor childhood health endured by most of these individuals is the frequent presence of linear enamel hypoplasias. Hypoplasias are disruptions in enamel formation that appear as transverse furrows or rows of pits on the teeth. They are nonspecific in nature and can be caused by a number of factors, including disease episodes and poor nutrition (Goodman and Rose 1990). Nearly all anterior dentitions displayed at least one hypoplasia, and most had multiple episodes. Episode severity ranged from slight to moderate.

Although a systematic paleopathological assessment will soon be undertaken, a preliminary examination suggests that conditions such as porotic hyperostosis, which is typically associated with childhood anemia (Stuart-Macadam 1995), and periosteal lesions related to infection, which commonly result from injury or from diseases such as syphilis (Ortner 2003), are quite rare in the Moran series. The collection does not exhibit any signs of long bone trauma as well. In contrast, the series recovered from St. Peter's Cemetery has several instances of each condition, which was hypothesized to be related to the enslaved status of many of those interred there (Owsley et al. 1987).

Although the conditions at New Biloxi were quite dire as infectious disease, most notably malaria, compounded by starvation, was rampant—and indeed many individuals probably arrived already sick from their transatlantic voyage (Giraud 1974; Usner 1992)—the general lack of skeletal indicators of poor adult health at Moran is not entirely unexpected. Since these sorts of conditions typically kill quickly, they would not be expected to leave skeletal lesions (Ortner 2001). The bone isotope analysis also supports a relatively short survival time for most who came to Biloxi and were buried at Moran. Although the colonists were promised wheat provisioning by the Crown, this did not take place (Giraud 1974). Therefore, most of the immigrants were likely relying on lowly regarded corn as their major staple, but it would have taken at least a few years to show up in their bone signatures (Katzenberg 2000). Since virtually everyone still displayed a C_3 signature indicating a diet of European cereals, this evidence attests to death relatively soon after arrival on the Gulf Coast.

Thus, the preliminary results of archaeological and bioarchaeological analysis of this French colonial cemetery is helping to illuminate one of the most tumultuous episodes in Mississippi history, namely, the staging effort to settle the Louisiana colony that took place at New Biloxi between 1720 and 1722. The findings so far have largely confirmed what the historical records suggested. Those who came to New Biloxi were overwhelming young and predominantly male, the very segment of society that would be most expected to leave their homeland in order to take their chances in the Louisiana colony. Their bones tell of lives that had already been hard, and sadly their fates only seem to have worsened in the New World, where they evidently perished from malnutrition and disease soon after arrival. They were buried simply, as the lack of grave goods would indicate, and perhaps somewhat hastily, as the apparently random spacing of the graves and the facedown position of one individual might suggest. The expectation of representation of varied ancestries among those interred still needs greater evaluation, and mitochondrial DNA analysis is currently being undertaken (Cook n.d.). Additional excavation is planned for the site, and as further burials are uncovered, the record of life and death in Nouveau Biloxi will hopefully become even more complete.

Acknowledgments

Many thanks are given to the Moran family for permission to excavate on their property. Funding has been kindly provided by the National Endowment for the Humanities, the Mississippi Department of Marine Resources, the Mississippi Department of Archives and History, and the

University of Southern Mississippi. Those contributing to this chapter include Amy Young and graduate students Barbara Hester, Danielle Cook, Miranda Page, and Tiffany Hensley, all with the University of Southern Mississippi. Historian Edmond Boudreaux of Biloxi has provided invaluable support throughout the entire project.

References Cited

Angel, J. Lawrence
1976   Colonial to Modern Skeletal Change in the USA. *American Journal of Physical Anthropology* 45:723–736.
Anonymous
1914a   Indian Skull Is Found in Biloxi in Grading Yard. *Biloxi Sun-Herald*, May 1.
1914b   Old Legend Tells of Spanish Gold: Some Say Buried in Biloxi. *Biloxi Sun-Herald*, May 7.
1970   Human Skeleton No. 12 Uncovered at Moran Site: Biloxi Artists Says [sic] History of These People Is Mystery. *Jackson Daily News*, January 1.
Bogin, Barry
1999   *Patterns of Growth*. 2nd ed. Cambridge University Press, Cambridge.
Boudreaux, Edmond
1997a   Chamber of Commerce Excavations. *Mississippi Coast Historical and Genealogical Society* 33(2): 49.
1997b   Biloxi Chamber of Commerce Excavations. *Mississippi Coast Historical and Genealogical Society* 33(3): 82–83.
Brain, Jeffrey P.
1979   *Tunica Treasure*. Peabody Museum of Archaeology and Ethnology Papers No. 71. Harvard University, Cambridge, Mass.
Buikstra, Jane, and Douglas Ubelaker
1994   *Standards for Data Collection from Human Skeletal Remains*. Research Series No. 44. Arkansas Archaeological Survey, Fayetteville.
Carter, Cindy P., Ashley Seidell, Donald P. Craig, Edmond Boudreaux, Krista Lynee Burleigh, Jason A. Gardner, Stacey A. Young, and Marie Elaine Danforth
2004   A Bioarchaeological Analysis of the French Colonial Burials at the Moran Gallery, Biloxi, MS. *Mississippi Archaeology* 39(1): 41–68.
Conrad, Glenn R., translator and editor
1970   *First Families of Louisiana*. 2 vols. Claitor's Publishing, Baton Rouge.
Cook, Danielle N.
n.d.   An Analysis of Ancestry at the French Colonial Moran Site (22HR511), Harrison County, MS. Master's thesis in progress, University of Southern Mississippi, Hattiesburg.
Crist, Thomas
n.d.   *St. Croix Island Archaeological Project: Preliminary Report*. National Park Service, U.S. Department of the Interior, Washington, D.C.

French, B. F.
1853 *Plan du Fort Projette au Nouveau Bilocxy, 1721*. Lamport, Blakeman and Law, New York.

Garber, Peter M.
2000 *Famous First Bubbles: The Fundamentals of Early Manias*. MIT Press, Cambridge, Mass.

Giraud, Michel
1966 *Histoire de la Louisiane Française, Tome III, L'Époque de John Law (1717–1720)*. Presses Universitaires de France, Paris.
1974 *Histoire de la Louisiane Française, Tome IV, La Louisiane Après le Systeme de Law (1721–1723)*. Presses Universitaires de France, Paris.

Goodman, Alan H., and Jerome C. Rose
1990 Assessment of Systemic Physiological Perturbations from Dental Enamel Hypoplasias and Associated Histological Structures. *Yearbook of Physical Anthropology* 33:59–110.

Greenwell, Dale
1970 Ancient Burials Discovered Next Door to Biloxi Lighthouse. *Down South* 19(6): 3, 8–9.
2008 Moran Burial Site (22HR511): Project Two of 1969 (Post-Hurricane Camille). D'Iberville Historical Society, D'Iberville, Miss.

Katzenberg, M. Anne
2000 Stable Isotope Analysis: A Tool for Studying Past Diet, Demography, and Life History. In *Biological Anthropology of the Human Skeleton*, edited by M. Anne Katzenberg and Shelley R. Saunders, 329–350. Wiley-Liss, New York.

Kolmos, John, and Francesco Cinnirella
2005 European Heights in the Early 18th Century. Discussion Paper 2005-05, Department of Economics, University of Munich. http://epub.ub.uni-muenchen.de/572/1/, european_heights_in_the_early_18th_century.pdf.

MacIntire, Carl
1970 Camille Exposes Bones. *Jackson Clarion-Ledger*, August 16.

McIntyre, Craig, and Michael Freeman
2008 Comprehensive Review of Copper Based Wood Preservative with a Focus on New Micronized or Dispersed Copper Systems. *Forest Products Journal* 54:27–36.

Novotny, Vladimir, Mehmet Y. Iscan, and Susan R. Loth
1993 Morphologic and Osteometric Assessment of Age, Sex and Race from the Skull. In *Forensic Analysis of the Skull*, edited by Mehmet Y. Iscan and Richard P. Helmer, 71–88. Wiley-Liss, New York.

O'Neill, Charles Edward
1966 *Church and State in French Colonial Louisiana*. Yale University Press, New Haven, Conn.

Ortner, Donald J.
2003 *Identification of Pathological Conditions in Human Skeletal Remains*. 2nd ed. Academic Press, San Diego, Calif.

Owsley, Douglas, and Charles E. Orser

1985–1986 *An Archaeological and Physical Anthropological Study of the First Cemetery in New Orleans, Louisiana*. Department of Geography and Anthropology, Louisiana State University, Baton Rouge.

Owsley, Douglas W., Charles E. Orser, Robert W. Mann, Peer H. Moore-Jansen, and R. L. Montgomery

1987 Demography and Pathology of an Urban Slave Population from New Orleans. *American Journal of Physical Anthropology* 74:185–197.

Page, Miranda D.

2007 Dietary Reconstruction through Stable Isotope Analysis at the Moran French Colonial Cemetery on the Mississippi Gulf Coast. Master's thesis, University of Southern Mississippi, Hattiesburg.

Rinehart, Charles J.

1990 *Crucifixes and Medallions: Their Role at Fort Michilimackinac*. South Carolina Institute of Archaeology and Anthropology, University of South Carolina, Columbia.

Roland, Dunbar, and Albert Godfrey Sanders

1927–1984 *Mississippi Provincial Archives*. Press of the Mississippi Department of Archives and History, Jackson.

Stuart-Macadam, Patty

1985 Porotic Hyperostosis: Representative of a Childhood Condition. *American Journal of Physical Anthropology* 66:391–398.

Thurston, Herbert

1908 Christian Burial. In *The Catholic Encyclopedia*. Robert Appleton, New York. http://www.newadvent.org/cathen/03071a.htm. Accessed February 15, 2009.

Trotter, Mildred, and Goldie C. Gleser

1958 A Reevaluation of Stature Based on Measurements Taken during Life and of Long Bones after Death. *American Journal of Physical Anthropology* 16:79–123.

Usner, Daniel H., Jr.

1992 *Indians, Settlers, & Slaves in a Frontier Exchange Economy: The Lower Mississippi Valley before 1783*. University of North Carolina Press, Chapel Hill.

Young, Amy

n.d. Report on 2009 Excavations at the Chamber of Commerce Site (22HR999), Hancock County, Mississippi. Manuscript on file, Department of Anthropology and Sociology, University of Southern Mississippi, Hattiesburg.

6

The Greatest Gathering

The Second French-Chickasaw War in the Mississippi Valley
and the Potential for Archaeology

ANN M. EARLY

In the spring of 1740, relations between residents of France's North American colonies, their Indian allies, and the Chickasaw in northeastern Mississippi reached a point of anticlimax when massed forces of the French colonists and their allies and entrenched villages of the Chickasaw achieved stalemate in what has been referred to as the second French-Chickasaw War. This event influenced the economic and political landscape of France's North American colonial centers for years, and produced both a mountain of contemporary documents and a potential material signature that can be approached by archaeological investigations. The documents come from the Herculean logistical challenges of mounting a transcontinental and multiracial force to neutralize the Chickasaw, and from the postevent recriminations, finger-pointing, ruminations, and posturing that went on for years after the spring of 1740. The archaeological signature of this enterprise remains to be documented, so this essay is a call for research rather than a report of results.

A number of historians have presented summaries of the two principal Chickasaw wars that took place between 1736 and 1740, and their contexts, usually within the framework of French Louisiana colonial politics or in the broader contest between France and England for economic and political supremacy of their North American colonies (Peyser 1982; Brasseaux 2000; Foret 1995; Caldwell 1938; Harris 1959; Phelps 1957). Original correspondence between planners and participants, and between colonial authorities and French administrators, is available in many locations.

Most accessible are the documents gathered in the published Mississippi Provincial Archives that are translated into English and preserved with their archival citations (Rowland and Sanders 1927, 1932; Rowland et al. 1984).

Eyewitness accounts of the wars also exist. Pierre Vitry, a Jesuit priest, served as chaplain to the contingent of Louisiana troops and support staff from New Orleans sent to Arkansas to construct Fort St. Francis in advance of the second campaign in October 1738. He remained with the expedition until the waning weeks of the campaign in the spring of 1740, and he wrote a diary recounting his experiences (Vitry 1929; Delanglez 1985b). A second diary reportedly written by an unidentified officer under Captain Nouailles d'Ayme describes the arrival of the French marines in Louisiana in June 1739, and their experiences until their retreat from Fort Assumption (near present-day Memphis, Tennessee) in February 1740 (Claiborne 1964:64–84; Anonymous 1859).

One member of the Canadian force, Joseph Gaspard Chaussegros de Léry, wrote a diary of his experiences in 1740 (de Léry 1923). De Léry was a member of a prominent Canadian family who became an important military and political figure, and who was a lifelong diarist (Roy 1940). In the late winter, he was a member of a group of Canadian French and their Indian allies under the leadership of Pierre Joseph Celeron de Blainville, who left Fort Assumption to test the Chickasaw defenses in a foray that never actually reached the villages, but did skirmish with a group of Chickasaw. Celeron persuaded the Chickasaw to send delegates to Fort Assumption to negotiate an end to what was by then a stalemate, a diplomatic move that brought the campaign to a more or less dignified end for the parties in the field. The French campaign against the Chickasaw continued for several years after the spring of 1740, but was waged with a much lower profile, largely through raids by Choctaw allies and other surrogates.

Governor Jean-Baptiste Le Moyne Sieur de Bienville composed his own report about the expedition for French authorities shortly after he returned to New Orleans from Fort Assumption (Rowland and Sanders 1927:447–463), and he kept a diary of his own (Bienville 1923:166–178). Numerous letters, reports, and other short documents written by him during and after the spring of 1740 have also been preserved. Brief reports and correspondence from other members of the expedition, like the surveyor and engineer François Broutin, are also known to exist.

Two eighteenth-century Louisiana historians witnessed some of the events of the first French-Chickasaw War and included both campaigns in their manuscripts, although neither participated in the 1738–1740 campaign. Jean François Benjamin Dumont *dit* Montigny gave what is now believed to be a highly colored account of the conflict in his "Memoire," a lengthy history of the colony's early years, and in his "Poeme," an even lengthier epic in verse that tells the same story (Delanglez 1985a; Dumont 1931). Dumont no longer lived in Louisiana at the time of the second war, but he gave an account of those events based on his access to a diary, possibly Vitry's, and other secondhand information. Dumont's "Memoire" has not been published, and "Poeme" has been published only once, in French. Antoine-Simon Le Page du Pratz also recounted the two campaigns from first- and secondhand information (Le Page du Pratz 1975) in his now widely available history.

The Background to War

When Pierre Le Moyne, Sieur d'Iberville and his associates established the Louisiana colony along the Gulf Coast in 1700, the Chickasaw were already a threat to Natives and Europeans alike in the Mississippi Valley and farther west. With firm and profitable relations with traders from English Carolina that were in place in the late seventeenth century, the Chickasaw raided travelers and Native communities for captives, skins, and other goods in great demand along the Atlantic coast. As England's chief proxy in the region, the Chickasaw infringed on French colonial development by offering both threats and enticements to Louisiana's Indian allies, especially the Choctaw, to change allegiances, and by posing a recurring risk to colonial travelers and merchants seeking to convoy goods along the region's principal waterways. Commerce and communication among French settlements from the St. Lawrence Valley to the Illinois Country and beyond to Louisiana depended on the ability to use these rivers (Johnson 2000).

It was the Natchez, however, who precipitated the first great crisis in colonial-Indian relations in Louisiana and brought the French-Chickasaw relationship to a flashpoint. The Natchez War of 1730 revenged the 1729 massacre of French colonial residents at the Natchez settlement and removed the Natchez as a threat to the safety and economic well-being of French settlers in the Mississippi Valley. In the first years of Louisiana settlement, the Natchez were the most dominant Indian society along the Mississippi River. Missionaries established a permanent presence near the village of the principal leader, and a fortified garrison and companion colonial settlement grew up in the same location. The 1729 uprising shocked the colony and demanded a military response. The ensuing attack by French colonials and their Indian allies destroyed Natchez society. Most of the population was dead or enslaved, or had fled either to the remote swampy Ouachita River valley west of the Mississippi or northeast to the shelter of Chickasaw villages in the upper Tombigbee River basin in what is today northeast Mississippi (Johnson 2000; Lorenz 2000; Rowland et al. 1984; Le Page du Pratz 1975).

Between 1730 and 1735, the Chickasaw emerged as the next great Native threat to the Louisiana colonists. One reason often given was the continuing presence of a small number of Natchez refugees who resided in Chickasaw communities out of the reach of French authorities. A more important and long-term reason for French animosity, however, was the continuing close relationship between Chickasaw and English traders from the Carolina colonies. This economic and political influence was marked by the Chickasaw exchange of animal skins, captives, and other goods for guns, horses, and other trade goods. English traders made overtures to Choctaw leaders through Chickasaw intermediaries and, under the noses of the French colonial authorities, gained a physical foothold in the region through their trading alliances. Their activities precipitated Chickasaw raids against neighboring tribes like the Quapaw, and threatened people and goods traveling between Illinois and Louisiana along the Mississippi River and its tributaries. The English allies even reportedly taught the Chickasaw European methods of fortifying their communities (Rowland and Sanders 1932:394, 693–694). This last report led to the complex logistical challenges and ultimate failure of the 1737–1740 war plan.

In 1736, Louisiana authorities organized a military exercise against the Chickasaw that was intended to "reduce" their status in the region. Colonial militia and Indian allies from Illinois and Louisiana were supposed to launch a coordinated, simultaneous two-pronged attack against the fortified Chickasaw villages. Through a series of misadventures and poor timing, the enterprise was a disaster for the colonials. It resulted first in the massacre of large numbers of Illinois militia and the death by torture of Pierre D'Artaguette, commander of the Illinois garrison, and a few others in the leader's party (Rowland and Sanders 1927:297–314, 316–320; Le Page du Pratz 1975). Written plans for the attack found on Artaguette's body, and probably translated by English traders, alerted the Chickasaw to Bienville's scheduled arrival from the south, and the Louisiana soldiers and colonists were ambushed and routed en route. Jean Frederic Phelypeaux, Count de Maurepas, minister of marine for Louis XV, was furious about the loss and ordered Governor Bienville and others to start immediately on plans for a second campaign; however, Bienville and his associates were already formulating a new and ambitious war plan to launch a second campaign against the Chickasaw (Rowland and Sanders 1927:320–326).

The Cast of Characters

The new expedition took more than two years to plan and organize. It involved shipping cannons, marines, artillery officers, and bombardiers from France; arranging the rendezvous of Canadian cadet contingents and Indian allies from Montreal, Fort Michilimacinac, and various St. Lawrence Valley settlements; and recruiting volunteer colonists, militia, and Indian allies from Illinois and the greater Great Lakes region. Louisiana colonial troops and their Indian allies were also part of the expedition.

The first staging area for the expedition was at the mouth of the St. Francis River on the Mississippi's west bank. Bienville had dispatched surveyors and engineers to scout the most effective route to the Chickasaw villages for a large expedition that would haul heavy cannons and other supplies needed for a major campaign. Ignace Broutin and Bernard de Verges surveyed the Mobile River approach to the Chickasaw. François Saucier and an associate were sent to chart the Yazoo River basin to evaluate its value as an approach as well. In the first of these reconnaissances, de Verges traveled to Arkansas Post on the lower Arkansas River, where he acquired Quapaw guides who led him across the Grand Prairie to the mouth of the St. Francis River in what is today northeast Arkansas. De Verges reported back to Bienville that the Quapaw claimed it was only 12 leagues east from that point to the Chickasaw villages, and that there was a usable road. This estimate was unfortunately less than half the real distance, and there turned out to be no road. On the strength of de Verge's report, however, and the subsequently poor prospects for the long overland

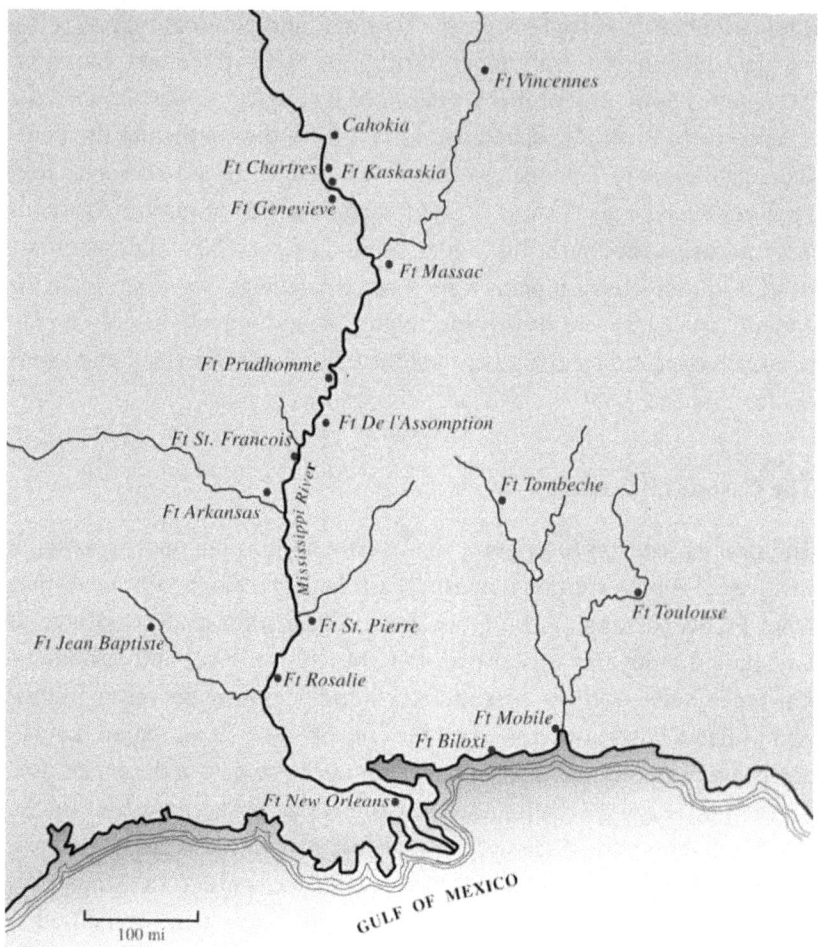

Figure 6.1. Map illustrating the locations of places mentioned in the text.

trek north up the Yazoo or Mobile River valleys, Bienville settled on a plan to marshal his forces on the Mississippi River at the mouth of the St. Francis and attack the Chickasaw from the west.

A detachment of 130 troops led by Jacques Coustilhas and accompanied by support personnel that included engineer de Verges, a surgeon, aides, a warehouse keeper, and Jesuit chaplain Pierre Vitry were sent to construct a fort at the St. Francis in December 1738 (Figure 6.1). This group, supplemented by a fluctuating number of Quapaw, spent the winter and spring at Fort St. Francis as people and supplies began arriving from all of France's North American settlements. By mid-1739, however, logistical problems in mounting an expedition to the Chickasaw villages through the roadless, swampy lowlands east of Fort St. Francis became evident, and a new staging area, Fort Assumption, was established on the bluffs at the mouth of the Margot, or Wolf, River. People and goods moved to and from this east-bank site until April 1740, although Fort St. Francis continued as a storage facility and bakery throughout the campaign.

A large convoy from Canada brought Charles Le Moyne, Baron de Longueuil, a nephew of Bienville, and about 600 men that included colonial soldiers and their officers, a corps of *habitants*, more than 300 Indian allies, and a support group that included two missionaries to the Iroquois, a chaplain for the French, various ancillary personnel, and an uncounted number of Native family members. The Indians came from at least 14 different tribal groups according to accounts made by Vitry and the anonymous French marine. The largest groups were Iroquois from two different villages. Also present were Potawatomi, Montagni, Nippising, Abenaki, Onondaga, Ottowa, Mascoutin, Sauteur, and small groups of individuals from several other Canadian and Great Lakes communities. Some Indian allies were recruited during the voyage from Montreal to replace others who began the trip but dropped out along the way. Throughout the winter, additional groups continued to arrive. Some contingent members, who were restless, tired of waiting for activity, or unsettled by the extended proximity of so many groups with uncertain or undefined social relationships, left for raids or for home (Vitry 1929:154–170; Delanglez 1985b:30–59; Wedel 1985; Brasseaux 2000).

The contingent from France was led by Colonel Nouailles d'Ayme, who, as senior military officer and French citizen, was officially head of the entire expedition although he had no experience with American Indians or colonial warfare. Contemporary protocol dictated that Nouailles d'Ayme outranked even Governor Bienville since the latter was Canadian-born (Delanglez 1985b). The arrivals included a battalion of both French and Swiss troops, their respective officers, and support personnel that included armorers, surgeons, and an unknown number of private servants. Supplies and equipment included the newly arrived cannons and ammunition as well as tents and all the other armaments and gear needed for a military campaign.

The contingent first made its way from la Balize (the mouth of Mississippi River) to New Orleans, arriving on October 6, 1739, two months behind schedule, where many of the number promptly became sick. Within a short time, 60 men were dead. The group rushed to embark for Fort Assumption in order to get away from the sickly atmosphere, but members continued to fall sick and die during the upstream journey (Claiborne 1964:64–73; Anonymous 1859). Upon leaving New Orleans, the French expedition took on additional personnel. There were slaves, French colonial militia and guides, and an ever-changing contingent of Indians from the small remnant tribes that remained on the outskirts of French colonial settlement in the lower Mississippi Valley.

Later in October, a convoy of boats from the Illinois settlements brought their commandant, Monseigneur De la Buissionnere; 40 soldiers; a group of settlers comprising a local militia; and a group of Indian allies from the Kaskaskia, Michigama, Petit Osage, and Missouri tribes. Commander Nouailles's anonymous diarist reports 117 Indians arrived in this group, nearly half of whom were Missouri. Subsequent boats arrived from the Illinois Country filled with salted beef and other necessary provisions throughout the winter of 1739–1740 (Claiborne 1964:73–80; Anonymous 1859). Among the participants were men who had survived the massacre of 1736 and who were eager for retribution.

Governor Bienville arrived in early November with a contingent of Louisiana soldiers and militia, support personnel, slaves, and Indian allies. By this time a forward base was established on high ground at the mouth of the Margot River, now the Wolf River, in the location of modern-day Memphis, and where the French and their Indian allies subsequently congregated.

Food and other supplies had been commissioned from the Illinois, Arkansas, and Natchitoches settlements. Significantly, Illinois and Louisiana communities were supposed to supply horses and oxen to haul the cannons and other equipment overland to the Chickasaw villages. Salted meat and other provisions arrived successfully, but the livestock arrived late, in no condition to be used, or not at all.

From mid-1739 to April 1740, the composition of the French-Indian expedition changed regularly as people and supplies moved to and from the staging area to villages and settlements in Canada, the Great Lakes region, Illinois, and Louisiana. It is not possible to track the size and makeup of the assembly from day to day, but Carl A. Brasseaux estimates, based on official records and diaries, that altogether 1,500 Europeans and 1,300 Indians participated and "constituted the largest French army ever assembled in Louisiana" (Brasseaux 2000:57). Free and enslaved Africans, women and children, servants and unofficial support personnel such as traders, missionaries, and other people attached to tribal groups and militia as well as small contingents of volunteers likely escaped enumeration in most instances and undoubtedly increased these numbers as well.

The Expedition

The challenges and limitations of coordinating activities on two continents with eighteenth-century communication technology and a dispersed chain of command were such that it is remarkable to realize that most elements of the plan came together in the approximate place and manner intended. At the same time, a series of intelligence and execution failures, some best seen as Murphy's Law in action, ultimately doomed the enterprise and left thousands of men and animals and tons of material camped on the Mississippi River in the spring of 1740 waiting for something to happen.

As an example of the unintended consequences of reconciling complex and incomplete information, Bienville was persuaded early in the planning that he needed more firepower than he had available in Louisiana to breach the Chickasaw village fortifications, an essential step in mounting a successful attack. An Abenaki informant recounted to Bienville the story of a futile English campaign against a fortified Catawba village because the attackers' cannons were too small. A Chickasaw slave reportedly told Governor Bienville in 1737 that the Chickasaw had, on advice of the English among them, fortified stockades around their villages to European standards, thus making it necessary to bring bigger guns from France in order to breach the walls (Rowland and Sanders 1932:394, 693–694). In addition, the French decided to prepare to tunnel under the fortifications and blow them up with mortars.

Once committed to this military plan, Bienville needed to secure the arms, supplies, and supporting troops from France. This delay took many months. In addition, the heavy guns would require the construction of equally heavy-duty carts, as well as livestock to pull them along the anticipated roadway. Horses and oxen had to be procured from Illinois and Natchitoches settlements, and personnel and supplies sufficient to build carts had to be at the staging area. Time necessary for transportation and assembly of the material was factored into the arrival schedule for personnel, extending further the mobilization time needed for the campaign.

I suspect that the Quapaw did not mean to deceive de Verges or Bienville when they gave inaccurate information about the access route between the Mississippi River and the Chickasaw villages; they had not tried this approach to their antagonists' villages themselves. The lack of a road was no less disastrous than the loss of most of the horses, cattle, and oxen driven from Natchitoches. Those animals that were not lost to predators, accident, and misfortune along the way arrived at Arkansas Post too weak to continue across the intermittently flooded landscape, and replacements had to be sought from Illinois on short notice. The chief Louisiana wrangler, named Magdenoch (MacDonald?), was later accused of being frequently both drunk and lost during the drive, but the Illinois stock did not arrive in much better condition (Bienville 1923:170ff.; Anonymous 1859:62ff.; Delanglez 1985b:n.72).

In September 1738, Captain Jacques Coustilhas set out from the lower Mississippi Valley with a detachment of 150 men that included 120 soldiers, some European or Creole workmen, and some Africans who were presumably slaves, to build Fort St. Francis in the vicinity of the mouth of the St. Francis River. Upon arrival in December, a forested tract was cleared large enough to build a fortified enclosure that housed officers' lodgings, barracks for enlisted men, two large warehouses, a powder magazine, and a three-oven bakery. Over the next five months people and goods continued to arrive from both upstream and downstream. It is likely that expedient residential and work facilities sprang up around the fort and up and down the river as carts were constructed and other preparations went forward.

By spring of 1739, it was apparent that there was no easy eastern route from Fort St. Francis to the Chickasaw villages, and a long stretch of trackless, saturated alluvial lowland lay between the Mississippi and the uplands farther east. Bienville's nephew, Gilles Augustin Payen de Noyan, commandant at New Orleans and a veteran of the 1736 debacle, and 70 troops secured a location on high ground on the east bank of the Mississippi upstream from Fort St. Francis and built a second headquarters, Fort Assumption, in the location of modern-day Memphis. This became the principal staging point for the expedition, becoming fully manned in October 1739, but Fort St. Francis maintained a garrison and a support role until the expedition was brought to a close in 1740.

In the fall of 1739, Canadian troops and tribal allies begin to arrive. Continuing to trickle in all winter, the contingent was led by Le Moyne and Commandant Pierre Joseph Céleron (also spelled as Céloron) de Blainville. Participant lists show what is likely an unprecedented commingling of Native groups. Allies were recruited from all French-influenced areas of North America. Some groups accompanied the official colonial military contingents, and others arrived independently. The eyewitness diaries and postcampaign correspondence indicate that both large and small contingents of Natives were arriving and departing at intervals throughout the course of the campaign. Maintaining harmonious relationships among these diverse and periodically antagonistic groups was probably one of the greatest challenges to campaign leaders while awaiting the late and much-delayed arrivals of the French marines and their cannons, and Governor Bienville and his party. The official diaries and documents offer periodic glimpses of intertribal relations and diplomatic activities, and some stresses are evident in the early departure of some groups before the campaign was declared over in March 1740. The Potawatomi grew tired of the wait and left for home in late December. Others were skeptical that the expedition members could drag cannons, carts, and many men through the lowlands 40 leagues to the Chickasaw villages, especially in wet weather, once reconnoitering parties disclosed the character of terrain and distance to their destination.

The winter passed with little military action and few sightings of the Chickasaw, who by this time were avoiding confrontations and making small nocturnal overtures to the expedition headquarters at Fort Assumption, where they left tokens of peaceful intentions. A Canadian contingent led by Céleron, with Iroquois and Choctaw support, executed one or two raids on Chickasaw patrols stationed in front of their fortified villages. The raids eventually led to direct negotiations that culminated in the Chickasaw turnover of a few French prisoners and Natchez refugees, the gift of a calumet, a suit for peace, and sufficient political cover for Bienville and his chief advisers to declare the expedition a success without a major confrontation. Contemporary documents indicate that the French and Canadians were by this time painfully aware that they would be unable to mount a full expedition overland to the Chickasaw villages and expect a military success. In effect, Bienville and his allies declared victory and returned home. As he left, Bienville ordered both Fort Assumption and Fort St. Francis to be breached so that they would not be available for reuse by the Chickasaw at a future date. The Europeans and colonists left it to the Choctaw to continue harassing Chickasaw villages, burning fields, and capturing horses and other stock, in their role as French proxies for several years to come.

What Does All This Mean in Terms of Archaeology?

The 1739–1740 Chickasaw campaign undoubtedly left behind a material signature that remains to be located and explored. The site of Fort Assumption may be beyond our reach under metropolitan Memphis, but maybe sealed deposits still remain under urban development. The landscape around the mouth of the St. Francis, on the west side of the Mississippi, has remained largely rural since the mid-eighteenth century, and is a mosaic of fields and forests today. If a river has not claimed it, the fort site may still exist. Residents, visitors, and incoming participants would have heavily used the landscape surrounding both forts. Satellite encampments may have been widely distributed in an effort to provide essential resources like water, game, suitable terrain for erecting shelters, and firewood to each party, and to avoid crowding groups of strangers whose compatibility was both fragile and expedient.

Archaeological studies of French colonial-era sites in eastern North America over the last half a century have focused on four types of settlements: Native American villages and encampments; forts that were established for strategic military, political, and economic purposes and were intended for long-term use; domestic settlements and town sites that sometimes grew in association with fortified locales and at other times were situated at some distance from military outposts; and trading posts. Many of these sites were at least in part contemporary with Fort St. Francis and offer important reference data regarding material culture assemblages associated with both Indian and European lifeways. Archaeological work at Fort St. Francis would add to this by including a major short-term, multiethnic community. Comparative data regarding the organization of the community as a whole, however, will be harder to find.

If found, sites associated with the second Chickasaw campaign hold the potential for exploring several issues. These include the degree to which Native communities had appropriated elements of European and colonial material culture and lifeways. Pierre Vitry described the Native allies arriving with the Canadians as having been recruited from Christian mission communities. Sites associated with different contingents would be potential laboratories for testing methods and abilities to detect not only the purpose of the settlement but also the ethnic or tribal identity of the residents. As places representing an important episode in Mississippi Valley colonial history, any sites located could also serve as the focal points for heritage tourism that would complement the chain of French colonial parks and places already established in the region.

Fort St. Francis, and its associated short-term multiracial population, is virtually unique as a settlement and archaeological site, and there are no close models of site plans from previous archaeological research to guide future fieldwork. Works Progress Administration–era excavations at Fort Massac, established on the Ohio River in southern Illinois in 1757 and abandoned seven years later, provide extensive and potentially important information about the organization and use of a site established for French colonial forces and Indian allies, albeit one established nearly 20 years later. Ironically, Fort Massac was established by some of the same people who took part in the second French-Chickasaw War and were once again, two decades later, engaged in a logistical chess game that involved the Chickasaw and their Indian and English allies (Walthall 1991:42–64).

Eight years before the construction of Fort St. Francis, another large contingent of French colonials and their Indian allies assembled to effect a military solution to threats from a hostile common enemy in what is today northeastern Illinois. This time the assembled force was directed against the Meskwaki during what is referred to as the second Meskwaki War, and it was the latter group that erected a defensive fortification that was used only briefly before the bloody encounter was terminated (Stelle 1992:265–307). Although the archaeological investigations in search of the site were on a much smaller scale than those at Fort Massac, the project reveals useful material culture and feature information, and also serves as an appropriate model for the organization and goals of a similar investigation directed toward Fort St. Francis.

In addition, in an unusual twist of fate, this sprawling, lackluster expedition produced a vast documentary record that still remains to be compiled, but could provide a rich counterpoint to archaeological research. Only a handful of the more accessible documents are cited in this article. Consider the effect of bringing together so many different people from far-flung settlements, and then sending most of them home without enduring a major loss of life in a real war situation. Many participants went on to live long and productive lives in France, Canada, Illinois, and Louisiana, and they left behind memoirs, diaries, personal and official correspondence, and other documents. Beyond the official bureaucratic documents in French and colonial archives, we have the production of secular, personal documents, and a third level of record keeping deriving from demobilization reports generated by the return of contingents like the Canadian cadets to Montreal. Indian agents and missionaries accompanying Native contingents are also likely to have written letters and reports that still reside in secular and ecclesiastical archives, or have found their way to private collections.

Three of the best contemporary accounts of the campaign are examples of the diverse locations of these documents. Jesuit Father Vitry's journal may have been sent to the minister of marine, but it resided in a private archive when it was found. The diary by an officer with the commandant of the French marines resided in the library of French geographer Philippe Buache for many years, and later was owned by American bibliophile James Carter Brevoort when John Gilmary Shea published it in 1859. The journal by the younger Chaussegros de Léry, resident of French Canada, is found in the de Léry papers in the Quebec provincial archives. More are undoubtedly waiting to be found, because they helped individuals like Dumont *dit* Montigny recount the expedition in both his epic poem and history.

References Cited

Anonymous
1859   *Journal de la Guerre du Micissippi Contre les Chicachas, en 1739 et finie en 1740, le Ièr d'Avril, par un Officier de l'Armée de M. de Nouaille.* Presse Cramoisy de Jean-Marie Shea, New York.

Bienville, Jean Baptiste Le Moyne, Sieur de
1923   Journal de la Campagne des Tcicachas (Chicachas). *Rapport de l'Archiviste de la Province de Québec pour 1922–1923,* 166–178. Imprimeur de Sa Majesté le Roi, Québec.

Brasseaux, Carl A
2000   *France's Forgotten Legion: Service Records of French Military and Administrative Personnel Stationed in the Mississippi Valley and Gulf Coast Region, 1699–1769.* CD-ROM Publication. Louisiana State University Press, Baton Rouge.

Caldwell, Norman W.
1938   The Chickasaw Threat to French Control of the Mississippi in the 1740's. *Chronicles of Oklahoma* 16(4): 465–492.

Claiborne, J. F. H.
1964   *Mississippi as a Province, Territory and State, with Biographical Notices of Eminent Citizens.* Vol. 1. Louisiana State University Press, Baton Rouge. Originally published 1880, Power and Barksdale, Jackson, Miss.

Delanglez, Jean S. J.
1985a   A Louisiana Poet-Historian: Dumont *dit* Montigny. In *A Jean Delanglez Anthology: Selections Useful for Mississippi Valley and Trans-Mississippi American Indian Studies*, edited by Mildred Mott Wedel. Garland, New York. Originally published 1937, *Mid-America* 19(1): 31–49.
1985b   The Journal of Pierre Vitry. In *A Jean Delanglez Anthology: Selections Useful for Mississippi Valley and Trans-Mississippi American Indian Studies*, edited by Mildred Mott Wedel. Garland, New York. Originally published 1946, *Mid-America* 28(1): 23–59.

De Léry, Joseph-Gaspard
1923   Journal de la campagne faite par le détachement du Canada sur les Chicachas en février 1740, au nombre de 201 Français et 337 Sauvages de Canada, Illinois, Missouris et 58 Chactas faisant en tout 596 hommes. *Rapport de l'Archiviste de la Province de Québec pour 1922–1923*, 157–165. Imprimeur de Sa Majesté le Roi, Québec.

Dumont de Montigny
1931   L'Etablissement de la Province de la Louisiane: Poème composé de 1728 à 1742 par Dumont de Montigny. *Journal de la Société des Americanistes de Paris* 23:273–440.

Foret, Michael J.
1995   The Failure of Administration: The Chickasaw Campaign of 1739–1740. The French Experience in Louisiana. In *The Louisiana Purchase Bicentennial Series in Louisiana History*, Vol. 1, edited by Glenn R. Conrad, 313–321. University of Southwestern Louisiana, Lafayette.

Harris, John Brice
1959   *From Old Mobile to Fort Assumption: A Story of the French Attempts to Colonize Louisiana, and Destroy the Chickasaw Indians.* Parthenon Press, Nashville, Tenn.

Johnson, Jay K.
2000   The Chickasaws. In *Indians of the Greater Southeast: Historical Archaeology and Ethnohistory*, edited by Bonnie G. McEwan, 85–121. University Press of Florida, Gainesville.

Le Page du Pratz, Antoine S.
1975 [1774]   *The History of Louisiana.* Louisiana State University Press, Baton Rouge.

Lorenz, Karl G.
2000   The Natchez of Southwest Mississippi. In *Indians of the Greater Southeast: Historical Archaeology and Ethnohistory*, edited by Bonnie G. McEwan, 142–177. University Press of Florida, Gainesville.

Peyser, Joseph L.
1982   The Chickasaw Wars of 1736 and 1740: French Military Drawings and Plans Document the Struggle for Lower Mississippi. *Journal of Mississippi History* 44(1): 1–26.

Phelps, Dawson A.
1957   The Chickasaw, the English, and the French 1699–1744. *Tennessee Historical Quarterly* 16(2): 117–133.

Rowland, Dunbar, and A. G. Sanders, editors
1927   *Mississippi Provincial Archives, French Dominion.* Vol. 1, *1729–1740.* Mississippi Department of Archives and History, Jackson.
1932   *Mississippi Provincial Archives, French Dominion.* Vol. 3, *1704–1743.* Mississippi Department of Archives and History, Jackson.

Rowland, Dunbar, A. G. Sanders, and Patricia Kay Galloway, editors
1984   *Mississippi Provincial Archives, French Dominion.* Vol. 4, *1729–1748.* Louisiana State University Press, Baton Rouge.

Roy, Pierre-Georges
1940   *Inventaire des Papiers de Léry Conservés aux Archives de la Province de Québec.* Vol. Troisieme, Archives de la Province de Québec, Québec.

Stelle, Lenville J.
1992   The 1730 Mesquakie Fort. In *Calumet and Fleur-de-Lys: Archeology of Indian and French Contact in the Mid-Continent,* edited by John A. Walthall and Thomas E. Emerson, 265–307. Smithsonian Institution Press, Washington, D.C.

Vitry, Pierre
1929   Journal du Père Vitry de La Compagnie de Jésus Faisant Fonctions d'Aumonier des Troupes Destinées à La Guerre Contre Les Sauvages Tchikachas en 1738, 1739, et le Commencement de 1740. *Nova Francia: Organe de la Société d'histoire du Canada* 4:146–170.

Walthall, John A.
1991   French Colonial Fort Massac: Architecture and Ceramic Patterning. In *French Colonial Archaeology: The Illinois Country and the Western Great Lakes,* edited by John A. Walthall, 42–64. University of Illinois Press, Urbana.

Wedel, Mildred Mott
1985   *A Jean Delanglez Anthology: Selections Useful for Mississippi Valley and Trans-Mississippi American Indian Studies.* Garland, New York.

7

Colonial and Creole Diets in Eighteenth-Century New Orleans

ELIZABETH M. SCOTT AND SHANNON LEE DAWDY

In this essay, we discuss the dietary evidence revealed by the analysis of animal remains from two sites in New Orleans, Louisiana, and how that evidence contributes to an understanding of the process of creolization. Faunal assemblages from the Madame John's Legacy (16OR51) and St. Augustine (16OR148) sites provide an opportunity to examine subsistence in both French and Spanish occupations of New Orleans between 1715 and 1800. The assemblages from Madame John's Legacy, an inn and a residence in the city, and St. Augustine, a plantation site just outside the city, allow us to address dietary differences related to socioeconomic position, ethnicity, and urban–rural location. In addition, we explore evidence for distinctions between colonial and Creole diets.

Site Descriptions

The Madame John's Legacy and St. Augustine sites are located within the present-day city limits of New Orleans. Both sites have standing architectural features as well as intact underground archaeological features dating to the early French colonial period (ca. 1718–1769), the Spanish colonial period (ca. 1769–1803), and the antebellum period (ca. 1803–1861). This essay is concerned with only the first two periods, however. The sites were excavated between 1996 and 1999 by staff of the Greater New Orleans Archaeology Program of the College of Urban and Public Affairs at the University of New Orleans (Dawdy and Ibáñez 1997; Dawdy 1998; Matthews 1999). Analysis of the faunal material from the sites was conducted in 2002 (Dawdy et al. 2002; Scott 2002).

Located in New Orleans' French Quarter, Madame John's Legacy is owned and managed by the Louisiana State Museum. The standing Main House, while rebuilt in 1788, is one of the few remaining examples of an architectural style common during the French colonial period. An earlier house on the same spot had been occupied by a French innkeeper from the 1720s to the 1770s, and then by the captain of the Spanish regiment from 1783 to 1788. Captain Manuel de Lanzos rebuilt the house in 1788 after a catastrophic fire struck the city in March of that year. His family continued to live on the site until 1813. Excavations led by Shannon Dawdy in 1997 revealed a number of courtyard and midden surfaces in addition to a well-preserved trash pit dating to the 1788 fire (Dawdy 1998). During excavations, it was noted that this trash pit was rich in animal bone and burned materials. For this reason, it was thought that the site could provide an excellent opportunity to study the diet and environmental adaptations of New Orleans' earliest inhabitants.

The St. Augustine site is located in a lot adjacent to St. Augustine Church in the Trémé neighborhood of New Orleans. One of the earliest plantation houses in the New Orleans area occupied this site, dating to the founding of the city under the Company of the Indies. The company established this "industrial" plantation in 1720 as a brickyard and tilery to provide building materials for the booming town. In the 1730s, the plantation was transferred to private ownership by the prominent de Morand and Prevost families, passing from French-born to Creole-born family members. They continued to operate it as a plantation and occasional brickyard until 1810. Between September 1998 and October 1999, Christopher Matthews directed excavations at the site (Matthews 1999). They revealed well-preserved colonial-era deposits along the back wall of the great house and what would have been the rear yard area. Layers of bricked courtyards and sheet-midden surfaces offered particularly rich contexts for faunal analysis.

Material Evidence of Creolization

Shannon Dawdy (2000) has proposed three phases of creolization in lower Louisiana and what they might look like materially: transplantation, closely linked to the French colonial period (1718–1769); ethnic acculturation, associated with the Spanish colonial period (1769–1803); and hybridization, associated with the antebellum American period (1803–1861).

We focus on the eighteenth century here, and thus will be examining the faunal remains in light of distinctions that might obtain for only the first two phases, transplantation and ethnic acculturation.

According to this model, in the transplantation phase, the first generation of foreign-born settlers builds houses and maintains a culture most closely matching that of the Old World. Even if unsuited to local conditions, they try to replicate foodways known from the home country. The second generation, or native Creoles, are the first to consistently integrate New World products and ideas into their daily lives. This should result in a diet that is adapted to the local environment and reflects practical considerations.

In the ethnic acculturation phase, "Creole" takes on an ethnic meaning of its own, and colonial material forms and household traditions become better defined. Some are a selection of Old World and New World ideas, and some are invented traditions, arising from the need to reinforce ethnic identity in the colonial setting. During this phase, new immigrants embrace the material identity of one of the dominant ethnic groups in the colony and leave behind Old World ways more quickly than did the first generation of settlers. Colonial architectural, consumer, and dietary traditions become better defined and somewhat conservative.

Scott has suggested elsewhere that the effects of economic position need to be included in our models of the creolization process (Scott 2007). Poorer colonists may not have had the financial means to make the kinds of choices about foods that middle- and upper-class colonists did. If those economic circumstances remained unchanged in later generations, then the diets of poorer households would be unlikely to undergo a creolization process such as that described above. It may well be that this creolization process occurred primarily among the middle- or upper-class colonists, such as those to be examined in this study.

The occupancy of Madame John's Legacy by the Pascal-Marin family, from ca. 1728 to 1777, encompasses the transplanted foreigner generation and the first native-born population, as does the 1715–1775 occupancy at the St. Augustine plantation. At Madame John's Legacy, the house/inn was run by a French immigrant, Elizabeth Real, during the early decades, but she was probably then assisted by her Creole daughter and grandchildren from the 1750s through 1770s (Dawdy 2000:112). At the St. Augustine plantation site, the Company of the Indies built the plantation and brickyard around 1717, but left in 1731. It was purchased by a former employee,

Charles de Morand, who continued its operation until he died in 1756. The plantation remained in the hands of the Morand family until 1775 (Matthews 1999:1-2). The later colonial occupation at Madame John's Legacy provides a glimpse of the ethnic acculturation phase. Between 1783 and 1803, the site was the residence of Manuel de Lanzos, a relatively wealthy Spanish officer; his Panamanian-born wife, Gertrudis; and their children (Dawdy 2000:113).

Zooarchaeological Methods

Identification of the faunal remains from these sites was conducted using the comparative collections of the Illinois State Museum in Springfield and the Georgia Museum of Natural History in Athens. Calculations of the minimum number of individuals (MNIs) represented for each taxon were figured based on the criteria of side, size, sex, tooth eruption, and fusion of skeletal elements (Reitz and Wing 1999:194-200; Purdue 1983). Meat weight estimates (biomass) were figured for the vertebrate remains using the techniques of skeletal mass allometry (Reitz and Wing 1999:221-231; Reitz et al. 1987). This method results in a conservative estimate of meat weight, since it predicts only the amount of meat that would have been adhering to the bones recovered. A least-squares regression formula was used, which calculates meat weight (live weight) from the bone weight. MNIs and biomass were calculated for each period at the site, that is, combining the data from all proveniences within each time period.

Results of the Analysis

Previous studies (e.g., Scott 1985, 1996; Martin 1986, 1988, 1991) suggested that faunal samples from French colonial deposits should exhibit use of a variety of wild species. It was not known, however, what the impact of the urban environment and urban marketing forces would have on French colonial dietary practices. All previous environmental studies of French Louisiana sites had been conducted on rural plantations or relatively small military settlements.

The results of this analysis do indeed confirm that French colonial residents used a variety of species in their environment, especially compared to British contemporaries. However, what was not necessarily expected was that almost all contexts from these New Orleans sites, including later

Spanish and antebellum deposits, would point to a diet rich in wild game and fish. This was somewhat surprising, given that New Orleans had, by the 1780s, taken on a respectable urban character, with over 5,000 residents and a well-developed market system for domestic produce. No consistent pattern emerged from the analysis to indicate that rural or urban setting had any effect on the origin of animal foods. Town dwellers up through the early antebellum period had access to, and an apparent interest in, wild game, particularly a wide variety of fish (both freshwater and saltwater), small mammals, and ducks. Often these species were obtained from Native Americans who brought foods to town to trade (Usner 1998:56–72), but they also could be obtained in the market and through hunting parties into the interior areas (Usner 1992:174, 208–209). The faunal assemblages at these sites provide material evidence for the consumption of many of the wild species that are mentioned in eighteenth- and nineteenth-century documents for the Louisiana colony.

The likelihood that plantation dwellers could economically raise their own domestic animals may have contributed to the somewhat higher biomass contributions in those contexts. However, there were plenty of cattle, pig, and sheep herds in Louisiana from at least the 1730s onward that could have supplied markets with meat from domestic animals (Usner 1992:176–190; Rushton 1979:127–131). In addition, until the construction of railroads in the 1880s, the Mississippi River was the chief means of transporting cattle and beef (Rushton 1979:131). Thus, the rural or urban location of these sites probably did not affect the residents' access to domestic meats.

Diet: Wild, Domestic, and Ethnic

It had also been expected that some ethnic dietary differences between the French, Spanish, and Anglo-American occupations may have been expressed in proportions of wild game to domestic meat. This held true for differences between the later Anglo-American occupations and the others, but not between the French and Spanish occupations. Wild species that were identified in the faunal collections include swamp rabbit, ducks, passenger pigeon, turtles, and several kinds of fish. The St. Augustine plantation occupation and the Spanish period de Lanzos occupation at Madame John's Legacy showed the greatest devotion to wild species (Figure 7.1). At the St. Augustine site, deer, opossum, turtles, and

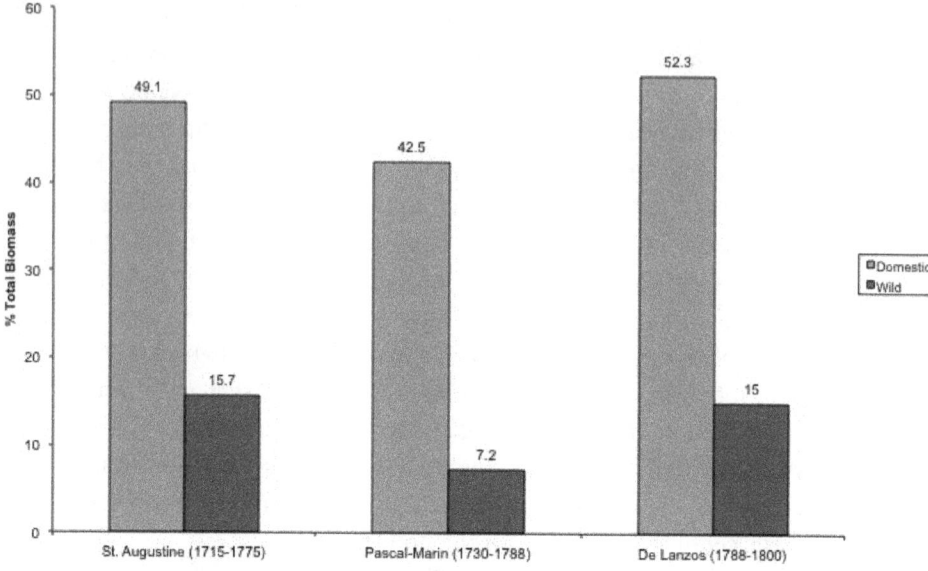

Figure 7.1. Percentages of biomass of total domestic and wild species recovered from excavations described in text.

fish accounted for 15.7 percent of the estimated meat weight (Figure 7.1). In the de Lanzos deposits at Madame John's, wild species account for a similar 15 percent of the total meat weight, but are more varied, including rabbits, ducks, turkey, passenger pigeon, turtles, and fish (Table 7.2). Thus, while one might think that the more rural location of the St. Augustine plantation would result in much greater use of wild resources than at the urban site, this does not seem to have been the case. One reason may be that the plantation was, in reality, just on the outskirts of the city, rather than in a more remote location. Another reason is that, as noted above, many wild birds and fish (and probably rabbits) were available in New Orleans' markets, such that city dwellers had easy access to them.

There are, however, a few indications that the more rural location may have influenced the *kinds* of wild species that were found at the plantation site (Table 7.1). Deer and opossum were found only at the plantation, and a greater variety of fishes were recovered at the plantation than in either period at the urban site. While all three assemblages included freshwater catfishes, sunfishes, and saltwater sheepshead, the St. Augustine plantation assemblage also included gar and bowfin (freshwater species) and jacks and flounder (saltwater species). Jacks inhabit shallow and deep

Table 7.1. Faunal remains, St. Augustine Plantation (16OR148), 1715–1775

Taxon	Adj #	Wt (g)	MNI #	MNI %	Biom kg	Biom %
Cow	14	366.2	2	8.0	5.79	46.6
Pig	7	11.5	2	8.0	0.25	2.0
Goat	1	0.9	1	4.0	0.02	0.2
Sheep/Goat	1	0.3			0.01	0.1
White-tailed deer	2	55.9	1	4.0	1.06	8.5
Unid. Large Mammal	70	162.4			2.85	22.9
Dog/Coyote	1	5.8	1	4.0	0.13	1.1
Unid. Rodent	2	0.0	1	4.0	0.00	0.0
Cf. Opossum	1	0.4	1	4.0	0.01	0.1
Unid. Mammal	136	53.5	___	___	1.06	8.5
MAMMAL SUBTOTAL	235	656.9	9	36.0	11.18	90.0
Chicken	2	1.0	1	4.0	0.02	0.2
Unid. Bird	95	20.0	2	8.0	0.35	2.8
BIRD SUBTOTAL	97	21.0	3	12.0	0.37	3.0
Pond slider	2	5.9	2	8.0	0.14	1.1
Unid. Turtle	1	0.5	___	___	0.02	0.3
REPTILE SUBTOTAL	3	6.4	2	8.0	0.16	1.4
Gar sp.	11	2.2	2	8.0	0.07	0.6
Bowfin	2	0.0	1	4.0	0.00	0.0
Freshwater Catfishes (Ictaluridae)	1	2.3	1	4.0	0.04	0.3
Catfishes (Siluriformes)	1	0.0	1	4.0	0.00	0.0
Sunfishes (Centrarchidae)	1	0.0	1	4.0	0.00	0.0
Jack sp. (*Caranx* sp.)	1	3.6	1	4.0	0.08	0.6
Sheepshead	1	0.6	1	4.0	0.02	0.2
Flounder sp. (*Paralichthys* sp.)	1	0.5	1	4.0	0.02	0.2
Unid. Fish	492	26.6	___	___	0.51	4.1
FISH SUBTOTAL	511	35.8	9	36.0	0.74	6.0
Unid. Bone	133	1.8				
Unid. Crustacean	1	0.1	1	4.0		
Unid. Bivalve	5	4.5	1	4.0		
Unid. Shell	5	0.9				
TOTALS	990	727.4	25	100.0	12.43	100.1

Note: MNIs refigured, biomass added (0.0=<0.1; 0.00=<0.01)

waters and occasionally enter fresh water; flounders live in estuaries and coastal waters; gars and bowfins inhabit backwaters and swamps, and gars occasionally enter brackish and marine waters. This suggests that plantation residents outside the city had greater access to a variety of fish habitats than did city residents, who probably relied on market selections.

The contexts at the St. Augustine site produced the only deer bones, suggesting that only in relatively rural contexts was this animal still

Table 7.2. Faunal remains, Madame John's Legacy (16OR51), de Lanzos occupation, 1788–1800 (fire and postfire)

Taxon	Adj #	Wt (g)	MNI #	MNI %	Biom kg	Biom %
Cow	66	1,507.9	3	5.9	19.89	34.9
Cow/Bison	8	167.9			2.69	4.7
Pig	34	333.6	2	3.9	5.26	9.2
Sheep/Goat	3	26.2	1	2.0	0.53	0.9
Unid. Large Mammal	1,065	1,147.2			15.66	27.4
Swamp Rabbit	12	7.8	3	5.9	0.18	0.3
Unid. Mammal	1,604	100.3	—	—	1.77	3.1
MAMMAL SUBTOTAL	2,792	3,290.9	9	17.7	45.98	80.5
Duck Group (Anatinae)	124	75.0	11	21.6	1.10	1.9
Ducks & Geese (Anatidae)	1	1.4			0.03	0.1
Turkey	2	5.0	1	2.0	0.09	0.2
Chicken	79	84.8	8	15.7	1.22	2.1
Turkey/Chicken	1	0.5			0.01	0.0
Passenger Pigeon	14	4.9	2	3.9	0.10	0.2
Rock Dove	57	15.8	5	9.8	0.27	0.5
Pigeons & Doves (Columbidae)	2	0.4			0.01	0.0
Passeriformes	1	0.1	1	2.0	0.00	0.0
Unid. Bird	711	87.9	—	—	1.27	2.2
BIRD TOTAL	992	275.8	28	55.0	4.10	7.2
Pond Slider	29	337.4	3	5.9	1.56	2.7
Pond Slider/River Cooter	2	80.2			0.60	1.1
Unid. Turtle	59	294.3	—	—	1.43	2.5
REPTILE SUBTOTAL	90	711.9	3	5.9	3.59	6.3
Bullhead sp. (*Ameiurus* sp.)	1	0.1	1	2.0	0.00	0.0
Blue Catfish	9	13.9	1	2.0	0.24	0.4
Cf. Blue Catfish	2	3.2			0.06	0.1
Freshwater Catfishes (Ictaluridae)	9	15.0			0.26	0.5
Catfishes (Siluriformes)	4	2.2			0.04	0.1
Bass sp. (*Micropterus* sp.)	1	0.3	1	2.0	0.01	0.0
Sunfishes (Centrarchidae)	1	0.2			0.01	0.0
Sheepshead	66	72.3	4	7.8	0.92	1.6
Porgies (Sparidae)	10	6.2			0.13	0.2
Red Drum	3	3.4	1	2.0	0.10	0.2
Cf. Red Drum	1	0.7	1	2.0	0.03	0.1
Freshwater Drum	1	0.2	1	2.0	0.01	0.0
Drums (Sciaenidae)	1	0.4			0.02	0.0
Unid. Fish	2,153	116.8	—	—	1.58	2.8
FISH SUBTOTAL	2,262	234.9	10	19.8	3.41	6.0
Unid. Bone	4,351	23.3				
Sea Urchins (Abaciidae)	3	0.1	1	2.0		
Unid. Shell	17	1.6				
TOTALS[a]	10,507	4,538.5	51	100.4	57.08	100.0

Notes: MNIs refigured, biomass added (0.0=<0.1; 0.00=<0.01)
a. Excluded 1 worked human tooth (0.8 g).

available for food. Although deer was by far the most important animal economically to the Louisiana colony in the French period, it does not appear to have been important to the New Orleans–area diet. It is quite likely, however, that the active trade in hides had greatly reduced deer herds in this densely populated section of Louisiana by the 1730s. Despite documentary references that bear oil was a significant component of the French colonial diet, no bear bones were found. Bear remains have been found at other French colonial settlements, such as Fort Pentagoet (Faulkner 1992), Fort Ouiatenon (Martin 1986, 1991), and Cahokia Township (Martin 1988, 1991). It is likely, however, that bear oil was obtained through trade with Native American groups, along with bear meat, venison, and tallow (Usner 1998:70), none of which would be visible in the archaeological record.

Comparing the two urban occupations at Madame John's, we see that the earlier French colonial residents depended on wild species much less than did the later Spanish-Panamanian residents. In the Pascal-Marin assemblage, 7.2 percent of the total meat weight is comprised of wild species, roughly half that of the de Lanzos assemblage (Tables 7.2 and 7.3). Among wild species, the French colonial deposits have a higher proportion of rabbit, while the Spanish deposits at Madame John's have a somewhat greater variety of birds and more fish (in terms of both biomass and diversity), as well as the only turtle remains. However, if this pattern is seen not as Spanish versus French, but as colonial versus Creole, the faunal results fit well with Dawdy's hypothesis that the second, Creole generation would embrace the native resources of the local environment more than the previous generations (Dawdy 2000). In fact, only one resident of the de Lanzos household was known to be born in the Old World, and that was the father, Captain de Lanzos. It is likely that his Afro-Creole slaves, his Panamanian-born wife, and his Louisiana-born daughters had the greater influence on what was placed on the dining table.

Although it is beyond the scope of this essay to discuss in detail, there is only slight evidence for change through time in the de Lanzos's diet. A large trash pit (Feature 12) was revealed in the courtyard of Madame John's Legacy, which contained large amounts of household refuse and animal remains that were burned in the catastrophic fire of March 1788. The faunal material does not suggest that entire animals or carcasses were being stored at the house and then accidentally burned in the fire. Instead, it suggests that the pit deposits represent a scooping up or gathering of

Table 7.3. Faunal remains, Madame John's Legacy (16OR51), Pascal-Marin occupation, 1730–1788 (prefire)

Taxon	Adj #	Wt (g)	MNI #	MNI %	Biom kg	Biom %
Cow	8	189.8	1	4.4	3.14	26.0
Cow/Bison	5	75.4			1.29	10.7
Pig	6	32.2	1	4.4	0.60	5.0
Cf. Pig	1	1.1			0.03	0.3
Unid. Large Mammal	57	225.1			3.62	30.0
Norway/Black Rat	1	0.3	1	4.4	0.01	0.1
Unid. Rodent	2	0.3			0.01	0.1
Swamp Rabbit	6	5.7	2	8.7	0.13	1.1
Rabbits & Hares (Leporidae)	1	0.5	1	4.4	0.01	0.1
Unid. Mammal	210	111.9	—	—	1.93	16.0
MAMMAL SUBTOTAL	297	642.3	6	26.3	10.77	89.4
Duck group (Anatinae)	37	15.7	7	30.4	0.26	2.2
Chicken	7	3.2	2	8.7	0.06	0.5
Passeriformes	1	0.1	1	4.4	0.00	0.0
Unid. Bird	170	33.2	1	4.4	0.53	4.4
BIRD SUBTOTAL	215	52.2	11	47.9	0.85	7.1
Blue Catfish	1	0.1	1	4.4	0.00	0.0
Freshwater Catfishes (Ictaluridae)	1	0.2			0.00	0.0
Sunfishes (Centrarchidae)	4	0.5	1	4.4	0.02	0.2
Sheepshead	2	3.2	2	8.7	0.05	0.4
Freshwater Drum	1	0.7	1	4.4	0.03	0.3
Unid. Fish	133	20.1	—	—	0.36	3.0
FISH SUBTOTAL	142	24.8	5	21.9	0.46	3.9
Unid. Bone	281	2.2				
Unid. Crustacean	1	0.2	1	4.4		
Unid. Shell	3	0.7				
TOTALS	939	722.4	23	100.5	12.08	100.4

Note: MNIs refigured, biomass added (0.0=<0.1; 0.00=<0.01)

general refuse after the fire, as secondary, and probably tertiary, deposits. The contents of Feature 12, then, represent refuse from the early years of the de Lanzos's occupation of the house, which they purchased in 1783, shortly after their arrival in the colony. The only significant difference in the assemblage from Feature 12 and the contexts dated 1788–1800 is the presence of turtle remains in the earlier Feature 12. At least three very large pond sliders are represented by the remains in Feature 12. No turtle remains are to be found at all in the postfire deposits (1788–1800) from the de Lanzos household, suggesting elimination of this food from their diet after only a few years. In most respects, however, the diet revealed in the 1788 fire trash pit is remarkably similar to the diet revealed in the 1788–1800 deposits, suggesting stability in the de Lanzos diet (even "conservatism") as suggested by Dawdy (2000) for the second stage in the creolization process.

Furthermore, the earlier French assemblages at Madame John's and at the plantation appear to have adhered to the most "European" diet. If we break down the Pascal-Marin (1730–1788) assemblage, we see some evidence of change through time. Although the assemblage from the first French-born occupants, the Pascals, at Madame John's Legacy (1730–1760) is too small to provide reliable conclusions (NISP=238; MNI=6), it reveals a dependence on inexpensive cuts of domestic meats supplemented with ducks and fish. In the 1760–1788 Pascal-Marin deposits, the diet diversifies somewhat, and includes rabbit and many different kinds of fish. This, too, would support an association between wild food consumption and creolization in later generations.

In all three households, domestic species contributed the greatest proportion of the estimated meat weight, ranging from 42 to 52 percent of the total biomass; these percentages are much higher if the unidentifiable large mammal is included with the domestic mammals. Domestic species here include cow, pig, sheep/goat, chicken, and rock dove (domestic pigeons). The last are considered to be domestic species, since they were introduced to North America by Europeans, and were likely to have been kept in *pigeonniers* by residents in or near New Orleans. Eighteenth-century market price lists of foods purchased in New Orleans include pigeons as well as turkeys and "French domestic duck" (Usner 1992:208–209).

Among the domestic species, however, some interesting differences appear between the sites. The French deposits suggest a reliance on and possible preference for beef over pork (Figure 7.2). In the Pascal-Marin assemblage at Madame John's, pork comprised 5.3 percent of the total meat weight compared with 36.7 percent for beef (see Table 7.3); in the St. Augustine plantation assemblage, pork comprised only 2 percent of the total meat weight, compared with 46.6 percent for beef (Table 7.1). Given the presence of several cow head and foot bones in the plantation deposits, it seems likely that cattle were raised and butchered on the plantation. At the slightly later French Main House at Nina Plantation (1820s–1851) in Pointe Coupee Parish, Louisiana, a similar preference is seen for beef (33.4 percent of meat weight) over pork (5.8 percent) and mutton (4.2 percent) (Scott 2001).

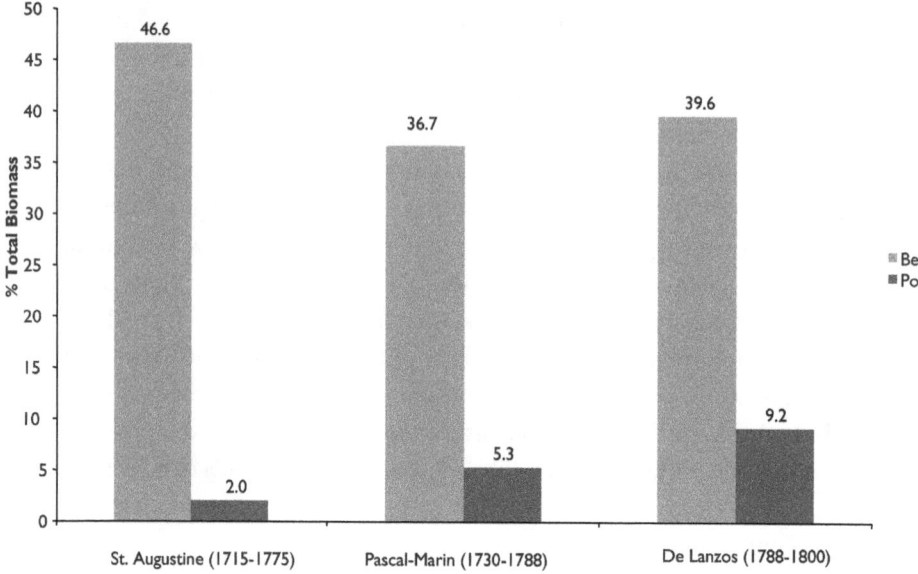

Figure 7.2. Percentages of total biomass of beef versus pork remains recovered from excavations described in text.

The Spanish deposits, however, suggest a greater reliance on pork. In the de Lanzos assemblage, pork comprised 9.2 percent of the total meat weight (Figure 7.2). When the de Lanzos assemblage is broken down, it appears that this preference for pork increases through time. In Feature 12, the fire trash pit, pig remains account for 5.3 percent of the total meat weight; in the 1788–1800 postfire deposits, pig remains account for 22.3 percent of the total meat weight. Studies of sixteenth- and eighteenth-century occupations in the southeastern United States suggest that the traditional Spanish preference for mutton had to be adapted to the conditions for raising livestock in the region. Pork and beef came to supplant mutton as the mainstay in the domestic meat diet. However, there is no clear-cut preference for pork, since some Spanish assemblages from southeastern U.S. sites are dominated by cow remains, and other assemblages are dominated by pig remains (Reitz and Scarry 1985:88–99). It might be noted that by the 1500s in Spain, eating pork had become a means of emphasizing that one was Catholic and not Muslim or Jewish (Sarasúa 2001).

At Madame John's Legacy, the Spanish deposits contained sheep and sheep/goat remains, but the French Pascal-Marin deposits did not. However, the French St. Augustine plantation deposits contained goat and sheep/goat; these remains also were found in another, smaller, French plantation assemblage in the New Orleans area (Scott 2002). This tentatively suggests that in the colonial period, sheep and goats may have been raised primarily for dairy products and wool, and that residents (whether French or Spanish) ate only old or surplus animals for their meat. Extensive documentation suggests that French Louisianans were attempting to re-create a dairy culture in the colony. It may be that they were finding these animals better suited to the local environment than were dairy cows. However, it may also be the case that sheep and goats did not thrive in the hot, humid environment of Louisiana, and therefore simply were not present in large numbers.

Strategies: Wild, Domestic, and Economic

Given the diversity of site functions and occupants at these sites, a measurement of socioeconomic status is difficult to obtain. The deposits left on these sites by enslaved laborers (both African and Native American), plantation owners, Creole sailors, aristocratic military officers, and struggling French immigrants may be as mingled as New Orleans' colonial populations were. Some generalizations are suggested, however, by the butchered cuts of meat. There appears to be some cross-cultural agreement on the meatier and more desirable portions of domestic animals, and zooarchaeologists have long used the distribution of meaty to bony portions in an assemblage as an indicator of the economic position of the site residents, especially in urban locations (e.g., Schulz and Gust 1983; Szuter 1996).

Among these households, the Spanish de Lanzos residence suggests the highest economic position based on the cuts of meat represented (Table 7.4 and Figure 7.3). Nearly 40 percent of the beef cuts were from the meatiest portions (loin, short loin, round, and rib), 41 percent from medium-ranked cuts, and 19 percent from the boniest portions. Pork also is represented primarily by high- and medium-ranked cuts (71.1 percent). Although very little mutton is present, it is primarily from the meatiest portions. Since the pig and sheep/goat remains from the St. Augustine plantation site are all foot bones, it is clear that cattle and deer provided most of the meat there (Table 7.5). The range of cattle portions represented in the assemblage suggests on-site butchering of whole animals, as might be expected. Overall, the meat cuts suggest a somewhat lower

Table 7.4. Meat cuts data, Madame John's Legacy (16OR51), de Lanzos occupation, 1788–1800 (fire and postfire)

Beef	# Cuts	% Beef
Loin (1-steak)	6	8.8
Short Loin	14	20.6
Chuck	2	2.9
Rump	2	2.9
Round	3	4.4
Brisket	3	4.4
Brisket/Short Plate	9	13.2
Rib	4	5.9
Rib/Brisket/Short Plate	5	7.4
Chuck/Rib (1-steak)	7	10.3
Foreshank	9	13.2
Neck	2	2.9
Foot	2	2.9
Beef Total	68	99.8

Pork	# Cuts	% Pork
Ham	2	6.5
Leg	2	6.5
Shoulder	4	12.9
Rib	8	25.8
Shoulder/Rib	3	9.7
Jowl	3	9.7
Foot	9	29.0
Pork Total	31	100.1
[Loose teeth]	[3]	

Mutton	# Cuts	% Mutton
Shoulder	2	66.7
Hindshank	1	33.3
Mutton Total	3	100.0

economic position compared to the de Lanzos household. The Pascal-Marin household appears to have had the lowest economic position of the three, based on the meat cuts represented (Table 7.6 and Figure 7.3). The beef and pork cuts are mostly medium- to poorer-quality portions; although the assemblage includes a pork loin and shoulder, no high-quality beef cuts are represented. This distribution of meat cuts does not fit with the archaeological and historical evidence of upper-middle-class residents during this period. It could reflect, however, the role of the property as an inn/tavern, where less expensive cuts of meat, soups, and stews may have been served to patrons.

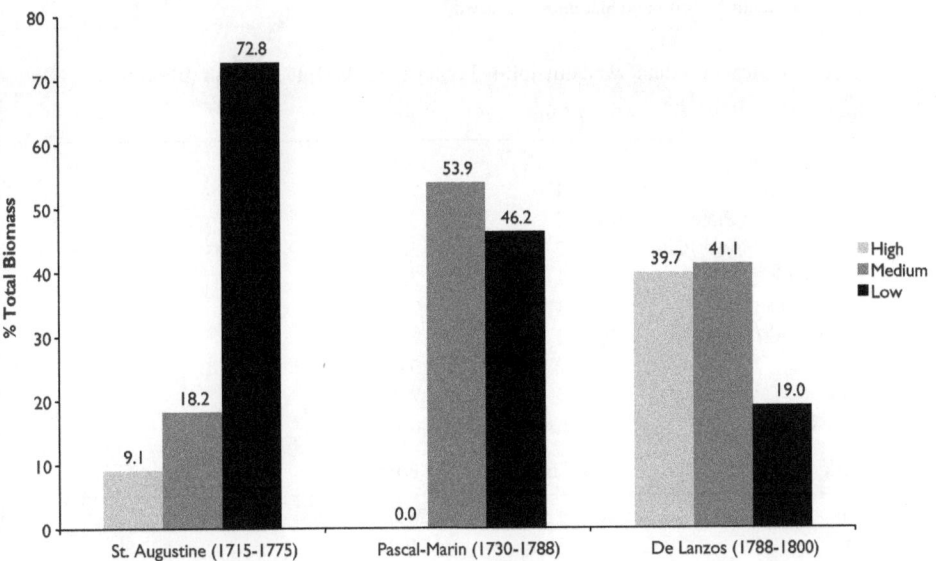

Figure 7.3. Percentages of total biomass of status-indicating cuts of beef recovered from excavations described in text.

Table 7.5. Meat cuts data, St. Augustine Plantation (16OR148), 1715–1775

Beef	# Cuts	% Beef
Loin	1	9.1
Chuck	1	9.1
Rib/Brisket/Short Plate	1	9.1
Hindshank (veal?)	1	9.1
Head	1	9.1
Foot	6	54.6
Beef Total	11	100.1
Pork	# Cuts	% Pork
Foot	2	100.0
[Loose teeth]	[5]	
Goat	# Cuts	% Goat
Foot	1	100.0
Mutton	# Cuts	% Mutton
[Loose teeth]	[1]	
Venison	# Cuts	% Venison
Shoulder	1	50.0
Hindshank	1	50.0
Venison Total	2	100.0

Table 7.6. Meat cuts data, Madame John's Legacy (16OR51), 1730–1788 (prefire)

Beef	# Cuts	% Beef
Chuck/Arm	2	15.4
Chuck/Rib	1	7.7
Brisket/Short Plate	2	15.4
Rib/Brisket/Short Plate	2	15.4
Foreshank	1	7.7
Hindshank	1	7.7
Hindshank/Hock	1	7.7
Neck	2	15.4
Foot	1	7.7
Beef Total	13	100.1
Pork	# Cuts	% Pork
Loin	1	20.0
Shoulder	1	20.0
Rib	1	20.0
Foot	2	40.0
Pork Total	5	100.0
[Loose teeth]	[2]	

Zooarchaeologists are not in agreement as to whether a high proportion of wild animals in an assemblage from a historical archaeological site indicates high status or low status, or how this may change according to culture/nationality. The results from this analysis suggest a complex picture indeed. The earliest plantation context at St. Augustine and the Spanish de Lanzos occupation at Madame John's Legacy are the richest in wild species. However, by other measures, occupants at St. Augustine were surviving at a significantly lower economic level than those of the de Lanzos household. This suggests that species diversity may be helpful as an indicator of status in strictly urban environments, but is not very helpful in more rural ones, where simple availability and the possibility of self-provisioning play a larger role than preference and status considerations. Furthermore, the fact that St. Augustine exhibited a range of low-, mid-, and high-status domestic meat cuts suggests that whole animals were butchered and consumed on site (seen especially in the head and foot elements present). Thus, socioeconomic measurements based on domestic animal consumption (that is, cuts of meat) may only be useful in strictly urban environments where consumers depended on the market butcher.

Our safest comparisons, then, might be between the two urban households, Pascal-Marin and de Lanzos, using both species diversity and meat cut data. In addition to the cattle and pigs that are present in both assemblages, the de Lanzos assemblage includes sheep/goat remains as well. Chicken and turkey provided the greatest meat contribution from birds, and domestic pigeons (rock doves) and passenger pigeon appear for the first time in the de Lanzos assemblage. The presence of these species, as well as the variety of fish remains and turtles, suggests a higher economic position for the de Lanzos than was true for the earlier Pascal-Marin inn and residence. This higher economic position is suggested by the meat cut data as well, as was just noted.

Discussion

This study was the first analysis of faunal material from any French colonial New Orleans site, and thus will help create a critically needed baseline for future studies. While extensive intersite comparisons are not possible in the space provided, a few thoughts in this regard might be offered here. Terrance Martin (1991:197) has noted several species that seem to be markers of French colonial occupation in the middle Mississippi Valley and Illinois Country, the northern end of the Louisiana colony. Among these are large blue catfish and large red-eared turtles, or pond sliders, which also were found in the New Orleans assemblages. Other species of catfishes and turtles were available in all of these locations, but French colonists seem to have preferred these species, and very large individuals, to the others. It might also be noted that, although the de Lanzos family was Spanish-Panamanian in origin, they were a minority among the predominantly French, Creole, and African residents in New Orleans. It is most likely that the markets of that city reflected the food preferences of the majority population, and that the kinds of fish or turtles or wild fowl the de Lanzos family bought reflected not Spanish food preferences but their choices among what was available at the largely French and Creole markets. And so we see large blue catfish and large pond sliders in their food remains, as in the French households.

Elizabeth Scott has argued elsewhere (1985, 1996, 2001) that French colonists in North America were more willing to incorporate wild species into their diets than were British colonists and Anglo-American residents in the same location. This is corroborated by the larger study of which the discussion here is only a part. The nineteenth-century Anglo-American occupations of these New Orleans sites are outside our focus on colonial and Creole diets, but it may be noted that Anglo-Americans used far fewer wild species than their predecessors (Scott 2002). Furthermore, this analysis confirms previous findings that Spanish colonists in the southeastern United States also were willing to incorporate wild species into their diets (e.g., Reitz and Cumbaa 1983; Reitz and Scarry 1985). Thus, both French and Spanish colonists tended to embrace a wide array of wild species that the British and Anglo-Americans did not.

It is true that some of this openness toward wild species is to be found in cultural food preferences brought from France and Spain. For example, wild game, wild birds, and fish are part of food traditions in rural France today (e.g., Guermont 1985) and of both Creole and Cajun food traditions in Louisiana (Esman 1985:52–53, 111, 113; Rushton 1979:167, 211–213). However, this study has emphasized that the incorporation of wild species into the diet in some colonial and postcolonial settings also may develop over time. In this case, diet is one means by which the creolization process may be seen archaeologically. This study has provided a unique opportunity to examine generational change and ethnic dietary preferences within New Orleans' dynamic Native American, French, African, Creole, Spanish, and Anglo-American households. It is hoped that future excavations will reveal additional eighteenth-century occupations and that the present study may provide a useful basis for comparison with that data.

Acknowledgments

This study would not have been possible without the support of the Greater New Orleans Archaeology Program of the College of Urban Affairs, University of New Orleans; National Park Service; Illinois State Museum; Georgia Museum of Natural History.

References Cited

Dawdy, Shannon Lee
1998 *Madame John's Legacy (16OR51) Revisited: A Closer Look at the Archaeology of Colonial New Orleans.* University of New Orleans, New Orleans.
2000 Understanding Cultural Change through the Vernacular: Creolization in Louisiana. *Historical Archaeology* 34(3): 107–123.

Dawdy, Shannon Lee, and Juana L. C. Ibáñez
1997   Beneath the Surface of New Orleans' Warehouse District: Archaeological Investigations at the Maginnis Cotton Mill Site (16OR144). University of New Orleans, New Orleans.

Dawdy, Shannon Lee, Christopher N. Matthews, Elizabeth M. Scott, and Gayle J. Fritz
2002   Preservation and Significance of Three Historic New Orleans Sites (16OR51, 16OR144, 16OR148) Based on Floral and Faunal Analysis. In *Greater New Orleans Archaeology Program End of Federal Fiscal Year Report, 2001–2002*, compiled by Juana Ibáñez, 7–14. University of New Orleans, College of Urban and Public Affairs, New Orleans. Submitted to the Office of Equal Opportunity, National Park Service, Washington, D.C.

Esman, Marjorie R.
1985   *Henderson, Louisiana: Cultural Adaptations in a Cajun Community*. Holt, Rinehart, and Winston, New York.

Faulkner, Alaric
1992   Gentility on the Frontiers of Acadia, 1635–1674: An Archaeological Perspective. In *New England/New France, 1600–1850*, edited by Peter Benes, 82–100. Boston University Press, Boston.

Guermont, C.
1985   *The Norman Table: The Traditional Cooking of Normandy*. Charles Scribner's Sons, New York.

Martin, Terrance J.
1986   A Faunal Analysis of Fort Ouiatenon, an Eighteenth Century Trading Post in the Wabash Valley of Indiana. Ph.D. diss., Michigan State University.
1988   Animal Remains from the Cahokia Wedge Site. In *Archaeology at French Colonial Cahokia*, edited by Bonnie L. Gums, 221–234. Studies in Illinois Archaeology, Vol. 3. Illinois Historic Preservation Agency, Springfield.
1991   An Archaeological Perspective on Animal Exploitation Patterns at French Colonial Sites in the Illinois Country. In *French Colonial Archaeology*, edited by John Walthall, 189–200. University of Illinois Press, Urbana.

Matthews, Christopher N.
2002   *Management Summary for Archaeological Investigations at the St. Augustine Site (16OR148)*. College of Urban and Public Affairs, University of New Orleans, New Orleans.

Purdue, James R.
1983   Epiphyseal Closure in White-Tailed Deer. *Journal of Wildlife Management* 47(4): 1207–1213.

Reitz, Elizabeth J., and Stephen L. Cumbaa
1983   Diet and Foodways of Eighteenth-Century Spanish St. Augustine. In *Spanish St. Augustine: The Archaeology of a Colonial Creole Community*, edited by Kathleen A. Deagan, 151–186. Academic Press, New York.

Reitz, Elizabeth J., and C. Margaret Scarry
1985   Reconstructing Historic Subsistence with an Example from Sixteenth-Century

Spanish Florida. *Society for Historical Archaeology Special Publications Series* No. 3.

Reitz, Elizabeth J., and Elizabeth S. Wing
1999 *Zooarchaeology*. Cambridge University Press, Cambridge.

Reitz, Elizabeth J., Irvy R. Quitmyer, S. S. Hale, Sylvia J. Scudder, and Elizabeth S. Wing
1987 Application of Allometry to Zooarchaeology. *American Antiquity* 52(2): 304–317.

Rushton, William Faulkner
1979 *The Cajuns: From Acadia to Louisiana*. Farrar, Straus, Giroux, New York.

Sarasúa, Carmen
2001 Upholding Status: The Diet of a Noble Family in Early Nineteenth-Century La Mancha. In *Food, Drink, and Identity: Cooking, Eating and Drinking in Europe since the Middle Ages*, edited by Peter Scholliers, 37–61. Berg, New York.

Schulz, Peter D., and Sherri M. Gust
1983 Faunal Remains and Social Status in 19th-Century Sacramento. *Historical Archaeology* 17(1): 44–53.

Scott, Elizabeth M.
1985 *French Subsistence at Fort Michilimackinac, 1715–1781: The Clergy and the Traders*. Archaeological Completion Report Series No. 9. Mackinac Island State Park Commission, Mackinac Island, Mich.
1996 Who Ate What? Archaeological Food Remains and Cultural Diversity. In *Case Studies in Environmental Archaeology*, edited by Elizabeth J. Reitz, Lee A. Newsom, and Sylvia J. Scudder, 339–356. Plenum Press, New York.
2001 Food and Social Relations at Nina Plantation. *American Anthropologist* 103(3): 671–691.
2002 Faunal Remains from the Madame John's Legacy (16OR51), St. Augustine (16OR148), and Maginnis Cotton Mill (16OR144) Sites, New Orleans, Louisiana. In *Greater New Orleans Archaeology Program End of Federal Fiscal Year Report, 2001–2002*, compiled by Juana Ibáñez, 26–69. University of New Orleans, College of Urban and Public Affairs, New Orleans. Submitted to the Office of Equal Opportunity, National Park Service, Washington, D.C.
2007 "Pigeon soup . . . and plover in pyramids": French Foodways in New France and the Illinois Country. In *The Archaeology of Food and Identity*, edited by Katheryn C. Twiss, 243–259. Occasional Paper No. 34. Center for Archaeological Investigations, Southern Illinois University, Carbondale.

Szuter, Christine R.
1996 A Faunal Analysis of Home Butchering and Meat Consumption at the Hubbell Trading Post, Ganado, Arizona. In *Images of the Recent Past*, edited by Charles E. Orser Jr., 333–354. AltaMira Press, Walnut Creek, Calif.

Usner, Daniel H., Jr.
1992 *Indians, Settlers, and Slaves in a Frontier Exchange Economy: The Lower Mississippi Valley Before 1783*. University of North Carolina Press, Chapel Hill.
1998 *American Indians in the Lower Mississippi Valley: Social and Economic Histories*. University of Nebraska Press, Lincoln.

8

Colonoware in Western Colonial Louisiana

Makers and Meaning

DAVID W. MORGAN AND KEVIN C. MACDONALD

> *The battle lines seem clearly drawn, and it is not clear to what end. The debate over who made colonoware appears to be a debate heading nowhere.*
>
> Singleton and Bograd 1995:26

In the archaeology of the colonial and antebellum African American experience, one of the most evocative artifact classes is low-fired earthenware. The blanket term usually applied to this category—"colonoware"—has entered the archaeological vocabulary rather uncritically despite its deeply contested meaning. Its origins go back to 1962, when Ivor Noël Hume (1962) coined the term "Colono-Indian ware" for shell-tempered earthenware recovered from excavations at colonial Williamsburg and Jamestown. These wares mimicked European vessel forms but had shell-tempered pastes comparable to local late prehistoric Algonquian wares. They were taken to represent low-cost Native American–made trade items acquired by Europeans, possibly for their slaves.

This assumption remained firmly in place until Leland Ferguson (1980) suggested that a large proportion of "colonoware" was likely to have been made by African slaves themselves. Ferguson (1992) noted that these low-fired earthenwares, although ubiquitous in East Coast colonial contexts, most commonly occurred in either the living or working areas of enslaved Africans. Indeed, the African (American) origins of such earthenwares were attested to in some documentary and oral historical accounts from the coastlands of Georgia and South Carolina. The presence of spalls and poorly fired pottery in seventeenth-century slave quarter assemblages at Pettus and Utopia plantations in Virginia was accepted as further evidence of local enslaved African manufacture (Ferguson 1992).

Thus, there was a shift in thinking, and "Colono-Indian ware" was rechristened "colonoware." In some areas, particularly parts of the Caribbean where Native populations were mostly extinct at the time of slavery, this term has morphed into such variants as "Afro-Colonoware," "Colono-African" pottery, "African-Jamaican-ware," and others. In 1988, James Deetz (1988:365) went so far as to assert that "most scholars working with Colono ware now agree that it was made by slaves, with its roots in a generalized West African Tradition."

Yet Noël Hume's original characterization of colonoware was not without merit, and more recently there has been a counterattack against the uncritical "Africanization" of these wares in North America (e.g., Mouer et al. 1999). Objections have turned upon documentary evidence for trade of earthenware vessels from Native Americans to colonists, as well as upon certain strong typological parallels of colonoware with indigenous wares of the contact period. Consequently, there has been a general retreat from making unsupported assumptions about the ethnic identity of colonoware potters in North America, and discourse has turned to colonoware as a "creolized" or culturally mixed phenomenon instead (Dawdy 2000; Loren 2000; Singleton and Bograd 2000).

Despite these recent developments, many uncritical assumptions about colonial low-fired earthenwares seem to remain. For one thing, there is an almost tacit tendency to view "colonoware" as a unitary phenomenon, despite caveats by Ferguson (1992:18) that it "is not an artifact 'type' and was never intended to be." Yet generalizations still are made about this series: it is generally undecorated, it occurs in slave contexts, it mimics European forms, and so on. We seem to forget about the economic adaptability of enslaved Africans and Native Americans; the diversity of systems of slavery in the New World; the variable distribution of African ethnicities both regionally and between individual plantations; and the relative isolation of plantation slave communities. We should expect to see many different, unique (micro)regional stories, rather than a single generalized phenomenon. We should marvel that there does seem to be so much in common between these assemblages, and we should contemplate what these broad similarities might imply. But first we should be sure that such interregional convergences really exist.

For this reason, we attempt in this chapter to do three things: examine how colonoware has been used as a category in Louisiana archaeology; consider the ways in which life in the French/Spanish colony—different in many ways from life in the English colonies—might affect the development and use of low-fired earthenwares; and consider methods one might use to explore inter- and intraregional diversity in this ceramic technology. We are particularly keen to avoid assumptions about what constitutes supposed Native American and African traits in such wares. For example, Ferguson (1992:83, 39) has argued that in colonial South Carolina, "certain Indian styles—like painting and complicated stamping—stand out from the plainer features of later artifacts," and that in St. Augustine, "pot rims were decorated with clay appliqué strips and punctations common in southeastern Indian pottery." This ignores that all of these motifs also are common to West African pottery traditions (see, e.g., Aiyedun 1988; Beier 1980; David et al. 1988; Gallay 1992; Gosselain 1994; Okpoko 1987).

Indeed, when the two authors, one an Americanist and the other a West Africanist, compared their comparative collections there was mutual shock at the degree of transcontinental overlap that exists: red slipping, painting, clay appliqué, punctate motifs, incising, comb stamping, brushing, and so forth, all on similar vessel forms. Only a few motif types like carved wooden stamps (Meyers 1999) and some cord roulettes seem to be distinctive for West African ceramics during the historic period. Likewise, there may be some hope in distinguishing ceramic traditions through different formation techniques (see Gosselain 1994). For example, coiled manufacture is typical of Native American pots and occurs frequently in the West Africa forest and Central Africa, but molding on convex and concave forms and the use of tournettes may be more indicative of Sahelo-Sudanic (Senegambian/Mande) manufacture (see Gosselain 1994). Real diligence and technical as well as decorative comparisons therefore are required before we can assume anything about colonoware makers, unless, of course, we wish to shrug our shoulders and walk away from the problem, labeling everything as "creolized" or uncritically dubbing it either an African or Native American phenomenon.

Thus, in our nascent research into colonial and antebellum plantations in Louisiana we have chosen to begin by critically examining extant Native American ceramic assemblages of the local contact and early colonial periods and comparing them against "colonoware" assemblages of the late colonial and early American periods. Through such an approach we hope to assess whether low-fired earthenware assemblages from ethnically unambiguous "Native" and ethnically ambiguous plantation contexts are one and the same. Moreover, by this attribute-based comparative analysis of "Native" and "plantation" assemblages, we hope to be able to gauge the degree of duplication or divergence between them stylistically, looking for traits that might indicate African contributions to Native traditions or vice versa. Most emphatically, we want to go beyond labeling all low-fired sherds as a single category, and show how they might be used to illustrate cultural dynamics between multiple identities.

Colonoware in Louisiana

While discussion of the meaning of North American colonoware has been lively on the eastern seaboard, there has been comparatively little contribution to it from those of us working outside of the boundaries of the former English colonies, with the notable exception of work in southwest Alabama (Cordell 2002; Silvia 2000, 2002; Waselkov 2000, 2002), west-central Louisiana (Avery 1995; Gregory et al. 2004; Hunter 1985, 1994a, 1994b; Loren 2000; MacDonald, Morgan, and Handley 2002/2003, 2006; Morgan et al. 2006), and south Louisiana (Dawdy 2000). What is surprising is that, considering their ubiquity at colonial period sites throughout lower French Louisiana, colonowares have not served as a research focus more often.

Recent archaeological research in lower French Louisiana continues to uncritically attribute all colonowares to Native American makers. At times the researchers have marshaled evidence for the claim based on ware and decorative attributes, but often the attribution is implicit or assumed. Seldom is there any discussion of a possible African contribution to what is locally classified as a monolithic ware type.

Consider, for example, the discussions surrounding the archaeology of the Spanish colonial presidio Los Adaes (16NA16). Hiram F. Gregory and his colleagues have provided an overview of the history of the fort and of the unpublished archaeological excavations spanning the 1970s to the 1990s (Avery 1995; Gregory et al. 2004), and they generally conclude from the archaeological material that "the cooperative nature of the relationship between the Spanish, French, and Caddoan groups at Los Adaes is abundantly clear" (Gregory et al. 2004:70). More than 30,000 sherds of low-fired non-European coarse earthenwares make up 85 percent of the ceramic assemblage. Only 15 percent of these are decorated, and most are fragments of bowls and jars, some of which replicate European stylistic elements, including shallow brimmed bowls and pitchers. The overwhelming majority of these low-fired earthenwares are attributed to the Caddo, with some 1 percent notionally deriving from the Natchez, Choctaw, or Mexican/Texas traditions. Yet both African slaves and individuals described historically as "Mulattos" are documented at Los Adaes (G. Avery, personal communication June 8, 2007), and a 1731 document states that 50 percent of the soldiers at Los Adaes were of mixed Spanish, Native American, and African ancestry (Avery 1997). An indigenous connection is clear, given the known intermarriage between Spanish soldiers and Caddoan women, and given the stylistic similarities of the decorated earthenwares with known Native American traditions; however, it is surprising that the authors attribute Native American identities to *all* of the potters with no discussion of other possibilities.

The invisibility of Africans and African descendents is echoed in Diana Loren's (2000) complementary discussion of colonial policy versus practice at the presidio and at the Chamard site (16NA100). Loren's work is a valuable investigation of the tensions of creole identity politics, but while she mentions that African slaves were known to have lived at the presidio, and she acknowledges the role of African heritage in creole identity formation, her discussion of the material culture at both sites is ultimately dichotomized as European versus Native American. The same holds true for her more recent examination of the depictions of eighteenth-century Spanish *casta* paintings in the light of archaeological materials from Los Adaes (Loren 2007). While Africans are central to the concept of "mixed bloods" expressed in the paintings, Loren's examination of the material record at the presidio compares Caddo traditions of dress, accoutrements, and architecture against Spanish ones. The Caddo connection is indisputable, but Africans, again, are invisible.

Take as a final example Shannon Dawdy's (2000) thorough, diachronic consideration of the evolution of "creole" as an identity in the New Orleans area, looking in particular at Madame John's Legacy house (16OR51) and Duplessis Plantation (16OR144) sites. Ceramics constitute one of the most important artifact classes present at Madame John's Legacy. In the circa 1728 to 1783 contexts associated with a French-born family, the pottery consists "almost entirely of French-made faience, Saintonge, and coarsewares," despite the high cost of their acquisition compared to the

Native American pottery, of which there is little. In a circa 1788 trash pit left behind by the second-generation native-born occupants of the house, by contrast, Dawdy encountered "twice as many ceramics of Native American manufacture than of French," illustrating the formation of "a 'native colonial'—or early creole—mindset." The situation is quite different at Duplessis Plantation. The circa 1788 to 1845 midden levels formed by second- and third-generation creole inhabitants produced a "complete absence of... Native American ceramic goods," which Dawdy (2000:116) interprets as a reflection of global market and political shifts rather than identity construction. Like the Los Adaes examples above, Dawdy's article was not intended to describe in any detail the ceramic attributes prompting her association of the colonowares with Native American manufacturers, so we hesitate to stretch our point too far; however, the unhesitating attribution of Native origins to colonoware, even in an article devoted to the complexity of creole identity formation in a city occupied by large numbers of free and enslaved Africans, is representative of the way colonowares have been uniformly interpreted in Louisiana's colonial contexts.

Potential Colonoware Makers in Colonial Louisiana

The authors cited above may be correct, but we believe it is essential to consider whether Louisiana colonowares might themselves be creolized, or indeed African, phenomena. To examine the colonoware question in colonial and antebellum Louisiana further, we draw upon largely unpublished data from recent work at late-eighteenth- and early-nineteenth-century plantations along a former channel of the Red River now referred to as the Cane River. Before examining those data, it is important to understand how the colonial history of this area shapes our understanding of who may have been colonoware's potential makers and users.

As Daniel Usner (1992, 1998) has illustrated, the French colony of lower Louisiana differed from the English colonies on the eastern seaboard in several fundamental economic and social respects. First, population growth within the colony by settlers, soldiers, and slaves was very slow. Until the late 1700s, Native Americans outnumbered non-Native Americans by a factor of about five to one, meaning that trade relations between colonists and Native Americans developed relatively freely because of less pressure on Native lands. Second, Louisiana was a low mercantile priority for the French regime, meaning the colony was poorly subsidized and adapted by developing a dependence on local trade for subsistence and material needs. Last, lower Louisiana's frontier location permitted great fluidity in interaction and exchange between ethnic groups (see also Avery 1995; Loren 2000, 2007).

The French recognized the importance of the Red River region early in their settlement effort. In October 1713, Antoine de Lamothe Cadillac, the colonial governor, wrote to Antoine Crozat, owner of the colonial trade monopoly, that he "has sent Sieur [Juchereau] de St. Denis with twenty-four Canadians and forty Indians to ascend the Red River with ten thousand livres worth of merchandise" in order to establish trade with Spain's New Mexico (Rowland and Sanders 1932:176), something that could be less easily accomplished at coastal ports because of trade prohibitions between the two rival powers. St. Denis ascended the river with his allies, and at the location of modern-day Natchitoches he established a colonial outpost/fort. This small garrison soon turned into a pivotal point on the frontier landscape, and consequently became a focus of interaction and cultural syncretism between numerous ethnic groups, including Native Americans, Spanish, French, and Africans. New identities developed out of multiethnic communities and households in and around the colonial settlement of Natchitoches, with the intermarriage between Spanish soldiers and Caddoan women at Los Adaes and the formation of the modern-day Cane River Creole of Color community being just two examples of many. The development of this area over the next century thus makes for an intriguing, complex backdrop for understanding the manufacture and use of colonowares.

Unlike on the East Coast, where the very presence of Native Americans as potential makers of colonoware is sometimes debated (e.g., Deetz 1999; Mouer et al. 1999), in lower French Louisiana Native Americans were very much a part of the daily cultural landscape. The early French explorers encountered at least 18 different Native American groups already residing in Louisiana, and numerous other ethnic groups migrated to Louisiana during the mid to late eighteenth century, including the Choctaw, Biloxi, Coushatta, Alabama, and Apalachee (Hunter 1985, 1994a, 1994b; Kniffen et al. 1987; Swanton 1911, 1946). By the 1760s and 1770s, the Apalachee, Avoyel, Taensa, Chatot, and Alabama had moved into the area south of Natchitoches along the Red River, between the Natchitoches garrison and the post known as Rapide, near modern-day Alexandria. This territory also became home to the Apalachee, Pascagoula, and Biloxi during the succeeding decades. Caddoan peoples such as the Natchitoches, Yatasi, Doustioni, Kadohadacho, and Ouachita simultaneously occupied much of the other land surrounding Natchitoches (Kniffen et al. 1987; Perttula 1992). This settlement situation changed in the 1820s and 1830s, when many Native American groups began migrating out of Louisiana into Texas because of Andrew Jackson's removal policy and the pressures exerted by the huge influx of mostly Anglo immigrants. The area around and north of Natchitoches in particular became a refuge for many Choctaw, who entered into lands traditionally occupied by Caddoan peoples (Kniffen et al. 1987; Perttula 1992). The departure of the Caddo made the Choctaw the most numerous Native American nation in Louisiana, "until *Choctaw* became nearly synonymous with *Indian* in much of Louisiana," and they resolutely deflected governmental efforts to force them into Oklahoma for many decades (Kniffen et al. 1987:95).

Usner (1998:35, Table 1, 61, 99, 108) has compiled historic data that allow us to look at the presence of some of these groups quantitatively. He suggests that Caddo and Avoyel populations in the Red River area rebounded from initial losses in the early 1700s to number about 4,200 people by 1775 (see Hunter 1994b for similar trends among the much smaller immigrant tribes of central Louisiana). By the 1780s, however, for the first time the Native American population in the lower Mississippi Valley as a whole was outnumbered by foreigners: colonial inhabitants, their slaves, and free people of color. By 1804, it is estimated that some 5,000 Native Americans lived in what is now Louisiana, while the non–Native American population of the state was at roughly 55,000 people in 1806 and climbed dramatically to about 150,000 by 1820. For comparison, in 1803 it is estimated that there were around 13,000 enslaved Africans in Louisiana, a number that had increased to 69,064 by 1820 (e.g., Berlin 1974:396–397). In summary, during the time period we are discussing here—the late 1700s and early 1800s—economic life was changing rapidly for the Native Americans of Louisiana. The competition between European colonial powers that Native Americans had so adroitly manipulated in the 1700s was at an end; Europeans and Africans were overwhelming them in unprecedented numbers; and the diverse frontier economy that had emerged with the French was being lost to expanding Anglo cotton production (Usner 1998).

The Choctaw and some other Native Americans rejected the wage-labor economy as a form of institutionalized slavery (Kniffen et al. 1987:97) and marginalized the cotton economy in their daily lives as a form of silent resistance (Usner 1998:95). They adapted to these new economic conditions by selling goods and labor on a seasonal basis at plantations and markets (Kniffen et al. 1987:97; Usner 1998:95). Various accounts exist of active trade in products such as bear oil, turtles, honey, deer hides, herbs, and baskets. We believe that pottery—preparation, serving, and commodity containers—also could be added to this list, a hypothesis that may be given credence by succession documents in the Natchitoches Parish courthouse spanning 1780 to 1810. Of the 2,302 vessels listed among the household inventories, some 81 were described as *terre sauvage* or *sauvage*, implying a Native American connection, and the contents most commonly listed in association with such vessels was bear oil (*huile d'ours*) (Handley et al. 2006). Furthermore, although the term "*sauvage*" would also have been attached to Africans in the nineteenth century, the Indian agent in the Natchitoches territory noted in 1806 specifically that it was Native American women who made and sold pottery vessels in Natchitoches (Sibley 1832). This local level of "invisible" commerce was so important that stores in Natchitoches went out of business at the time of Caddo removal (Kniffen et al. 1987:96).

As alluded to above, much of the Native American barter economy remained centralized on Natchitoches and its hinterlands, as it had in prior decades, despite the establishment in 1804 of the American government's Indian trading house. In 1813, the superintendent of the trade house, William Linnaird, complained that the "vagabond Indians found always behind plantations & near fields" were drawn there by the prospect of work as hunters or stock tenders for planters (Usner 1998:106). Linnaird's comment again gives us an anecdotal perspective on the frequency of interaction between Native Americans, plantation owners, and enslaved people despite the supposed centralization of trade. The arrangement so vexing to the official trade house representative was so common that "there is scarcely a planter in the Parish who cannot converse in one or more Indian tongues" (Usner 1998:106). The Mobilian trade jargon emerged as a common language in the area (Hunter 1994b:40), and others also have noted that it was still spoken around Louisiana even in the first decades of the 1900s (Kniffen et al. 1987:124–125).

Although we must consider the possibility that Native Americans made a considerable proportion of the low-fired earthenwares at Cane River plantations given the social history of Louisiana, we also must consider the likelihood that African slaves or their descendants made some of these earthenwares for reasons elucidated by our colleagues working in Georgia, Virginia, and South Carolina (e.g., Ferguson 1980, 1992; Hill 1987). Indeed, one might argue that this possibility is even more likely in Louisiana than in the English colonies, since the majority of slaves brought into lower French Louisiana in the eighteenth century had suffered from comparatively little ethnic randomization. Between 1719 and 1743, 65.9 percent of enslaved Africans who landed in Louisiana came from Senegambia, and the remainder came almost entirely from the Kingdom of Kongo and the Bight of Benin. Those arriving from Senegambia were predominantly of Mande heritage and shared common lingua franca such as Bambara. There were even coherent Bambara revolts, or attempts at revolt, between 1729 and 1731 in close concert with the Natchez (Hall 1992).

The occurrence of ethnically coherent resistance, recognized as such by the French administration, demonstrates two things of relevance to this study: first, strongly recognizable African ethnicities/identities survived in first-generation slave contexts in Louisiana, and, second, such coherent cultural groups interacted frequently with Native American populations. Furthermore, this interaction was not just an early 1700s phenomenon. At the beginning of the nineteenth century the American government viewed this long-standing tradition of Native American and African slave interactions with increasing suspicion. The government grouped Native Americans, slaves, and free people of color together legislatively in an attempt to regulate the economic and social behavior of those it marginalized (Usner 1998:87, 104).

There are other factors that make the study of African cultural elements particularly interesting in Louisiana. To begin, there is the excellent record keeping of French and Spanish officials as to the "nations" of enslaved Africans (Hall 2000). There are thus useful ethnic indices that may be derived for plantations under archaeological study. Another important factor is the high rate of manumission in the region of Louisiana during the colonial period. Approximately 7,585 Africans—one-fifth of the African American population of Louisiana—were living as free individuals in Louisiana in 1810 (Berlin 1974). This proportion gradually decreased in succeeding decades as the state became Anglicized. This leads to further potential research questions, such as: Did free Africans use colonowares? Were the slaves of free African masters more or less likely to use colonowares? These, then, are the cultural contexts for our archaeological research program along the Cane River.

Archaeology on the Cane River

Since 2001, we have investigated two late colonial/early American plantation sites in the Natchitoches area, both originally owned by the same family (Figure 8.1). The first site is the Maison de Marie Thérèse, also known colloquially as the Coincoin Plantation, and known in official state documents as the Whittington site (16NA241). As the unofficial names imply, this is the plantation home of Marie-Thérèse Coincoin, a free

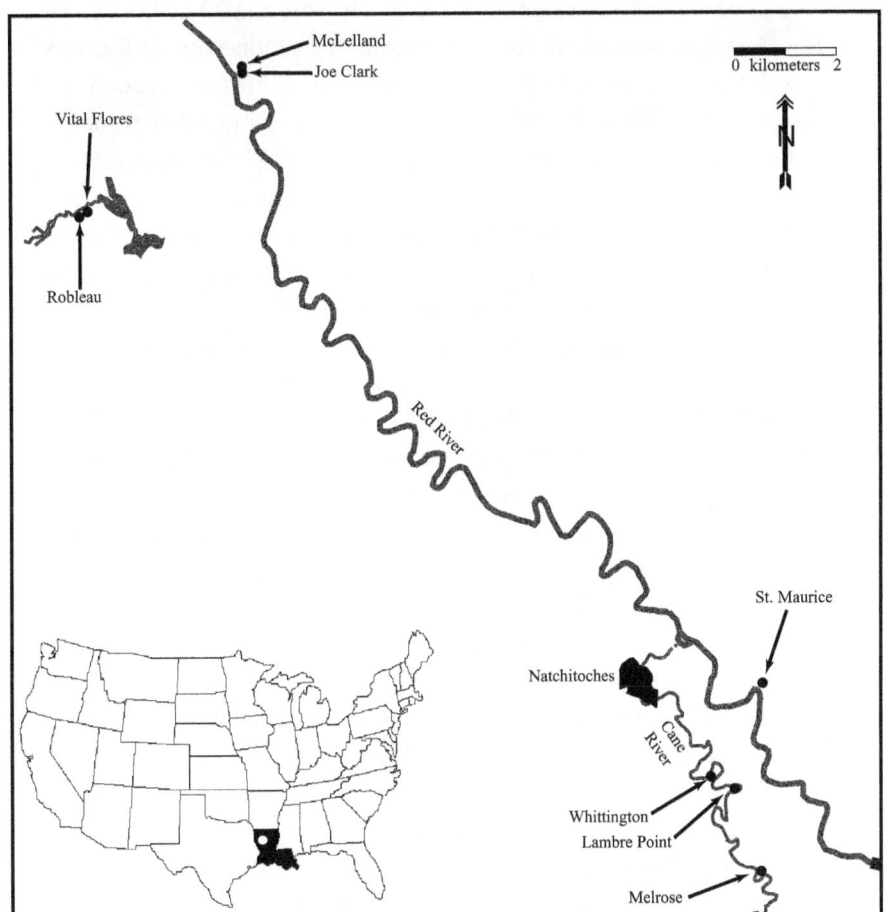

Figure 8.1. Map of Cane River plantations and Native American sites discussed in text.

woman of African descent who received a tract of land in 1788 along the Cane River. Using the labor of at least 16 African slaves, Coincoin developed and expanded this original tract into a 68-acre plantation between 1788 and circa 1816. These slaves included at least one adult who self-identified as being of the "Kissi nation," two adults who said they were of the "Kongo nation," and nine Louisiana-born children (MacDonald, Morgan, and Handley 2002/2003, 2006).

In 2001 and 2002, we used remote sensing instruments, systematic pedestrian survey, systematic shovel tests, and a series of three 2 by 2 m and three 1 by 1 m test excavations to identify potential subsurface architectural remains and a large midden deposit at the Coincoin Plantation site. In 2005, we returned to excavate a trench covering some 16.25 m², along with four 0.5 by 1 m test units. Our excavations produced post features, clay wall features, and more of the midden exposed in 2002. In 2006 and 2007, we continued our fieldwork using a suite of geophysical instruments to better target the exposure of an additional 117 m², which resulted in the full excavation of the previously investigated midden, along with the discovery of two structures and several significant landscape features. Most germane to this essay is the total resulting assemblage of 3,115 pottery sherds, 1,258 of which (40.4 percent) are colonowares.

Lest these be mistaken for debris from an older Native American component, it bears mentioning that no stone artifacts were present at the site and that many of the low-fired earthenware sherds occurred in clear association with colonial European artifacts in the intact midden feature.

Furthermore, we are fortunate in that the Coincoin Plantation site was not occupied sequentially over the historic period, unlike many of the plantations on the Cane River. It is decidedly a single-component occupation, as the ceramic and other data attest. Ignoring colonowares for the moment, creamware sherds account for 55.1 percent (n=919) of the rest of the identifiable Euro-American ceramic assemblage (n=1,668);[1] pearlware makes up 22.8 percent (n=380); and tin-enameled wares, almost all faience typed as Rouen Plain, account for 15.1 percent (n=252). In other words, these three ceramic types on their own make up 93.0 percent of the identifiable noncolonoware pottery, and these types have a manufacturing lifespan of circa 1760 to 1815, almost exactly the lifespan of the plantation. The discrete occupation of the site is supported by the presence of hand-wrought nails and cut nails with clenched necks, as well as minority pottery types, like Saintonge Plain (n=2, or 0.1 percent). Other ceramic ware types, like stoneware (n=16, or 1.0 percent) and redware (n=55, or 3.3 percent), have manufacturing periods broad enough to encompass the entire historic period, but pottery sherds clearly postdating the plantation period, including whiteware/ironstone (n=37, or 2.2 percent), semiporcelain (n=6, or 0.4 percent), and yellow ware (n=1, or 0.1 percent), are sparse. The latter wares combined represent only 2.7 percent of the identifiable noncolonoware collection, and these post-1830 sherds likely were introduced from the nearby standing structure that remains in use today.

The second site we have investigated is Melrose Plantation (16NA591), which is located several miles downriver from Coincoin Plantation. Melrose Plantation was reportedly established in 1796 by one of Coincoin's sons, Louis Metoyer. Our archival research and subsequent excavations beneath and around Yucca House, the oldest remaining structure on the property, date it to no earlier than circa 1813, *contra* a long-standing myth dating it to the late 1700s (MacDonald et al. 2006; Morgan et al. 2006). This structure would have continued in use throughout the Metoyer ownership of the property into the 1840s.

In 2001, we used remote sensing instruments to identify potential subsurface architectural remains and midden deposits at Melrose. Then, in 2002 we opened excavations over a total of 33 m² adjacent to Yucca House and other early-nineteenth-century structures, discovering mostly landscape features. Later that year we teamed up with Aubra Lee of Earth Search, Inc. to excavate an additional 9 m² under and around Yucca House, with excavations targeting sensitive architectural contexts, such as within an earthen fireplace base, under doors and windows, near central piers, and within a drip-line midden feature. Despite the presence at Melrose in the 1830s of four times as many slaves as at Coincoin Plantation, our total excavations in 2002 yielded only two low-fired earthenware sherds, less than 0.1 percent of the total pottery assemblage (MacDonald et al. 2006).

Besides our Coincoin and Melrose research, work at sites along the Cane River dating to the eighteenth and early nineteenth centuries has gone almost entirely unpublished. The state of Louisiana's regional archaeologist for the Northwest District, Jeffrey Girard (1997), has conducted relevant work as part of his recording and monitoring duties. Other work has been compliance driven (cf. Miller and Wood 2000; Morgan 2005), conducted

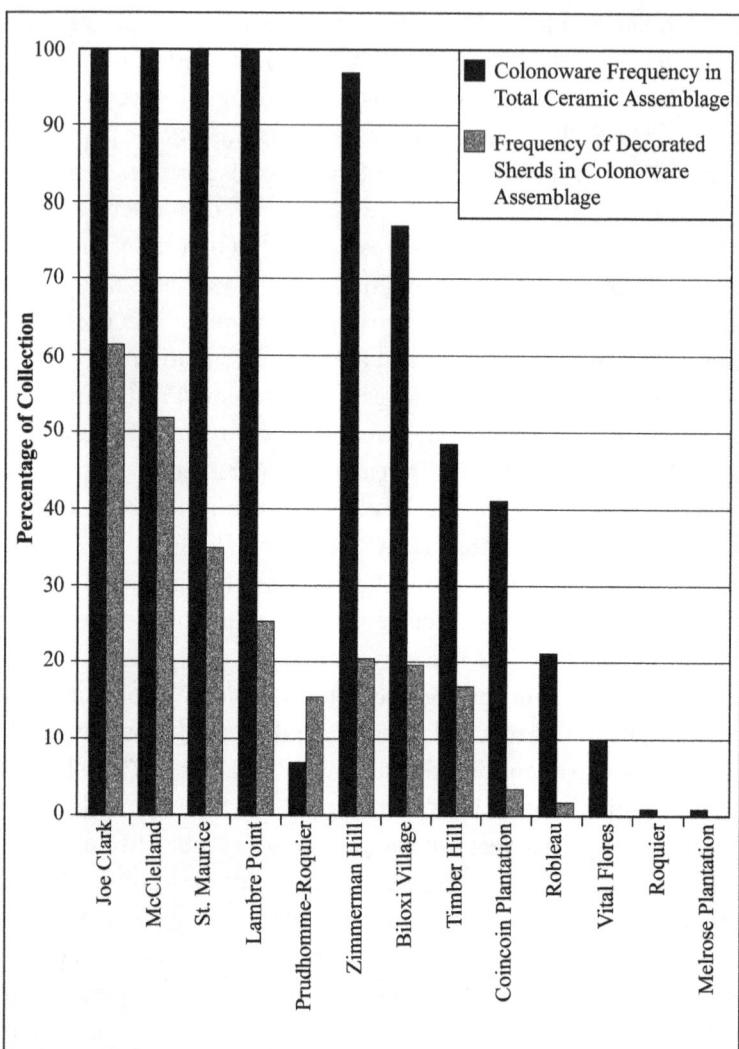

Figure 8.2. Frequency of all colonowares described in the text (sites are arranged left to right in approximate chronological order from oldest to most recent).

as salvage projects, carried out during thesis research (cf. Mathews 1983; Shaw 1983), or performed as part of field schools undertaken by Northwestern State University of Louisiana. To place our results in a wider regional context, we have tapped into this body of "gray" literature, which allows an initial glimpse at some striking material culture patterns.

Low-Fired Earthenware along the Cane River

As a first foray into examining Louisiana colonoware, we tabulated information on low-fired earthenwares from 10 sites. These represent both colonial period plantations and Native American sites spanning roughly 1650 to 1850 (Figures 8.2 and 8.3). If these are representative, then one of the trends in low-fired earthenwares noted in the eastern United States seems to hold in northern Louisiana: there was a steady decline over the

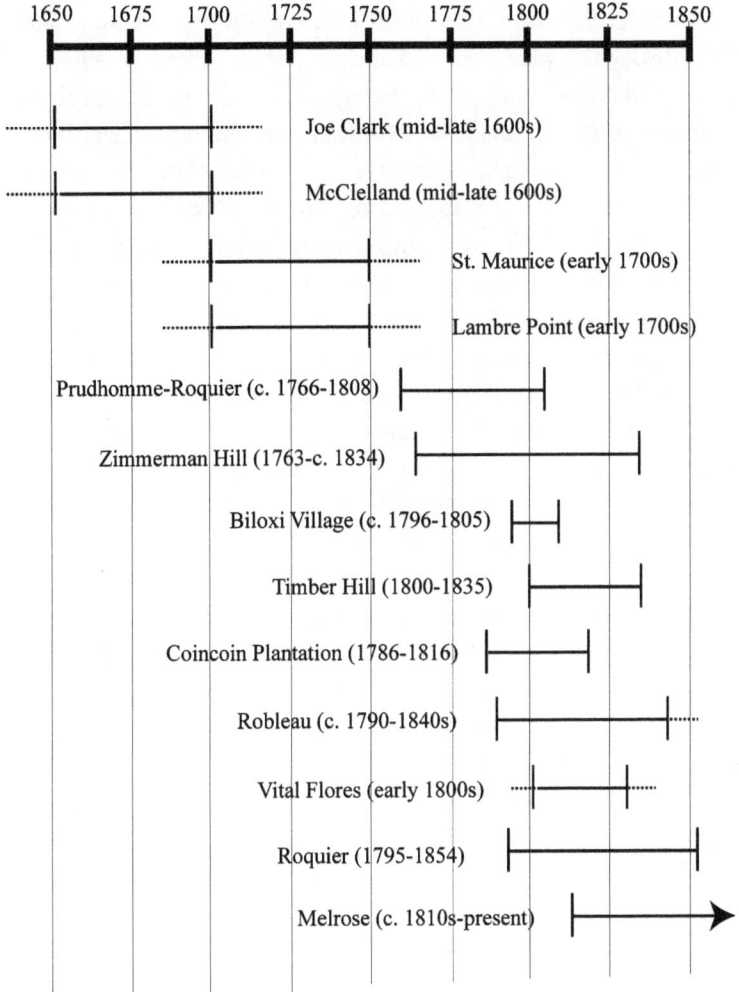

Figure 8.3. Approximate chronological distribution of sites under comparison.

course of the historic period in the relative quantity of low-fired earthenwares (see Singleton 1988). To this we may add the fact that the frequency of decoration also appears to decrease over time.

Turning first to the relative quantity of local low-fired earthenwares versus Euro-American ceramics, in the late 1600s and early 1700s, prior to the establishment of the Natchitoches post, European pottery is absent in aboriginal contexts, when Native American inhabitants of the area had only passing contact with Europeans. For example, two pieces of brass were the only European artifacts found at the seventeenth-century Caddoan farmsteads forming the Joe Clark (16BO237) and McLelland (16BO236) sites, which produced 449 and 7,120 sherds, respectively (Kelley 1997; see also Kelley et al. 1996). European influences thus probably did not affect pottery manufacture at these sites in the mid to late 1600s. The same seems also to have been the case a few decades later. Surface collections and excavations at the St. Maurice site (16WN265), a multicomponent historic site, yielded only a single creamware sherd in association with early 1700s Caddoan material, including 144 sherds, 50 flakes, 18 fire-cracked rocks, 2 bifaces, and 2 cores (Girard 1997). Surface collections and auger tests at the Lambre Point site (16NA544), another early 1700s Caddo habitation, produced only a single possible European artifact—a scrap of iron—along with faunal remains, 61 sherds,[2] 77 flakes, 4 flake bifaces, and an unstemmed triangular arrowpoint (Girard 1997).

By the late 1700s and early 1800s, however, the Cane River colonial plantations were firmly established, and in these contexts colonoware use was more evenly balanced against use of Euro-American wares. Turning from Native American contexts to Euro-African ones, the next datum in this chronological sequence is a circa 1766 to 1808 kitchen midden at the Prudhomme-Roquier site (16NA240) (Mathews 1983:69, Table 4), which provides a frequency of low-fired non-Euro-American coarse earthenware that seems inordinately low: 7 percent (n=75). We believe this may be due to the fact that Prudhomme-Roquier, situated in what was downtown Natchitoches, is the only urban home in the sample. As we move along in time, low-fired earthenwares from our excavations at Coincoin's 1786 to 1816 plantation make up slightly less than half of the assemblage (n=1,258, or 40.4 percent).

Quantities of colonoware appear to have declined in the years spanning the turn of the nineteenth century. For example, they make up 21 percent (n=1,733) of the assemblage from the circa 1790 to 1840s

Robleau site (16DS380), a homestead in the Bayou Na Bonchasse community located north of Natchitoches (Girard 2002:14–51). At the Vital Flores site (16DS389), a Bayou Pierre homestead near Robleau that dates to the early 1800s (Girard 2003:43–48), low-fired earthenwares form only 10 percent (n=3) of what is a problematically small assemblage. At the Roquier site (16NA299), a 1795 to 1854 cotton plantation home on the outskirts of Natchitoches (Mathews 1983:70, Table 5), local earthenwares make up less than 1 percent (n=20). An even lower percentage is found at the circa 1796 to 1830s Yucca House (Melrose Plantation) during the same period (n=2).

In summary, when comparing contact period and early colonial Native American pottery assemblages with late colonial and early American period Euro-African pottery assemblages, it is apparent that low-fired earthenwares go from being the only available ceramic in northwest Louisiana in the mid-1600s to a seemingly obsolete ware by about 1830, a trend Hunter (1994a:38) has also observed. One potential problem with this analysis is that the late 1700s to middle 1800s sites in the sample represent only multiethnic occupations with a strong Afro-European presence. There are no known examples of late 1700s to early 1800s Native American homesteads or villages in the Cane River–Natchitoches area with which to compare. Consequently, we draw from nearby northeast Texas and central Louisiana to introduce the Timber Hill (41MR211), Zimmerman Hill (16RA335), and Biloxi Village (16RA60) sites into our sample.

Timber Hill, also known as Sha'chahdínnih, was a village site that represents "the last settlement in the traditional Caddo homeland occupied by the great Kadohadacho confederacy" (Parsons et al. 2002:1). It existed between 1800 and 1835, and the occupants represent the Kadohadacho, the Nanatsoho, the upper Nasoni, the upper Natchitoches, members of other Caddoan groups, and Caddo-European creoles. At Timber Hill, the villagers used Euro-American pottery but continued to produce low-fired earthenwares of their own historical tradition. Euro-American pottery makes up 48 percent (n=383) of the assemblage, while Native American wares comprise 52 percent (n=413).

The Zimmerman Hill site in central Louisiana is a multicomponent site that served as the principal Red River village of the Apalachee from 1763 to circa 1834 (Hunter 1985, 1994b). It is a useful datum point in this comparison, but it also is problematic, because of the length of its occupation (circa 71 years) compared to the other late colonial and early American period sites, whose mean span of occupation was circa 37 years. In contrast to Timber Hill, colonowares dominate the assemblage. They form 95.4 percent (n=591) of the pottery affiliated with the Apalachee occupation, while imported pottery (tin-enameled wares, redware, creamware, and pearlware) make up the other 4.6 percent (n=27).[3] Hunter (1985:112) attributes the paucity of European goods to a supply shortage during or just after the American Revolution, which the Apalachee countered by continuing "to produce native equivalents, especially ceramics."

The Biloxi Village site in central Louisiana was identified and surveyed by Hunter (1994a) in 1990. Spanish-period colonial documents suggest an affiliation with the eponymous Biloxi, who probably dwelled there from roughly 1796 to 1805. Hunter's surface collections at the site produced a small sample of colonowares (n=76) and Euro-American sherds (n=23). Many of the former were assigned to type-varieties of the Choctaw Chickachae series (Blitz 1985; Gregory and Avery 2006; Voss and Blitz 1988), which may raise the possibility of sequential occupations of the site by different peoples or more complex concurrent social interactions between them (Hunter 1985). Regardless of specific tribal affiliation, in this Native American context colonowares outnumber refined earthenwares by three to one.

In summary, the proportion of colonowares characterizing Zimmerman Hill, Biloxi Village, Timber Hill, and Coincoin is broadly similar. Colonoware in each instance makes up roughly half or more of the pottery in use at the site, and as a whole these frequencies are markedly higher than those recorded from the nearly coeval Robleau, Vital Flores, Roquier, and Melrose sites (21 percent or less). This may reflect small chronological differences, but the great disparity in colonoware frequencies does not seem to correspond to the slight difference in mean site age between the two groups. Ethnicity, we suggest, also is a factor.

When Hunter (1994a:38) published the Biloxi Village data, he asserted that the relative frequencies of colonowares to Euro-American wares were "disproportionate to those from other contemporaneous Indian or Euro-American sites in the region." The data presented here suggest that Hunter's sense of how common colonowares are in Euro-American contexts is accurate, but in other contexts his Biloxi Village data are not as atypical as he believed. In other words, what the Timber Hill, Coincoin, Biloxi Village, and Zimmerman Hill sites all have in common is that they represent predominately Native American or African contexts, with all of the socioeconomic and cultural implications such a difference in identity may entail (e.g., Hunter 1994b:40). For example, understanding why colonowares are common at sites with an overwhelming Native American and/or African presence entails considering their occupants' potentially more limited access to expensive, imported refined earthenwares; the role of material culture in identity formation and retention; and the interplay between dietary choices and food preparation technology.

There is a parallel decorative trend to be found within this declining series of colonowares (see Figure 8.2). As Euro-American wares came to dominate the vessels being used at plantations, urban homes, and Native American villages, the amount of decorated low-fired earthenwares became increasingly sparse. Over half of the pottery assemblages at the two mid- to late-1600s Caddoan sites are decorated (61 percent, or n=273, at Joe Clark; 52 percent, or n=3,280, at McLelland). This number drops to somewhere between 25 and 35 percent of the assemblages for two Caddoan sites occupied in the early 1700s (35 percent, or n=51, at St. Maurice; 25 percent, or n=15, at Lambre Point). Continuing this progression, excavation of the Zimmerman Hill site produced 122 decorated sherds, which represent some 21.6 percent of the Apalachee assemblage spanning the late 1700s and early 1800s. Only 16 percent (n=63) of the pottery from Timber Hill is decorated. Likewise, only 19.7 percent (n=15) of the small sample of 76 sherds derived from the ground surface of the Biloxi Village site is decorated. The quantity drops further when French/African and Creole/African kitchen contexts are factored in: 15 percent (n=11) at Prudhomme-Roquier and 2.9 percent (n=36) at Coincoin.[4] The dates for the latter four contexts—Timber Hill, Biloxi Village, Prudhomme-Roquier, and Coincoin—together span 1766 to 1834. Decorated low-fired earthenwares are, for all intents and purposes, nonexistent at the Robleau, Roquier, and Vital Flores sites (1 percent, or n=25, at Robleau), which together span 1796 to 1854. Likewise, neither of the two sherds we recovered from Melrose Plantation is decorated.

Evaluating the Makers of the Cane River "Colonowares"

Above we outlined some trends in the relative quantity and decoration of low-fired earthenwares in the Cane River and surrounding regions. In order to interpret them properly, it would be helpful to have some notion as to whether these ceramics were made by Native Americans and/

or Africans. The approach of this preliminary study is to contrast plantation earthenwares with local earthenwares from what may be considered ethnically Native American sites. The seventeenth-century sites of McClelland and Joe Clark provide a good baseline, as they represent Caddoan households occupied prior to intensive Euro-African contact. The assemblages from these sites are of predominantly simple bowls, short-rimmed jars, and carinated bowls decorated primarily using a stylus of some sort to incise or punctuate the vessel's exterior (Kelley 1997:37–60). Ridged pottery (that is, Belcher Incised, with narrow vertical ridges created by parallel incisions with a round-tipped tool or fingertip) is the most common decorative type (Kelley 1997:44–45). The next most common decorative Caddoan motif is simple linear or complex curvilinear incised designs, the latter forming concentric circles and waves. The paste of the Caddoan ceramics at these sites is mostly shell tempered (55.7 percent, n=3,099), followed in frequency by grog-tempered sherds (42.9 percent, n=2,389) (Kelley 1997:42, Table 7). Very small quantities of sand-tempered sherds and sherds exhibiting temper combinations of shell and bone, grog and bone, and grog and shell make up the remainder (1.4 percent, n=78).

Moving nearer Coincoin Plantation in time and space, we next consider Lambre Point, an early-eighteenth-century Caddo occupation located 3.25 km away from Coincoin Plantation (Girard 1997). We had the opportunity to reexamine this small assemblage as part of this study (Table 8.1). The sherds are much more rarely decorated than those of the seventeenth-century Caddoan sites, featuring only simple stylus-based incised motifs and a total absence of ridging. Additionally, temper was less varied, with shell temper being dominant (89 percent, or n=54). Pots from this site all were simple bowls or collared jars that were coil-built, thin-walled, and fired in an oxidizing or mixed (oxidizing/reducing) atmosphere.

The low-fired earthenwares encountered during our work at Coincoin Plantation have strong similarities to those at Lambre Point and to other documented historic period Native American pottery assemblages (Table 8.2).[5] Decorated sherds are rare, numbering only 36 (2.9 percent), and were tempered with shell, bone, sand, and/or their combinations, with shell temper being most common. Most of the decorations consist of engraved, curved lines that often demarcate zones of engraved cross-hatching. Ten could comfortably be classed to the type Natchitoches Engraved (Figure 8.4), which is affiliated with the historic period Caddoan tribes in the Natchitoches area as well as with the Natchez, Choctaw, Apalachee,

Table 8.1. Low-fired earthenware attributes at the Lambre Point site (early 1700s)

		Surface Treatment		Total	
		Plain	Incised	n	%
Temper	Grog	0	1	1	1.6
	Sand	3	3	6	9.8
	Shell	43	11	54	88.5
Total	n	46	15	61	100
	%	75.4	24.6	100	

Table 8.2. Low-fired earthenware attributes at Coincoin Plantation (ca. 1788–1816)

		Surface Treatment						Total	
		Plain	Decoration						
			Combed	Engraved	Incised	Slipped	Indet.	n	%
Temper	B-Sh	—	—	1	—	—	—	1	0.1
	Sh	277	—	11	1	4	6	299	24.1
	Sa-Sh	159	—	1	2	4	8	174	14.0
	Sa	30	—	1	2	4	2	39	3.1
	B-Sa-Sh	9	—	—	1	—	—	10	0.8
	Bone	2	—	2	—	—	—	4	0.3
	B-Sa	1	1	—	—	—	—	2	0.2
	Indet.	19	—	—	—	—	—	19	1.5
	<1.28 cm	709	—	—	1	—	—	710	57.2
Total	n	1,206	1	16	7	12	16	1,258	100
	%	97.2	0.1	1.3	0.6	1.0	1.3	100	

Notes: B-Sh = mixed bone and shell
Sh = shell (These data on temper types by surface treatment are preliminary. A petrographic study is under way, and a possible elemental analysis using X-ray fluorescence may also be conducted. Additionally, a traditional analysis of vessel form, firing atmosphere, and thickness is near completion.)
Sa-Sh = mixed sand and shell
Sa = sand
B-Sa-Sh = mixed bone, sand, and shell
B-Sa=mixed bone and sand

and Coushatta (Gregory and Avery 2006). In terms of ceramic chronology, it is surprising to note the dominance of sherds similar to Natchitoches Engraved among the decorated colonowares we recovered, since up to this point it was thought to have largely fallen out of use by the late eighteenth century (Hiram F. Gregory, Jeffery S. Girard, and George Avery, personal communication March 9, 2007), with the exception of a few sherds recovered from the Robleau site (Girard 2002).

Figure 8.4. Example of a Coincoin Plantation (16NA241) colonoware sherd, assignable to the type Natchitoches Engraved. Specimen 180, Unit LE 12-5.

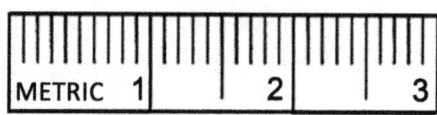

Slipped sherds are the next most common (n=12) among the decorated colonowares, with slip colors including red/brown (n=9), black (n=1), and white/cream (n=2). Red slipping is something of a horizon marker across the aboriginal Southeast in the historic period, which may reflect the movement of people across the landscape as they adapted to interaction with Europeans, as with the Apalachee movement from Florida to Alabama to Louisiana during the eighteenth century. Given the presence of red slipping in West African traditions, it is tempting also to link the widespread historic presence of red slips in the Gulf South with African influences. In the Natchitoches region, specific red slip parallels may be found in the Old Town Red *var. Rapides* and Chicot Red types that Donald Hunter (1985) described among the Apalachee assemblages excavated at the Zimmerman site (see also Brain 1979, 1988, 1989; Phillips 1970; Williams and Brain 1983), or also the types Chickachae Red and Chickachae Red and Black (Hunter 1994a) classified at the Biloxi Village site.

Another pair of sherds from this small sample also may have value as an identity marker. One bone/sand-tempered specimen exhibits three to four closely spaced, parallel curved lines combed across its surface. It appears to fit the type Chickachae Combed (Blitz 1985; Collins 1927; Galloway 1995; Haag 1953; Penman et al. 1980; Voss and Blitz 1988), which is attributed to the Choctaw in Mississippi and which has been found at Los Adaes and other historic Native American sites in the Natchitoches area. Gregory and Avery (2006) correlate the type in northwest Louisiana with the Adaes, Apalachee, Choctaw, Coushatta, Natchez, Natchitoches, and Yatasi. The second sherd of the pair exhibits two sets of four engraved or combed, parallel lines. The motif would fit the type Kemper Combed, which is currently viewed in Mississippi as part of the Choctaw ceramic complex (Voss and Blitz 1988). The singular specimen from Coincoin Plantation, however, is executed on a bone-tempered paste and appears more engraved than sharply incised, which technically puts it outside the type's definitional boundaries in several respects. Given the variability, it may have Choctaw affiliations, or it may connote a connection with the freehand incised equivalents in the Natchez tradition, like Fatherland Incised (Voss and Blitz 1988).

The incised or dragged stylus sherds prove more difficult to assign to any particular type, as they bear one or more incisions from which an overall pattern could not discerned. That said, it bears noting that they would by no means seem out of place among general Native American or West African pottery traditions.

The bulk of the remaining (plain) sherds are indistinguishable in paste, thickness, firing, and coiled formation from the Lambre Point Caddoan sherds that can be classified as unspecified varieties of Mississippi Plain or Bell Plain (Phillips 1970). Of the plain sherds larger than 1.28 cm (1/2 inch) whose temper types we were able to classify (n=478), some 57.9 percent (n=277) are tempered exclusively with shell, and another 33.3 percent (n=159) are tempered with a mixture of sand and shell. Many of the sherds in the latter set have pastes replete with very fine sand that may be part of the clay matrix, rather than intentional inclusions. Together, shell- and shell/sand-tempered sherds account for 91.2 percent of the plain colonoware. Plain sherds tempered solely with sand make up a distinct minority (n=30, or 6.3 percent), and they tend to exhibit well-smoothed, compact surfaces often displaying remnant burnishing marks. Bone and mixtures of bone and other tempers characterize the pastes of the remaining identified plainwares (n=12, or 2.5 percent) above 1.28 cm in size.

In short, there are strong correspondences between the Coincoin colonowares and known Native American decorated types of the historic period, particularly as they relate to the Caddo and possibly the Apalachee, Choctaw, Natchez, and Coushatta. Moreover, there is Sibley's (1832) account linking pots directly to Native American women, as described previously. If Native Americans are linked closely to the bear grease–filled colonoware jugs and jars known from the archival documents (Handley et al. 2006; Waselkov 2000), and if they made the handful of engraved and combed sherds in the Coincoin collection, then did they also manufacture the other colonoware forms? Maybe not. Perhaps we should ask why Africans would not also have had a hand in the manufacture of undecorated storage, cooking, and serving vessels.

Identifying a possible Native American parallel does not automatically discount the possibility of African production. Indeed, to draw from Timber Hill, Zimmerman Hill, Biloxi Village, and Coincoin, it may be that both Native Americans and Africans shared a common preference for, or perhaps only had economic access to, vessels made locally from traditional methods and materials. What about the enslaved Africans working on plantations alongside enslaved Native Americans, the nearest to the Coincoin Plantation being those on the adjacent property owned by Pierre Metoyer, Coincoin's former common-law husband? What about those seasonal, transitory laborers that Linnaird found so vexing? Could those Native Americans also have been making pottery with Africans? Consider also the fact that every single adult on Coincoin Plantation was African, and that red-slipped pottery is found across almost all West and Central African pottery traditions in the historic period. Sand-tempered wares also were manufactured in West and Central Africa in the historic period, and sand-tempered sherds make up a distinct, albeit small, component of the Coincoin assemblage. Could these also be African-made? The variability, we argue, should serve to remind us that we are dealing with a multicultural landscape, and that the simplest of pottery vessels—unrefined and undecorated coarse earthenware of local manufacture—may be instrumental in helping us understand how such diversity is negotiated and normalized in the creolization process.

Where might African potters fit into this scenario? The African women on Coincoin Plantation who may have served as potters were likely of the "Kongo Nation." Of course, attributing Kongo or Bakongo ethnicity to such named individuals would be misleading, given the multiethnic nature of this vast region, and the fact that the dominant Bakongo frequently enslaved less powerful neighbors such as the Teke (e.g., Miller 2002). Consequently, it is worth briefly examining the broader corpus of contemporary and historic pottery studies within the region of the old Kingdom of Kongo. In west-central Africa, cord roulettes are relatively rare (Soper 1985). Instead, most documented decoration on late prehistoric, historic, and contemporary pottery consists of dragged or stabbed comb, as well as incised and punctate designs carried out with a stylus (e.g., de Maret 1974; Huffman 1989; Lanfranchi and Clist 1991; Pinçon and Ngoie-Ngalla 1990). Kongo region vessel forms encompass great variability, but include collared jars, pots with mildly everted rims, and simple rimmed globular vessels (Pinçon and Ngoie-Ngalla 1990). Studies of pottery technology among the contemporary Teke, Kongo-Manyanga, Kongo-Dondo, and Kongo-Ndibu show that three out of these four groups use no temper in their pottery, with one (Kongo-Manyanga) using crushed rock. Likewise, all of these groups use variations of the coil method for the formation of vessels (Gosselain 1994).

In other words, Kongo region pottery traditions share remarkably close parallels with historic period Native American traditions in Louisiana, with the exception of a seeming neglect of temper. It is perhaps worth noting that it was the presence of a notable minority of untempered sherds at the Biloxi and Apalachee village sites that prompted Hunter's (1985, 1994a, 1994b) creation of a number of new type varieties. It is thus tempting to link the importance of "sand-tempered" or potentially "untempered" sherds at Coincoin Plantation to the craft products of these women of "Kongo Nation." We are not sanguine about promoting such a supposition at this point because of the small size of our sample of sand-tempered sherds, the few people at Coincoin Plantation who might have produced them, and the regular appearance of sand-tempered wares in minority frequencies in Native American contexts. Suffice to say it raises intriguing possibilities for future research. To this end, it would also be useful to explore the ethnic and gender composition of enslaved populations of neighboring plantations in relation to their low-fired local earthenware assemblages. Here one thinks particularly about the substantial properties of Pierre Metoyer and Ailhaud de St. Anne that flank Coincoin Plantation. The potential for low-level trade in locally produced earthenwares between these plantations might also be a possibility.

For the moment, however, we are left with the impression that the late-eighteenth-century Coincoin assemblage shares most of its attributes in a straightforward manner with preexisting or contemporary local Native American pottery traditions. Yet there could also be African input to this assemblage, which may include the amplification of African techniques, such as red slipping, or the assimilation of African practices into Native American traditions. Noticeable variations, or noise, in the Coincoin assemblage when compared to the relatively coherent Lambre Point assemblage, for example, may reflect this subtle influence.

Discussion

Thus far discussions of colonoware have centered on the archaeology of the former English colonies. Little has been heard about the issue from the vantage point of Louisiana. We began our work in the Cane River area with the understanding that lower French Louisiana's frontier region might be an ideal situation in which to look for African continuities in pottery. We also began it with the knowledge that this French and Spanish colonial border region had unique economic ties to the Native American populace, as well as a relatively permissive stance toward interethnic interaction. In short, we believed that Cane River archaeology might demonstrate that earthenware pottery of the seventeenth through early nineteenth centuries had multiple makers and occurred in numerous social and economic contexts.

Our preliminary examination suggests instead strong correspondence between most late colonial- and early American–era earthenwares and those produced by Native Americans. We say this with some reluctance, because on an intuitive level we still feel it likely that Africans and their descendants in the Cane River area would not have obtained all the earthenware they used from Native Americans. The possibility remains that African, or more specifically Kongo, influences may be indicated at Coincoin Plantation by the presence of unusually high numbers of sand-tempered or "untempered" sherds among all those Caddoan-like shell-tempered wares.

As to the noticeable decline in the frequency and decoration of earthenwares in colonial- and American-era pottery assemblages over time, we think an explanation of the first trend is fairly clear and involves several concurrent factors. First, the 1820s marks the beginning of an exodus of Native Americans from Louisiana, a process that ultimately culminated in the removal of the local Caddo to Oklahoma in the 1830s. Second, the few Native Americans that remained were virtually hidden by the roughly 150,000 largely Anglo newcomers to Louisiana who arrived in the first two decades of the 1800s. The visibility of the Native Americans' vended products, possibly including pottery, attenuated along with the visibility of the Native Americans themselves. Third, the nineteenth century marks a period of production of inexpensive new American wares. Stoneware production accelerated markedly in the 1780s and into the 1800s (Guilland 1971:37, 73), and whiteware and ironstone production also began during the early 1800s, which may have undercut the market for cheap utilitarian vessels, a position probably held by the low-fired earthenwares (Noël Hume 1969; Price 1982; Yakubik 1990). Finally, inasmuch as there may have been an African contribution to Louisiana colonowares, factors such as increased generational removal from Africa, increased ethnic randomization, and increased acculturation in the nineteenth century would have acted, as elsewhere, to diminish the production of African material culture (e.g., Singleton 1988).

There may be several reasons why we also observe a trend for decreasing decoration of low-fired earthenwares over time, even in strictly Native American assemblages. One possibility is overt economics. Market demand among the colonial and American planters may have been for unadorned vessels. For instance, Native potters may have emulated certain European vessel forms, presumably because such vessels held greater trade value and/or conferred higher social status. If they emulated vessel form, they probably emulated vessel decoration, too, especially when it required less effort from the potter.

In a more speculative vein, another possibility is that this market pressure may have coincided with a subtle defiance on the part of Native Americans. Native Americans may not have wanted the pots obtained by outsiders to possess elements of their own symbolic grammar and lexicon. If African slaves played a role in pottery manufacture, whether as the pupils of Native Americans or as independent producers, this same argument may hold.

Last, we may be observing a functional difference. If we accept the rough axiom that coarse wares are typically unadorned, and that plain coarse wares represent utilitarian cooking/preparation vessels, then we may be seeing a truncation in the traditional continuum of pottery forms. In other words, Europeans were providing the tablewares—the prestige wares—and the inexpensive local colonowares were for nondisplay contexts.

In conclusion, we are for the moment obliged to see social and cultural dynamics in the Native American world playing a primary, though not an exclusive, role in the utilization and stylistic properties of colonowares in northwestern Louisiana. A clarification and expansion of the role of Africans in earthenware use and/or manufacture awaits continuing research.

Acknowledgments

Funding for this project has generously been provided by the U.K. Arts and Humanities Research Council, the British Academy, the U.S. National Endowment for the Humanities, the Cane River National Heritage Area, the National Park Service's Delta Initiative, and the Institute of Archaeology of University College London. We are extremely grateful to Mr. and Mrs. B. F. Bouser and Henry E. Metoyer for both permitting and supporting our research efforts on their properties. We also are indebted to many local partners, including the personnel at the Cultural Resource Office of Northwestern State University of Louisiana, the Creole Heritage Center, Cane River Creole National Historical Park, the National Center for Preservation Technology and Training, the Natchitoches Parish Courthouse, and the Cane River National Heritage Area.

Notes

1. We were unable to comfortably identify 189 of the 1,857 Euro-American sherds recovered from 2002 to 2007. Most often the problem was our inability to identify a given refined earthenware as creamware or pearlware. Therefore our counts of the latter ware types are, if anything, slightly conservative, as we eliminated these 189 from our percentages when characterizing the collection as a whole.

2. Girard enumerates in his 1997 article only the 56 sherds recovered in 1996, but he refers to subsequent visits in which he collected additional material, which is why our reinspection of the sherd collection in 2004 results in a different quantity (n=61).

3. Counts are drawn from Hunter's type-variety descriptions, in which he lists 564 plain and decorated sherds. He states that some 15 "decorated ceramics, exhibiting incising, engraving or brushing are extremely scarce in this assemblage" (Hunter 1985:85). He dismisses 2 from his discussion because of their prehistoric age, leaving a sample of 13 decorated sherds. He distinguishes these from the 109 red-filmed or black-filmed sherds. Ignoring the latter, he describes in his type-varieties some 33 incised, engraved,

or brushed sherds. It is unclear which he excludes to derive his number of 13. We rely on his judgment and thus use the latter figure, instead of the enumerated 33, suspecting that he has eliminated some of the Maddox Engraved sherds as prehistoric by virtue of their design motifs.

4. Of the collection of 1,258 colonoware sherds, 36 are clearly decorated. Possible decorations were noted on an additional 16 sherds, but, given the uncertainty, they are not counted in this analysis. Including them would expand the quantity of decorated sherds to 52, or 4.1 percent, which does not change the course of the observed trend.

5. These data were preliminary when submitted for publication. Since then a petrographic analysis has been conducted, as has a traditional study of vessel form, firing atmosphere, rim shape, and thickness.

References Cited

Aiyedun, D. K.
1988   Pottery Making in Ibaja, Igbomina Area, Kwara State. *Nigerian Field* 53:76–88.
Avery, George
1995   More Friend Than Foe: Eighteenth Century Spanish, French, and Caddoan Interaction at Los Adaes, a Capital of Texas Located in Northwestern Louisiana. *Louisiana Archaeology* 22:163–193.
1997   *1997 Annual Report for the Los Adaes Station Archaeology Program.* Department of Social Sciences, Northwestern State University of Louisiana, Natchitoches. Submitted to the Louisiana Division of Archaeology.
Beier, G.
1980   Yoruba Pottery. *African Arts* 13:48–53.
Berlin, Ira
1974   *Slaves without Masters: The Free Negro in the Antebellum South.* New Press, New York.
Blitz, John Howard
1985   *An Archaeological Study of the Mississippi Choctaw Indians.* Mississippi Department of Archives and History Archaeological Report No. 16. Mississippi Department of Archives and History, Jackson.
Brain, Jeffrey P.
1979   *Tunica Treasure.* Papers of the Peabody Museum of Archaeology and Ethnology, Vol. 17. Harvard University, Cambridge, Mass.
1988   *Tunica Archaeology.* Papers of the Peabody Museum of Archaeology and Ethnology, Vol. 78. Harvard University, Cambridge, Mass.
1989   *Winterville: Late Prehistoric Culture Contact in the Lower Mississippi Valley.* Archaeological Report No. 23. Mississippi Department of Archives and History, Jackson.
Collins, Henry B.
1927   Potsherds from Choctaw Village Sites in Mississippi. *Journal of the Washington Academy of Sciences* 17:10.

Cordell, Ann S.
2002   Continuity and Change in Apalachee Pottery Manufacture. *Historical Archaeology* 36(1): 36–54.

David, N., J. Sterner, and K. Gavua
1988   Why Pots Are Decorated. *Current Anthropology* 29:365–389.

Dawdy, Shannon Lee
2000   Understanding Cultural Change through the Vernacular: Creolization in Louisiana. *Historical Archaeology* 34(3): 107–123.

Deetz, James
1988   American Historical Archaeology: Methods and Results. *Science* 239:362–367.
1999   Archaeology at Flowerdew Hundred. In *"I, Too, Am America": Archaeological Studies of African-American Life*, edited by T. A. Singleton, 39–46. University Press of Virginia, Charlottesville.

de Maret, Pierre
1974   Un Atelier de Potière Ndibu au Bas-Zaire. *Africa-Tervuren* 20:49–54.

Ferguson, Leland
1980   Looking for the "Afro-" in Colono-Indian Pottery: Archaeological Perspectives on Ethnicity in America. In *Archaeological Perspectives on Ethnicity in America*, edited by R. L. Schuyler, 14–28. Baywood, Farmingdale, N.Y.
1992   *Uncommon Ground: Archaeology and Early African America, 1650–1800.* Smithsonian Institution Press, Washington, D.C.

Gallay, A.
1992   Traditions Céramiques et Ethnies dans le Delta Interieur du Niger (Mali): Approche Ethnoarchéologique. *Bulletin du Centre Genevois d'Anthropologie* 3:23–46.

Galloway, Patricia K.
1995   *Choctaw Genesis 1500–1700.* University of Nebraska Press, Lincoln.

Girard, Jeffrey S.
1997   Historic Caddoan Occupation in the Natchitoches Area: Recent Attempts to Locate Residential Sites. *Louisiana Archaeology* 8(3): 19–31.
2002   *Regional Archaeology Program Management Unit 1: Thirteenth Annual Report.* Northwestern State University of Louisiana, Natchitoches.
2003   *Regional Archaeology Program Management Unit 1: Fourteenth Annual Report.* Northwestern State University of Louisiana, Natchitoches. Submitted to the Louisiana Division of Archaeology.

Gosselain, Olivier
1994   Identites Techniques: La Travail de la Poterie au Cameroun Méridional. Ph.D. diss., Université Libre de Bruxelles.

Gregory, Hiram F., and George Avery
2006   Using American Indian Pottery to Identify Historic Period Sites in Northwest Louisiana. Paper presented at the Annual Meeting of the Louisiana Archaeological Society, Monroe.

Gregory, Hiram F., George Avery, Aubra L. Lee, and Jay C. Blaine
2004   Presidio Los Adaes: Spanish, French, and Caddoan Interaction on the Northern Frontier. *Historical Archaeology* 38(3): 65–77.

Guilland, Harold F.
1971 *Early American Folk Pottery*. Chilton Book, Philadelphia.
Haag, William G.
1953 Choctaw Archaeology. *Southeastern Archaeological Conference Newsletter* 3(3): 25–28.
Hall, Gwendolyn Midlo
1992 *Africans in Colonial Louisiana: The Development of Afro-Creole Culture in the Eighteenth Century*. Louisiana State University Press, Baton Rouge.
2000 *Databases for the Study of Afro-Louisiana History and Genealogy 1699–1860: Computerized Information from Original Manuscript Sources*. Baton Rouge, La., CD-ROM.
Handley, Fiona J. L., David W. Morgan, and Kevin C. MacDonald
2006 Things and Words—Bringing Together the Material and Historical Records of the Isle Brevelle, Cane River, Natchitoches, Louisiana. Paper presented at the annual Contemporary and Historical Archaeology in Theory Conference, Bristol, U.K.
Hill, M. H.
1987 Ethnicity Lost? Ethnicity Gained? Information Functions of "African Ceramics" in West Africa and North America. In *Ethnicity and Culture: Proceedings of the Eighteenth Annual Chacmool Conference*, edited by R. Auger, M. F. Glass, S. MacEachern, and P. McCartney, 135–139. Archaeological Association, University of Calgary, Calgary.
Huffman, Thomas N.
1989 Ceramics, Settlements and Late Iron Age Migrations. *African Archaeological Review* 7:155–182.
Hunter, Donald G.
1985 The Apalachee on Red River, 1763–1834: An Ethnohistory and Summary of Archaeological Testing at the Zimmerman Hill Site, Rapides Parish, Louisiana. *Louisiana Archaeology* 12:7–127.
1994a The Biloxi on Bayou Boeuf: An Ethnohistory and Analysis of Surface Collections from the Biloxi Village Site (16-Ra-60), Rapides Parish, Louisiana. *Mississippi Archaeology* 29(2): 18–43.
1994b Their Final Years: The Apalachee and Other Immigrant Tribes on the Red River, 1763–1834. *Florida Anthropologist* 47(1): 3–46.
Kelley, David B.
1997 *Two Caddoan Farmsteads in the Red River Valley*. Research Series No. 51. Arkansas Archeological Survey, Fayetteville.
Kelley, David B., Donald G. Hunter, Paul S. Gardner, Daniel C. Weinand, Angela Tiné, and Larry L. Tieszen
1996 The McLelland and Joe Clark Sites: Protohistoric-Historic Caddo Farmsteads in the Red River Valley of Northwest Louisiana. *Southeastern Archaeology* 15(1): 81–102.
Kniffen, Fred B., Hiram F. Gregory Jr., and George A. Stokes
1987 *The Historic Indian Tribes of Louisiana: From 1542 to the Present*. Louisiana State University Press, Baton Rouge.

Lanfranchi, R., and B. Clist, editors
1991   *Aux Origines de l'Afrique Centrale.* Sepia, Paris.

Loren, Diana DiPaolo
2000   The Intersections of Colonial Policy and Colonial Practice: Creolization on the Eighteenth-Century Louisiana/Texas Frontier. *Historical Archaeology* 34(3): 85–98.
2007   Corporeal Concerns: Eighteenth-Century *Casta* Paintings and Colonial Bodies in Spanish Texas. *Historical Archaeology* 41(1): 23–36.

MacDonald, Kevin C., David W. Morgan, and Fiona J. L. Handley
2002/2003   Cane River: The Archaeology of "Free People of Color" in Colonial Louisiana. *Archaeology International* 6:52–55.
2006   The Cane River African Diaspora Archaeological Project: Prospectus and Initial Results. In *African Re-Genesis: Confronting Social Issues in the Diaspora*, edited by J. B. Haviser and K. C. MacDonald, 123–144. UCL Press, London.

MacDonald, Kevin C., David W. Morgan, Fiona J. L. Handley, Emma Morley, and Aubra Lee
2006   The Archaeology of Local Myths and Heritage Tourism: The Case of Cane River's Melrose Plantation. In *A Future for Archaeology: The Past in the Present*, edited by R. Layton, S. Shennan, and P. Stone, 127–142. UCL Press, London.

Mathews, James H.
1983   Analysis of Ceramics from Three Eighteenth- and Nineteenth-Century Sites in the Locale of Natchitoches, Louisiana. Master's thesis, Northwestern State University of Louisiana, Natchitoches.

Meyers, Allan D.
1999   West African Tradition in the Decoration of Colonial Jamaican Folk Pottery. *International Journal of Historical Archaeology* 3:201–223.

Miller, Christina E., and Susan E. Wood
2000   *Oakland Plantation: A Comprehensive Subsurface Investigation.* Southeast Archeological Center, National Park Service, Tallahassee, Fla.

Miller, Joseph C.
2002   Central Africa during the Era of the Slave Trade, c. 1490s-1850s. In *Central Africans and Cultural Transformations in the American Diaspora*, edited by L. M. Heywood, 21–69. Cambridge University Press, Cambridge.

Morgan, David W.
2005   *Phase II Archaeological Investigations at the American Cemetery (16NA67), Natchitoches Parish, Louisiana.* Report submitted to the Louisiana Division of Archaeology and the American Cemetery Association of Natchitoches. Report on file at the Louisiana Division of Archaeology and the Cultural Resource Office, Northwestern State University of Louisiana, Natchitoches.

Morgan, David W., Kevin C. MacDonald, and Fiona J. L. Handley
2006   Economics and Authenticity: A Collision of Interpretations in Cane River National Heritage Area, Louisiana. *George Wright Forum* 23(1): 44–61.

Mouer, L. Daniel, Mary Ellen N. Hodges, Stephen R. Potter, Susan L. Henry Renaud, Ivor Noël Hume, Dennis J. Pogue, Martha W. McCartney, and Thomas E. Davidson
1999   Colonoware Pottery, Chesapeake Pipes, and "Uncritical Assumptions." In *"I, Too, Am America": Archaeological Studies of African-American Life*, edited by T. A. Singleton, 83–115. University Press of Virginia, Charlottesville.

Noël Hume, Ivor
1962   An Indian Ware of the Colonial Period. *Quarterly Bulletin of the Archaeological Society of Virginia* 17(1): 2–12.
1969   *A Guide to Artifacts of Colonial America*. University of Pennsylvania Press, Philadelphia.

Okpoko, A. I.
1987   Pottery-Making in Igboland, Eastern Nigeria: An Ethnoarchaeological Study. *Proceedings of the Prehistoric Society* 53:445–455.

Parsons, Mark L., James E. Bruseth, Jacques Bagur, S. Eileen Goldborer, and Claude McCrocklin
2002   *Finding Sha'chahdínnih (Timber Hill): The Last Village of the Kadohadacho in the Caddo Homeland*. Archeological Reports Series No. 3. Texas Historical Commission, Austin.

Penman, John T., Priscilla M. Lowrey, and Samuel O. McGahey
1980   *Archaeological Survey in Mississippi, 1974–1975*. Mississippi Department of Archives and History, Jackson.

Perttula, Timothy K.
1992   *"The Caddo Nation": Archaeological and Ethnohistoric Perspectives*. University of Texas Press, Austin.

Phillips, Philip
1970   *Archaeological Survey in the Lower Yazoo Basin, Mississippi, 1949–1955*. Papers of the Peabody Museum of Archaeology and Ethnology, Vol. 60 (2 vols.). Harvard University, Cambridge, Mass.

Pinçon, B., and D. Ngoie-Ngalla
1990   L'unité Culturelle Kongo á la Fin du XIXe Siécle. L'apport d'études Céramologiques. *Cahiers d'Etudes Africaines* 118:157–178.

Price, Cynthia R.
1982   *19th Century Ceramics in the Eastern Ozark Border Region*. Monograph Series No. 1, Reprinted. Center for Archaeological Research, Southwest Missouri State University, Springfield.

Rowland, Dunbar, and A. G. Sanders, editors
1932   *Mississippi Provincial Archives: French Dominion, 1704–1743*. Vol. 3. Mississippi Department of Archives and History, Jackson.

Shaw, Billy Wayne
1983   A Ceramic Chronology for the Whittington House Site: 1780–Present. Master's thesis, Northwestern State University of Louisiana, Natchitoches.

Sibley, John
1832   Historical Sketches of Several Indian Tribes in Louisiana, South of the Arkansas River, and between the Mississippi and River Grande. *American State Papers, Class II, Indian Affairs* 1:721–731.

Silvia, Diane E.
2000   Indian and French Interaction in Colonial Louisiana during the Early Eighteenth Century. Ph.D. diss., Tulane University, New Orleans.
2002   Native American and French Cultural Dynamics on the Gulf Coast. *Historical Archaeology* 36(1): 26–35.

Singleton, Theresa A.
1988   An Archaeological Framework for Slavery and Emancipation. In *The Recovery of Meaning: Historical Archaeology in the Eastern United States*, edited by M. P. Leone and P. B. Potter Jr., 345–370. Smithsonian Institution Press, Washington, D.C.

Singleton, Theresa A., and Mark D. Bograd
1995   *The Archaeology of the African Diaspora in the Americas.* Guides to the Archaeological Literature of the Immigrant Experience in America No. 2. Society for Historical Archaeology, Ann Arbor, Mich.
2000   Breaking Typological Barriers: Looking for the Colono in Colonoware. In *Lines That Divide: Historical Archaeologies of Race, Class, and Gender*, edited by J. A. Delle, S. Mrozowski, and R. Paynter, 3–21. University of Tennessee Press, Knoxville.

Soper, Robert
1985   Roulette Decoration on African Pottery: Technical Considerations, Dating, and Distributions. *African Archaeological Review* 5:29–51.

Swanton, John R.
1911   *Indian Tribes of the Lower Mississippi Valley and Adjacent Coast of the Gulf of Mexico.* Bureau of American Ethnology Bulletin No. 43. Government Printing Office, Washington, D.C.
1946   *The Indians of the Southeastern United States.* Bureau of American Ethnology Bulletin No. 137. Government Printing Office, Washington, D.C.

Usner, Daniel H., Jr.
1992   *Indians, Settlers, & Slaves in a Frontier Exchange Economy: The Lower Mississippi Valley before 1783.* University of North Carolina Press, Chapel Hill.
1998   *American Indians in the Lower Mississippi Valley: Social and Economic Histories.* University of Nebraska Press, Lincoln.

Voss, Jerome A., and John H. Blitz
1988   Archaeological Investigations in the Choctaw Homeland. *American Antiquity* 53(1): 125–145.

Waselkov, Gregory A.
2000   Bear Oil in the Colonial Southeast. Paper presented at the 57th Annual Southeastern Archaeological Conference, Macon, Ga.

Waselkov, Gregory A., editor
2002   French Colonial Archaeology at Old Mobile: Selected Studies. *Historical Archaeology* 36(1).

Williams, Stephen, and Jeffrey P. Brain
1983   *Excavations at the Lake George Site, Yazoo County, Mississippi, 1958–1960.* Papers of the Peabody Museum of Archaeology and Ethnology, Vol. 74. Harvard University, Cambridge, Mass.

Yakubik, Jill-Karen
1990   Ceramic Use in Late Eighteenth Century and Early Nineteenth Century Southeastern Louisiana. Ph.D. diss., Tulane University, New Orleans.

9

Living on the Edge

Foodways and Early Expressions of Creole Culture on the French Colonial Gulf Coast Frontier

MEREDITH D. HARDY

The study of the material culture—in particular, those artifacts associated with the acquisition, preparation, presentation, and consumption of foods—allows archaeologists to study the social processes that resulted in the deposition of material remnants of past lives, and to attempt to place these processes within a cultural framework. We excavate and analyze ceramic sherds and broken pieces of metal pots, knife blades, and bottle glass, and classify them according to a dizzying array of criteria, looking for patterns of their physical distribution across a landscape (whether across a site or a region). This framework is not rigid or static, and over time various cultural elements, like beliefs and objects, are developed, adopted, exchanged, preserved, or lost. However, many times the meanings originally associated with these elements are often misunderstood or misused, and new meanings are created, while in other instances people used goods for their own purposes, with intent that differed from their original intended functions. That is why it is important not to study objects in isolation but processes of change (Hodder 1995).

Through documentary searches we may discover points of the origin and manufacture of goods and commodities, how they were moved from point A to point B, where they were purchased, and even to whom they were willed upon their owner's death. But archaeology is the study of people of the past, not just their possessions. It is important to step back from the artifacts and examine context. How were these objects being used? Why these objects, or cuts of meat, or species of animals? How were the foods prepared and served, and why did people go to such effort to obtain particular things? And what do these actions indicate about the social and cultural worlds of the actors involved? Do they inform about social relations between consumer and provider, between home owner and food preparer, between master and slave?

The first Louisiana colonists did not have the luxury of selectively including new, exotic foods into the nouvelle cuisine as did those in the home country. The difficulties in obtaining the ingredients called for in published culinary works forced the colonists to improvise and create a new cuisine, a combination of the techniques of the Old World with the foods of the New World, a "creole" in every sense of the word. For example, the bouillabaisse of Provence incorporated local shellfish, fish, and even game, in addition to thickening agents like filé (ground sassafras). Foods introduced from Africa and the Caribbean, like okra and some chilies, were also included. When combined with legal and illegal trade for commodities such as ceramics, and a market economy in which the demands of the colonists superseded both the French and Spanish Crown's rules of trade, a creolized cultural tradition began to develop.

It is important to here state what is meant by the term "Creole" in the Louisiana context. In Louisiana, "Creole" came to mean "native born," anyone following the first generation of French, then Spanish immigrants who were born in the New World. In the eighteenth and nineteenth centuries, distinctions were made between Creoles of Color and French Creole. The term did not come to be used as a self-definer until after the rapid influx of Americans in the nineteenth century threatened to drown the culture, and political power, of Creole elites in the region. In New Orleans, Creole came to be associated with both native-born of French or Spanish descent and light-skinned African Americans with a heritage of free status in the region; in this latter instance, Creole was intentionally used as a definer between those who were born free and emancipated slaves, and often inferred higher social status. Finally, Creole as a cuisine came to be representative of all cultures—African, French, Spanish, Canary Islander, German (and other Europeans), English, Anglo-American, Native American—involved in this process of interaction, interface, and exchange.

Creolization theory can be used as an explanatory framework to interpret those situations in which superstrate/substrate relations result in the development of a new culture, a new Native culture, with its own language, customs, and traditions, as opposed to instances of borrowing or total replacement. The speed at which these relations develop can be evidenced by the degree to which various cultural elements are used or ignored, adopted and altered, and assigned new or multiple meanings. We must remember, though, that cultures develop and change according to unique histories and trajectories, experiences, and circumstances (Bourdieu 1977). While we can use models as frameworks for culture change and development, they are only frameworks. And they can be used in this case to investigate the development of foodways and culinary traditions as components of larger cultural changes.

In this chapter, I examine a broad foodways system that developed in one particular region that has, until the last 15 years or so, received little attention—the French colonial coast of the Gulf of Mexico, Louisiana, during the late seventeenth and eighteenth centuries. It was during this time that France became the culinary, cultural, and artistic capital of Europe, resulting in the explosion during the 1650s through the 1700s of *la cuisine bourgeoise*. I incorporate non-French influences—West African, Haitian and pan-Caribbean, Native American, and Spanish, among others—in the development of regional foodway traditions of creole cuisine known today as Louisiana or Gulf Coast Creole. I then examine the ceramics that were used in the preparation and serving of these foods that are recovered from archaeological contexts. Included in this discussion is an examination of the styles and decorative elements of the Regency and rococo artistic movements that were reproduced onto French ceramic tablewares, namely faience, and brought with the colonists and settlers to Louisiana. Many of the stylistic elements present on these eighteenth-century wares appear to indicate an affiliation with regions of southern France and the Mediterranean. The purpose of this chapter is to provide historical and cultural context to the artifacts that we as archaeologists recover in our investigations: ceramics, cookware, faunal and botanical remains, and architectural remnants such as chimneys, hearths, and brick stoves.

Much of the following discussion is based on previous studies that I have conducted on foodways and the distribution of ceramics across the French Gulf Coast region. These studies have centered in large part on firsthand analysis and available ceramic and faunal data gathered from published reports on archaeological sites within this region: 419 Decatur Street, New Orleans; the Hermann-Grima House, New Orleans; Rodriguez Plantation; Chalmette Battlefield; the French Warehouse, Ship Island, Mississippi; and Old Mobile (Figure 9.1) (Beavers and Lamb 1990,

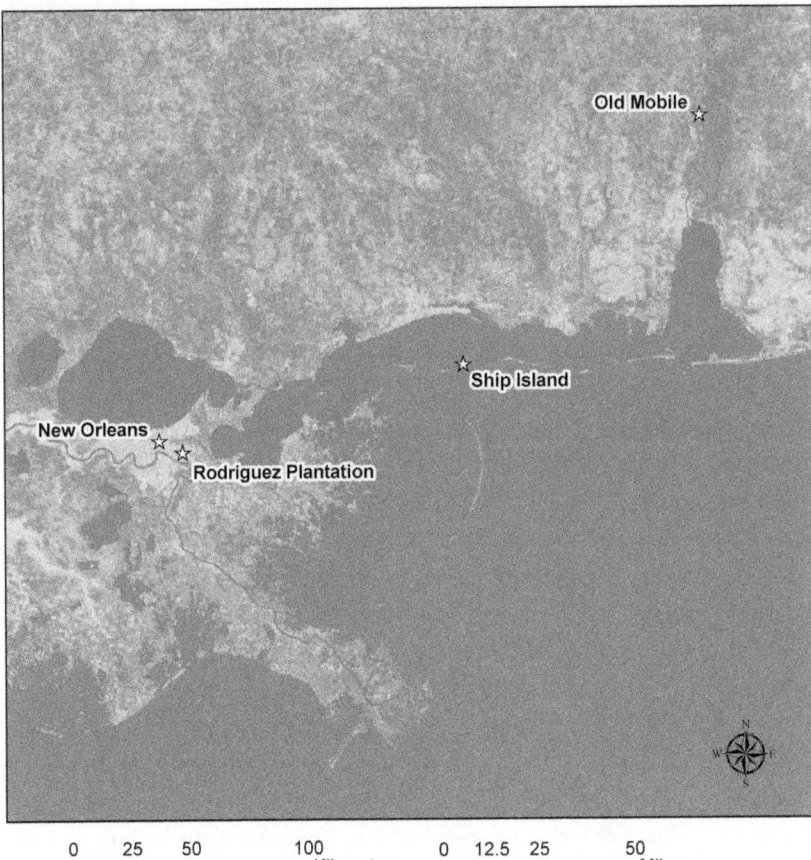

Figure 9.1. Map of the region showing the locations of archaeological sites discussed in text. Created by the author.

1993a, 1993b; Birkedal and DeMarcay n.d.; Davis and Giardino 1983; Hammersten 1990; Hardy 1998, 2002, 2004; Hardy et al. 2004; Lamb and Beavers 1983; Shenkel 1977; Waselkov 1991).

Introduction to Foodways

Ceramics have been the primary means by which archaeologists have identified cultural affinity and identity. These material fragments of past cultures are representative of both expressions of particular worldviews and the social aspects of individual lives, such as socioeconomic status and trade (Rice 2006). But as ceramics are indicative of customs and beliefs as they develop and change over time, they are only a singular physical component within the larger sphere of social interaction and exchange. The consumption of food, and the methods of preparation and presentation associated with this act, is one example of the everyday rituals and customs used to define cultures and social groups. Foods are identified as healthy or poisonous, and preferences for tastes are established. These preferences, over time, acquire a social significance and aura of prestige or commonality that are often illustrative of the social status of a consumer (Douglas 1966). The consumption of particular foods can indicate social membership and exclusion, and demarcate boundaries that may otherwise be invisible. The status associated with particular foods is not static, but changes as new items come into vogue, foods become more readily available or scarce, and social groups associated with particular foods assume various status ranks. By studying foodway systems, or the means, styles, and manners in which food is acquired, prepared, served, and consumed, one can infer status, religious associations, means of self identification, ingenuity, adaptation, loss, and preservation (Anderson 1970). Foodways serve as powerful metaphors of group identity and incorporate symbols laden with multiple layers of meaning.

In Louisiana, the ongoing interaction and interdependence between the French, Spanish, Africans, and Native Americans fostered the development of a creolized system of food production, preparation, and consumption (Fleetwood and Filipelli 2004:9; *Times Picayune* 2002:5). These foodways were largely based on the desires of many of the colonists to imitate the lifestyles and obtain the material culture of the noble classes.

Setting the Table

The origins of the foodways and cultures of Louisiana resulted from a process of interaction and exchange between French and Spanish settlers, planters, and merchants and various indigenous groups, African slaves, and later European and American arrivals. When combined with spheres of trade and a market economy, a creolized tradition of food acquisition, preparation, and presentation developed. The French origins of this style derived from the baroque, mannerism, Regency, and rococo philosophic and artistic movements of the sixteenth through the eighteenth centuries.

Greatly influenced by the Italian Renaissance of the fifteenth and sixteenth centuries, the French Renaissance was based on conceptions of laws of nature created by God—logic and order, discipline, and aesthetic beauty. The Renaissance pulled from classical Greek and Roman ideals of symmetry, form, and proportion, and gradually gave way to the more natural yet opulent and grandiose expressions of the mannerism and baroque artistic movements of the sixteenth century. Regional trends soon developed; to the north, the artistic and architectural expression was more restrained and "academic" than in southern regions of Provence and the Mediterranean coast, which were typified by light and airy uses of color, line, and form.

By the end of the first quarter of the eighteenth century, the French baroque and Regency styles had given way to the rococo (Lane 1948:22–23). Compared to the baroque period, the rococo period was one of refinement and linearity, with asymmetrical natural motifs like rocks and shells, scrolls, leaves, branches, and flowers, in addition to chinoiserie, Chinese, and Oriental-inspired designs increasing in popularity.

The Development of *la Grande Cuisine*

As France was becoming the artistic and stylistic center of Europe, it was also developing into Europe's culinary capital. The arrival of Catherine de Médicis to France, in 1533, is often heralded (incorrectly) as the beginning of the French culinary revolution. Throughout the sixteenth century, communication and the exchange of ideas were obviously ongoing practices and processes between developing Renaissance Italy, late medieval France, and the rest of northern Europe and the Mediterranean region.

The ways in which foods were prepared and served changed greatly during this time. These refinements grew out of the monasteries of the Middle Ages, and haute cuisine developed in the noble and aristocratic courts (Flandrin 1999a:408–409). The trend was toward a simpler style of cooking in order to enhance the natural flavors of the various ingredients. Four of the major developments that led to the establishment of *le grande cuisine* were: the increased and accepted consumption of vegetables; the use of roux (butter in the north, oil in the south) as a thickening agent for sauces and soups; the increased importance of soup; and a decrease in the amount of spices used.

Foods of the early baroque period were highly spiced, and meats were served with sweet sauces and fruits. Prior to the 1600s, cooking was directly related to medicine and health (Flandrin 1999c:423, 431). During the seventeenth century, cooking developed into an "art form," when efforts were made to harmonize flavors, and gastronomy was emphasized over dietetics. During this period, the separation of sweet and savory flavors was a distinctive feature of French cooking. This arose partially because of the dramatic increase in sugar consumption during the sixteenth century. This trend changed during the seventeenth century, when sugar was used with decreasing frequency to enhance meats, fowl, and vegetables, and began to be used to sweeten fruits, pastries, coffee, tea, and chocolate (Wheaton 1996:55). By the beginning of the eighteenth century, though, sweet foods had been relegated to the final course so as to not mask the natural flavors of meats and vegetables (Mintz 1985:363, 367).

Higher-status meals during the early Renaissance consisted of up to eight courses, and were dominated by meats and breads, but by the eighteenth century meals had been reduced to three or four courses. The first course was comprised of soups, appetizers, and sauces, while the second consisted of roasted meats, salads, and side dishes of vegetables. A third course that repeated the second was optional. The fourth was dedicated to sweet desserts, pastries, and fruits. A great variety of dishes were offered so as to meet individual dietary needs. The preferences of the upper classes gradually shifted from heavy meats and sauces loaded with a profusion of spices to lighter meats, such as fowl and fish, served with delicately seasoned sauces and more vegetables and fruits. By 1650, larger birds like swans, cranes, and peacocks were no longer available in markets or mentioned in cookbooks, being replaced largely by turkeys (Flandrin 1999a:404, 1999b:359).

During this same time, lower-status meals, traditionally consisting of gruels thickened with bread, and poorer cuts of meats (Gross meats), namely beef, and vegetables and fruits, were replaced by stews seasoned with local spices and garden herbs. During the eighteenth century, seafoods were eaten in greater quantities during non-Lent times, and meats were preferred over fowl (Hyman and Hyman 1999; Wheaton 1996:63).

The disparities between the cuisines of the large aristocratic kitchens and the smaller kitchens of the bourgeoisie that began around 1650 increased through the eighteenth century. In short, the aristocrats developed an infatuation with the "simple life" and began to eat like the middle classes, while the bourgeoisie were eating slightly dated aristocratic cuisine (Wheaton 1996:232). Following these lines, by the 1740s a nouvelle cuisine was developing that emphasized "simplicity" and "purity" of natural flavors, but included the preparation of more expensive fresh ingredients.

There were regional differences, too. For example, southern French diets incorporated oils, especially olive oil; garlic; fruits; vegetables; and, later, the American tomato. Provençal cuisine is typically identified with particular herbs, such as rosemary, thyme, marjoram, sage, and lavender; bouillabaisse and fish stews; and vegetables, especially eggplant, zucchini, and onions. It became known for its use of strong, abundant spices and sweet sauces made of grapes, prunes, pears, and other fruits, and sugar, indicative of Arabic influences on neighboring Spanish cuisine (Rosenberger 1999:221). Languedoc is perhaps best known for cassoulet, a "casserole" of white beans and meats, primarily pork, duck in confit, and lamb. This is similar to Spanish dishes such as *olla podrida*, meat stews thickened with a wide variety of vegetables and beans, which were cooked in three-legged pots.

In northern regions like Normandy and Brittany, butter was and is the primary fat, and onions and shallots, rather than garlic, provide the primary flavor. Northern cuisines also relied more heavily on other dairy products (cream and cheeses) than southern regions, and did not readily incorporate wine into recipes. Some seventeenth- and eighteenth-century recipes called for both butter and fat. Oils were used initially by aristocratic and bourgeoisie cooks (Flandrin 1999a:409). There were parallels between religious affiliation and the use of dairy products or oil; the northern regional use of butter increased while the influence of the Catholic Church decreased, while in southern Europe olive oil remained the mainstay, as did the Church's influence (Flandrin 1999a:417, 1999b:372).

Traditions, Cookbooks, and the Institutionalization of Practice

With the advent of the printing press, cookbooks became available to a growing audience, covering such varied topics as cooking techniques, how to lay a table, and how to peel and cut fruits. From ca. 1480 to 1800, at least 50 books dedicated to culinary traditions and techniques were printed. The first books dedicated to specific types of foods, like pastry, were also written during this time. In particular, two cookbooks have risen to the forefront as representative of these changes. In 1651, François Pierre la Varenne wrote *La Cuisinier Francois*, which methodically organized cooking for the first time and made the developing haute cuisine available to the bourgeoisie (Hyman and Hyman 1999:395). La Varenne has been attributed with founding the classical school of French cooking. Other cookbooks included François Massialot's *Le Cuisinier roïal et bourgeois* (1691), which was renamed *Le Nouveau Cuisinier royal et bourgeois* and expanded to three volumes between 1712 and 1730 (Hyman and Hyman 1999:394–395, 398; Wheaton 1996:151). This book was aimed at experienced cooks and provided few measurements for ingredients. Finally, Nicolas de Bonnefons also addressed the prosperous middle classes with two works, *Le Jardinier François* (1651) and *Les Delices de la Campagne* (1654).

With the rise of the bourgeoisie during the reign of Louis XV, there was also a growing desire for objects that reflected the lifestyles of the nobility without the cost. In 1746, Menon's *La Cuisiniere Bourgeoise* appealed to these broad audiences, especially to women, by introducing cooking methods once reserved for the nobility to the middle classes (Wheaton 1996:98). Menon and other cookbook writers of the eighteenth century stated that the middle classes could eat like the nobles if they had the proper pots and pans, went to the market every day, and knew how to make a good bouillon (Wheaton 1996:209; Tannahill 1988). In turn, the nobles were aspiring for the "simplicity" of the middle classes (Wheaton 1996:195). The noble classes served their meals on gold and silver wares, while the middle classes had to settle for ceramic wares glazed in lead, or tin-enamels known as faience. While at first the nobility used faience rarely, viewing the ware as "vulgar," circumstances would quickly change these perceptions. As a result of French involvement in the War of the Grand Alliance (1689–1697) and the War of the Spanish Succession (1701–1714), "the nobility were required to send their gold and silver plate to the mint.... Largely as a result of these decrees, France became the dominant force in European faience throughout the eighteenth century.... [W]ithin a few decades it had become also a fashionable pastime" (Caiger-Smith 1973:115).

Tools of the kitchen included a wide variety of vessels and utensils of ever-increasing specialization, such as large stockpots, skillets, and chafing dishes, of metal and clay (Figure 9.2). Meals were prepared on open hearths, in pots hanging over the fire from an iron arm, and meats were often roasted on a spit (Blanchette 1981:30; Flandrin 1999a:414). The kitchens of the middle and lower classes typically did not have ovens, but these groups cooked on open hearths, and in embers and ashes. Breads and

Figure 9.2. *The Kitchen Table*, by Jean Siméon Chardin, 1757. Courtesy of the Boston Museum of Fine Art.

pastries were typically purchased from a *pâtisserier*, who did have the necessary ovens. Larger, wealthier houses had brick ovens built into the kitchen chimney.

Some households had a brick *potager* and several small charcoal stoves or braziers. A *potager*, or "stew stove," was a brick masonry raised counter with several openings containing iron grills or baskets that acted like burners (Wheaton 1996:101). These grills held charcoal, and heat could be adjusted. They were built near or below windows for ventilation, but later versions had a flue that was shared with a kitchen chimney. These stoves were illustrated in architectural pattern books by the middle of the eighteenth century, and by the early nineteenth century were incorporating specialized grates, such as ones for poaching fish. Originally, though, they were intended for cooking soups and stews by placing the pot on the grill. Copper braziers (or chafing dishes) stood on legs over charcoals, and were used for foods that required higher heat.

Ceramic vessels were preferred for slow cooking of both wet and dry dishes (Blanchette 1981:30). Wet meals included stews, sauces, creams, and other items that were prepared in hollow wares, such as the pot-terrine, *huguenote*, platters, and casseroles. Dry meals were mostly meats (or pâtés), prepared in a variety of ways—on platters, cooked twice (once on a spit, and then placed in a terrine or covered clay pot), or in *pâtisserie* (pastries), which did not require a vessel for cooking but for serving. Other vessels were used for making jellies, preserves, and other cold foods.

Thus, these cultural developments and practices were brought to the New World via the explorers, voyageurs, and colonists who were charting coastlines and establishing settlements and storehouses along the Gulf of Mexico. The expansion of trade systems in the French colonies of the New World introduced a wide variety of new, exotic, luxury foods into the kitchens of the French nobility, though many of these items, like tomatoes, potatoes, and corn (maize), took over two centuries to be accepted. Other foods from the colonies were readily embraced, like turkey, beans (*Phaseolus vulgaris*), and cacao (Flandrin 1999b:361). The amounts and varieties of cooking and serving vessels, like the chocolate pot, expanded in accordance with these new foods.

Non-French Foodway Traditions

Before food production by the Louisiana colonists became successful, these settlers were dependent on local Native Americans for their survival (Mitchell 1994, 1998; Usner 1992). Much of what we know of Native American foods from this time is based on historical observations by Antoine Simon Le Page du Pratz, whose *History of Louisiana*, initially published in 1758 and translated into English in 1774, provides a unique insight into the natural flora and fauna of the region. These observations, while amusing in some ways, are useful for a couple of reasons. First, the descriptions of the animals illuminate both their presence and relative abundance in the region. Second, his observations made while living among the Natchez provide some of the only insights regarding the practices and lifeways of one of the few remaining Mississippian chiefdom societies, and it was these people who showed the first European settlers of the region how to collect, hunt, and prepare the local foods when provisions from France did not arrive.

The Spanish influence on this culinary tradition comes largely from pan-Mediterranean trade going back to Moorish times. Spanish cuisine of the time was not necessarily differentiated by status, with the exception of members of the court, who ate a wide variety of highly spiced foods. Spanish influences (with introductions from the Americas, the Middle East, and the Arabian peninsula) included olive oil, rice, citrus, almonds, sugar, tomatoes, peppers, garlic, saffron, eggplant, and cacao (Flandrin 1999a:417); Arabic contributions, dating from the thirteenth through the fifteenth centuries, included rice, spinach, eggplant, apricots, lemons, and bitter orange.

In many African food traditions, meat is used as a flavoring and is not the primary component of a meal. Among many West African peoples, fish were a large part of the diet. One-pot meals, like stews and soups with fish, crab, and other seafoods, were combined with starchy pulps of palm nuts or groundnuts (peanuts) and other vegetables. Guinea fowl was also used. Islamic areas tended to have diets based on beans, sorghum, and brown rice, while other peoples, such as the Yoruba, ate stews and soups with okra and spinach. The influence of African cooking ways and foods can be seen throughout the Caribbean and the Gulf Coast–Louisiana. Foods that bear these traditions include Foo Foo (based on fufu), *moros y cristianos*, pelau, dirty rice, and, of course, gumbo and jambalaya (Fleetwood and Filipelli 2004:8; Mitchell 1993:3–5).

The one-pot meal, however, should not be exclusively associated with Native American, African, or European originality or influence (Mitchell 1994:7, 1998:13). It is a practical means of cooking on many levels: it saves energy (fuel), the meal can serve many people, and it requires few tools to prepare and few wares to serve and consume—you only need a ladle, bowl, and spoon. The one-pot meal can be viewed as a point of commonality, a common denominator between many traditions of food preparation with which cooks from different cultures can communicate and learn, adopt new foods, and experiment.

The first Louisiana colonists did not have the luxury of selectively including new, exotic foods into the nouvelle cuisine as did those in the home country (Mitchell 1991:3). The difficulties in obtaining the ingredients called for in published culinary works forced the colonists to improvise, using locally available foods and herbs, substituting new species of fish and game. By the late eighteenth century, markets were established that carried a wide variety of foodstuffs. Captain Basil Hall observed the diversity of items available for purchase in the markets of the late eighteenth century: "Peas, cabbages, beet roots, artichokes, French beans, radishes . . . spotted seeds . . . potatoes both of the sweet and irish kind, tomatoes, rice, Indian corn, ginger, blackberries, roses and violets, oranges, bananas, apples, fowls tied in three by the legs, quail, gingerbread, beer in bottles, and salt-fish" (Crete 1978). Fowl and game were sold in markets in the early eighteenth century, and by the first quarter of the nineteenth century marked preferences were notable; for example, chickens and turkeys were preferred to duck and geese (Hilliard 1972).

Again, regional culinary styles began to develop. Urban and rural styles of cooking developed based largely on market availability of food and goods used in both service and preparation (Mitchell 1999:4–5). Urban Creole cuisine came to be defined by the incorporation of separate courses, and a plate for each course could have several separate foods. There were many ceramic and metal pieces that would comprise a table service, and many pieces of cookware were designated for specific recipes and foods. Urban Creole cuisine maintained a closer allegiance to southern French cooking, with heavy emphases on use of oils and garlic and tomato sauces; a heavy use of herbs like bay, marjoram, rosemary, sage, and thyme; the use of wine in preparation; and the creation of separate sauces for individual dishes and meats. Dairy products such as cheese were also more heavily used in urban areas, but initially were not a major component of the diet. However, by the time the first Creole cookbook was published in 1885, butter and cream comprised an almost defining role in the developing urban Creole cuisine, reflecting an increasing use of butter as a base for sauces in French cuisine (Flandrin 1999a:417).

In contrast, rural or country cooking did not rely so heavily on markets but on what could be obtained by the consumers themselves by hunting, fishing, and trapping (Mitchell 2004:4). Meals tended to be prepared in single large pots or terrines and incorporated game, fowl, fish, and shellfish—the bounty of the bayou. Portions were served in dishes or bowls, and often were accompanied with rice.

Following the Louisiana Purchase in 1803, the doors to Anglo-American trade were opened. It did not take long for Americans of English, Dutch, and other European ancestry to descend on the region. By the mid-nineteenth century and especially after the Civil War, a rapid Americanization had occurred, and Louisianans and coastal residents began to fear their local Creole cultures were being overwhelmed.

In the 1870s, the first Creole revival movements began, with the first use of the word "Creole" as a self-imposed label of identity. In 1885, Lafcadio Hearn published *La Cuisine Creole*, the first collection of Creole recipes (receipts). Hearn defined what makes Creole cuisine unique, beyond the blending of French and Spanish West Indian (and by this time Italian and Mexican) influences: "Economy and simplicity govern... and its many savory dishes are rendered palatable more as the result of care in their preparation, than any great skill or expensive outlay in the selection of materials" (Hearn 1990:1).

In 1901, the *New Orleans Times Picayune* published a version of these collected recipes in *The Picayune's Creole Cook Book*. The introduction to the second edition states that this collection "is the only book of the kind," and claims that every recipe in the collection had been tried and tested, "given as the result of the personal practical experience and success in the Creole Kitchen." The first edition was distributed across the United States and quickly sold out. The introduction to the first edition clearly stated that "especial care has been taken to rescue from oblivion many fine old-fashioned dishes, and bring them back into general use... special attention has been given to the simple, every-day home dishes of the Creole household, while those that tempted the gourmet and epicureans in the palmist days of old Creole cookery have not been omitted" (7).

A third compilation of recipes was published by Célestine Eustis in 1904, *Cooking in Old Creole Days*. An interesting observation was made in the introduction that was not described in the earlier publications—the role of song in the preparation of particular dishes. The singing of these songs was largely practical, in addition to just "passing the time." For example, the time it took to sing two verses of some hymns was the time required to boil an egg. The author stated that this tradition was practiced by African and slave-descendant cooks, and recorded many of these songs as an "effort to preserve the folklore of the far Southern cook" (xiv), traditions that even then were disappearing without a written record.

Trade, Resources, and the Availability of Food

The coastal marshes, swamps, and bottomland hardwood forests of the Gulf Coastal Plain of Louisiana are some of the most biologically productive regions in the world (Hardy et al. 2004) (Figure 9.3). Despite the high biodiversity and wide range of resources, the first French settlers of the region nearly starved to death. From the establishment of the first colonies in the region, settlers withstood a multitude of hardships, both natural and human incurred. Problems of remote location and reliability

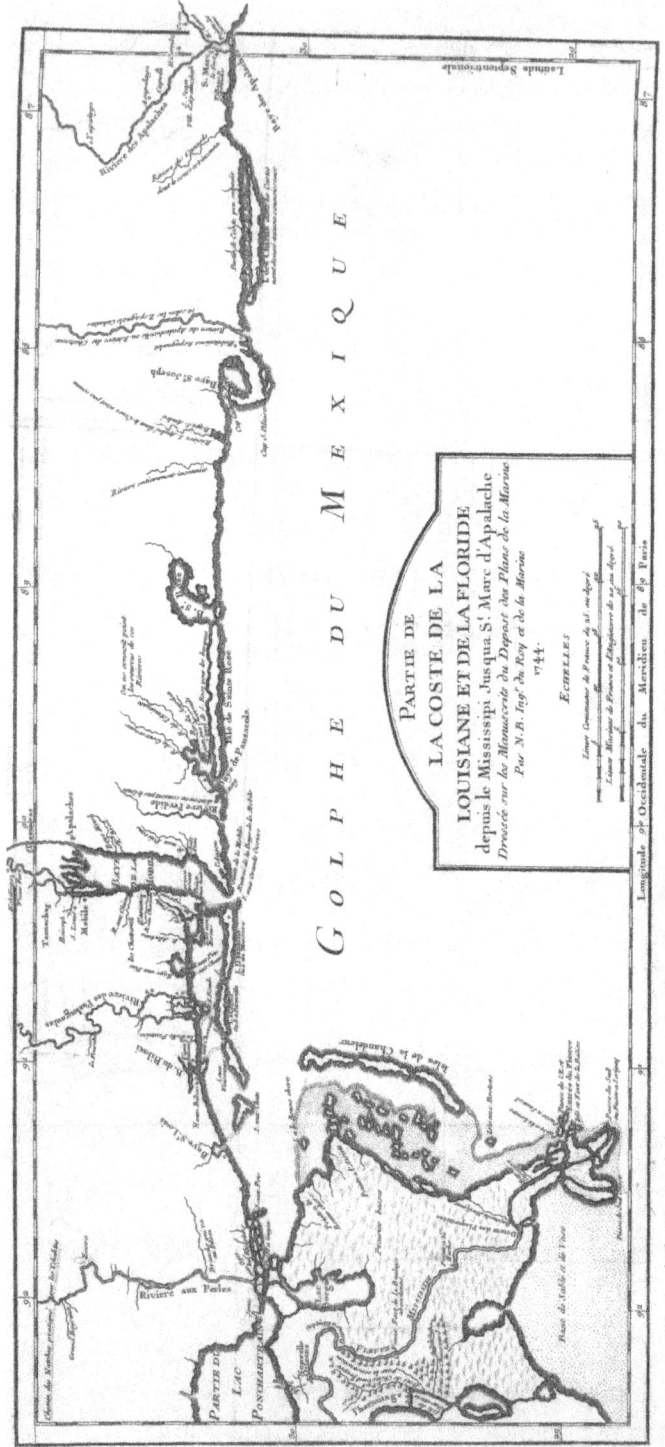

Figure 9.3. *Partie de la Coste de la Louisiane et de la Floride*, 1744. Courtesy of the Rucker Agee Map Collection, Birmingham (Alabama) Public Library.

of shipping were only partially responsible for the colonists' troubles; some of their problems were self-perpetuating. In particular, the majority of the first settlers were not planters familiar with planting in warm, humid climates, but were military personnel, artisans and skilled laborers, and former prisoners.

The initial French settlers to the region were often dropped off with provisions, with promises of return visits in the next year. Before food production by the colonists became successful, these settlers were dependent on local Native Americans for their survival, though they could hardly keep the settlers supplied. These indigenous groups traded their surpluses for European-made goods. Eventually, the Europeans successfully cultivated rice, corn, pumpkins, and sweet potatoes. Agricultural food production by the Europeans in the Louisiana territory did not begin in earnest until the arrival of a slave labor force. By the 1720s, several thousand slaves had been brought to the Louisiana colony. Cattle and pigs were also brought by the first settlers. The year 1725 was the turning point regarding the success of agriculture and pastoralism, with herds of cattle increasing, the presence of slave labor to work the fields, and trade with Native Americans. These multiple economic facets served as "the foundation of the frontier exchange economy" (Unser 1992:149). Even after the French colonists finally established profitable methods of agricultural production, local American Indian groups continued to bring produce, meats, and skins for trade. These American Indian merchants offered a wide variety of items: venison, waterfowl, game, wild fruits, herbs, and spices. African slaves were also allowed to sell produce and game they had grown in provisioning grounds or hunted on their off time (Giraud 1987; Usner 1992:149).

However desperate the colonists' economic situations were, they still needed goods in order to survive. English merchants, determined to increase their economic hold on the New World by expanding their markets, quickly filled the position of "supplier." They were willing to accept local crops in payment for their own goods. In this infancy of the Industrial Revolution, the mass production of goods kept prices low to make them affordable to the colonists, and thus began a contraband trade that would last throughout the rest of this region's history. Illegal trading was ignored and actually encouraged, especially when produce, which would otherwise rot on the docks, could be exchanged for goods like flour, wine, and ceramics (Clark 1970).

Another source of trade goods that helped the first settlers to survive were the outposts and settlements of the Illinois territories farther up the Mississippi River. These posts often supplied flour, pelts, smoked meats, and a variety other goods. By the 1760s, Louisiana was transforming into an agricultural export economy. By the end of the eighteenth century, the Superior Council felt obligated to establish regulations regarding the distribution of foods, so it could follow sales and extract and collect tariffs (Brown 1979).

New Orleans soon developed into the urban center of the region; it was the entrepôt for regionally produced cotton and sugar, and the funnel through which a majority of the commercial output from the entire Mississippi-Ohio-Missouri-Tennessee watershed was siphoned (Hardy 1998, 2002, 2004).

Thus, the cultural developments that defined the nobility and upper classes were brought to the New World via the explorers, voyageurs, and colonists who were charting coastlines and establishing settlements and storehouses along the Gulf of Mexico. The expansion of trade systems in the French colonies of the New World introduced a wide variety of new, exotic, luxury foods into the kitchens of the French nobility, though many of these items, like tomatoes, potatoes, and corn (maize), took over two centuries to be accepted. Other foods from the colonies were readily embraced, like turkey, coffee, tea, and cacao (Flandrin 1999b). The amounts and varieties of cooking and serving vessels expanded in accordance with these new foods. These creolized food traditions, however, could not be realized without the wares and tools for preparation, service, and consumption.

Ceramics of the Era

As a result of War of the Grand Alliance and the War of the Spanish Succession, France's treasury was so depleted that King Louis XIV ordered the nobility to send their gold and silver plate to the mint to be melted down and stamped into coinage. As observed by Saint-Simon, within a week "all leaders of society had equipped their tables with faiences," and prices for these wares escalated (Lane 1948:12, 17). As a consequence, advancements in ceramic production and decorative technologies put France in the forefront of tableware manufacture. This position of prestige remained fast until the second half of the eighteenth century, with the development of mass-produced refined earthenwares in England.

The technique used by factories producing tin-enameled earthenware throughout Europe was the *grand feu*, a single firing of a vessel that fused the glaze and painted decorations to the clay surface (Boone 1998; Giacomotti 1963:11; Lane 1948:1). Only a few oxide pigments painted onto the enamel could withstand the intense heat: cobalt (blue), copper (green), antimony (yellow), manganese (browns and purple), and iron (orange to brown). In the 1740s, *faienciers* began to experiment with various firing techniques and glaze compositions in order to reproduce the delicate pinks, crimsons, violets, greens, and gold found on Chinese hard-fired porcelains (Giacomotti 1963:11). By 1750, *petit feu* glazing, based on the firing techniques used for porcelain, was developed.

During the seventeenth century, and especially from 1640 to 1680, many of the decorative motifs used on faience were heavily influenced by the Italian baroque, reflecting the opulence of the early reign of Louis XIV. The shapes of wares initially imitated gold and silver vessels, but by the 1720s had become simpler in form, especially in pitchers, platters, and tureens. Ceramic wares also reflected the influence of the Kang Hsi period (1622–1722) in China, introduced to Europe in the 1640s. Blue-and-white chinoiserie designs were widely imitated throughout the Netherlands and Normandy during the second half of the seventeenth century. *Faience populaire*, a white faience (*faience blanche*) that was plain or simply decorated, was readily available to members of the bourgeoisie and lower classes. Consisting of simple border patterns painted in bright hues of blue, orange, or yellow, these wares were produced for mass consumption (Lane 1948:12, 17). *Faience blanche* was the lifeblood of the faience industry, as most of the upper bourgeoisie and noble classes desired imported porcelains and more elaborately decorated wares.

By the end of the seventeenth and the beginning of the eighteenth centuries, decorative designs were influenced by both the rigid, formal manner of the *style Academie* and the grandiose, fluid feel of the Italian high baroque. The greatest influence on the decoration of ceramic wares was Jean Bérain, who was appointed to the cabinet of Louis XIV in 1674 and eventually achieved the title designer to the king in the Department of Occasional (Boone 1998; Giacomotti 1963:32; Lane 1948:26). It was his job to create fireworks displays; design gardens, festivals, costumes, and room interiors; and plan and decorate royal gatherings. His influence on ceramic decorations reflected a formal, symmetrical balance while incorporating romantic curves, spirals, urns, grotesques, and floral elements. Perhaps the most recognizable component of the developing *style Bérain* on ceramics was the *style rayonnant*, a rim pattern consisting of pendants that radiated toward the center of vessels, or downward on upright vessels. These pendants included spirals, and foliate or floral designs in white on a blue ground (or vice versa), again reflecting the influence of seventeenth-century Chinese porcelains. Other decorative elements included the *lambrequin*, or trefoil with spirals reserved on a blue ground.

During the early eighteenth century, the *style raynonnant* was further stylized, combining *ferronerie* (ironwork) with swags and garlands of fruit. The resulting *style Régence* (1715–1723) incorporated light and delicate frameworks and curves with naturalistic, organic forms (Caiger-Smith 1973; Giacomotti 1963; Lane 1948). From ca. 1709 to 1740, the centers of many ceramic vessels were decorated with simple designs of flowers, fountains, coats of arms, or other motifs within a circle or medallion.

Beginning in the 1720s to roughly 1750, the demand for blue-and-white wares yielded to a trend for polychrome designs. Initially, chinoiserie motifs continued to be produced but in the colors of *grand feu* palette.

The primary regional centers of manufacture for tablewares during much of the seventeenth century were Nevers and Lyon. Later in the seventeenth and eighteenth centuries, influential faience centers included Rouen and Lille in the north, Moustiers and Marseilles in the south, and Strasbourg in the east (Caiger-Smith 1973; Giacomotti 1963; Lane 1948).

Faience production at Nevers was heavily inspired by the Italian baroque, especially Rome. In addition to the heavy and elaborate baroque influences, Nevers was also known for two other styles of ceramic decoration. From 1630 to ca. 1710, though, the Nevers *faienciers* are perhaps best known for their use of intense blue or yellow grounds onto which white, orange, or yellow designs were painted, a style called *bleu persan*, but polychromes using greens, blues, and yellows and incorporating chinoiserie-inspired bird and floral designs were also created (Giacomotti 1963:20–22; Lane 1948:12).

In general, it can be said that the "Rouen style" and others of Normandy reflected the symmetrical and balanced ornaments of the *style Bérain*, incorporating and developing the *style rayonnant* as a primary decorative element. During the late seventeenth century, rich blue-and-white designs were coupled with a distinctive brick or "sticky" red, used as an outline, to vein leaves, or as hatching to fill spaces. The Saint-Cloud factory dominated the blue-and-white Rouen style until the beginning of the eighteenth century, and this style is distinguished by a characteristic black or manganese outlining of designs and the absence of the Rouen red. Rouen ceramics were typically composed of dark red clays that contained bits of shell (*Littorini littoriea*), which cause imperfections when glazing (Giacomotti 1963:30). The early glazes incorporated molten tin or pewter that gave the "white" ground a bluish green tone, though by the 1720s these imperfections were corrected and true whites were being produced. Because of imperfections in these metals the glazes often crazed.

To the south, the *faienceries* of Provence (Moustiers, Marseilles, and others) were very influential in the development of the *style Bérain*. What distinguishes the designs of southern France was the incorporation of light, airy, and naturalistic elements. Outlines were soft and lines curved. Many of the potters, most notably those from Marseilles and southeastern France, embraced and quickly mastered the *petit feu* technique.

Moustiers became one of the prominent faience production centers, and was renowned for a lightness and thinness of wares and smooth and bright glazes. Some *faienceries* embraced the polychromes that were influenced by the majolica factories of neighboring Spain and Italy, especially in Alcora, Spain, while others continued to produce blue-and-white wares and *grand feu* colors. By the 1740s, many elements of the *style Bérain* lost favor to the hanging festoons, floral garlands and swags, asymmetrical shells, foliated scrolls, and arabesques of the rococo, though grotesques and other motifs continued to be used by Moustiers painters (Giacomotti 1963:132; Lane 1948:25–27).

Along the Mediterranean coast, the *faienciers* of Marseilles became best known for their incorporation of *petit feu* glazing, especially yellow backgrounds and floral designs. The decorative elements were oriental in feel with organic, asymmetrical, and naturalistic qualities.

To the east, the Strasbourg potters were instrumental in the development of the use of *petit feu* glazing, namely pinks, crimsons, and greens (Giacomotti 1963:11, 195). Designs were based on botanical prints.

More functional, multipurpose faience was also produced throughout the eighteenth century and into the nineteenth century, especially in Rouen. Brown faience, or *brun de Rouen*, consisted of a black/brown manganese-based lead glaze on the exterior and white tin-glazed enamel on the interior (Giacomotti 1963:36), and was intended to be heat resistant, its underside glazed so it could be used for preparing foods on hot surfaces. Many of these interiors were painted with simple designs found on *faience blanche*, making them suitable for both food preparation and service. The brown faience industry kept Normandy alive during the second half of the 1700s, though potters who made brown could not, by royal decree, make white faience (Barton 1981; Blanchette 1981:44).

Typically, nonservice, utilitarian, or multipurpose wares, like brown faience, Albisola slip wares, stonewares, and lead-glazed ceramics, were multifunctional and would be found in kitchens and storage areas. Many were coarse redwares, but other varieties of coarse earthenwares had thick bodies, had buff to pink pastes, and were lead glazed (Barton 1981; Yakubik 1990; Yakubik et al. 1989). Some wares were slipped, either over the entire vessel prior to the application of the lead glaze or decorated with a trailed slip. Glaze colors were varied, ranging from green to brown to yellow to transparent.

Many of these wares were produced in southwestern France at La Chapelle-de-Pots, Saintes, Charentes Maritime (Yakubik et al. 1989). The Saintonge potteries had been producing fine ceramics since the mid-thirteenth century. During the late seventeenth through eighteenth centuries, both the product and focus of the Saintonge market changed; they began to produce utilitarian wares specifically designed for the needs of the New World. These new forms, such as large bowls, plates, jars, porringers, and terrines, were integral to preparing the recipes of the nouvelle cuisine, even if many of the ingredients were not available. They are typically buff to pink earthenwares with interiors covered in a bright, "apple green" glaze.

Other coarse ceramic wares that were reportedly common during the early eighteenth century were produced in Albisola, Liguria, Italy. They consisted of a dark brown lead glazed with a black or dark brown slip trailed on the interior, and have been called both Albisola Slipped and Northern Italian Brown and Black wares by several archaeologists (Barton 1981; Yakubik et al. 1989). These wares were imported to the New World, and have been recovered in archaeological contexts across coastal Gulf of Mexico and up the Mississippi River. Olive jars were also used extensively, especially in southern France, and as the oil is found throughout the Mediterranean, the jars themselves do not necessarily indicate a Spanish cultural presence in the archaeological record.

Archaeological Evidence for Diet and Consumption

Faunal Evidence

Studies of animal remains recovered from archaeological contexts across the Gulf Coast region have yielded several patterns in consumption habits. In previous studies, I have demonstrated that for eighteenth-century French colonial sites, domesticated animals were preferred as foods, and wild game was occasionally used to supplement the diet (Hardy 1998, 2002, 2004). Table 9.1 illustrates the number of individual specimens (NISP) from some of the sites listed earlier in this essay.

Table 9.1. Comparison of faunal remains (NISP) from various sites mentioned in the text

Fauna List	Hermann-Grima House 1996	419 Decatur Street	Esplanade/Rampart Street	Rodriguez	Ship Island
Mammalia	163	2901			300
Mammalia, Large	239				9
Mammalia, Medium	91				
Mammalia, Small	4				
Bos taurus	22	404	289	25	25
Cervidae		60			
Sus scrofa	3	184	76	6	15
Ovis/Capra	6		73	1	
Procyon lotor					9
Artiodactyla	5			2	
Aves or Laomorpha	39	442		6	216
Aves, Large					12
Aves, Medium					4
Anatidae	11	10			
Eudocimus albus	1				
Gallus gallus	9		279		
Fulica americana	1				
Meleagris gallopavo	6				
Testudines		10			7
Kinosternidae	3				
Reptilia					1
Serpentes					20
Osteichthyes	43	583			309
Ariidae		5			
Siaenidae		36			
Mugilidae		27			
Archosargus probatocephalus	7				
Sciaenops ocellatus	6				
Carcharhinidae					9
Unidentified Vertebrate	11			62	1625

Mammals are often well represented in archaeological contexts, especially cow, sheep/goat, and pig. The great amount of cow that was consumed in these Gulf Coast sites varies from the pig preference models for the southern diet, as identified by Hilliard (1972). This perhaps reflects cultural preference as opposed to economic pressure, though the model is also based on the assumption that the amounts of pork and beef remains recovered are an accurate reflection of what was actually consumed. The frequencies of various types of domesticated and wild animals are possibly indicative of differences between rural and urban contexts. Prior to 1762, much of the cattle was supplied illegally to the port of New Orleans via the cattle trade, which came east from Texas, through Los Adaes and Natchitoches, Louisiana, and down the Mississippi River.

Fowl, both domesticated (chickens) and wild (ducks, geese, white ibis, and wild turkeys), played an important role in the colonists' cuisine, though significantly less than other meats. Fish, such as sheepshead and redfish, were also common food items, to about the same degree as poultry. According to historical sources, the colonial diet was supplemented by the occasional musk or mud turtle, the only reptile deemed palatable by du Pratz.

The evidence for butchering practices is taken from the faunal sample of the Hermann-Grima House excavations (1996). The sample examined was taken from excavation units located in and around the eighteenth-century kitchen. A total of 86 specimens were found to have cut marks or other evidence for butchering activities. The majority of these cut marks (n=50) were witnessed on large unidentified mammal specimens (n=50), followed by unidentified medium-sized mammals, and *Bos taurus* (cows).

Evidence for butchering activities is often observed archaeologically by cut, hack, and saw marks on individual specimens, and can serve as evidence of the socioeconomic status of the consumer. For example, on eighteenth-century French sites along the Gulf Coast the practice of sawing meats was apparently rare and would have been available only to those of the upper classes (Table 9.2). More detailed analysis and comparisons with data from additional archeological sites have the potential to reveal patterns of consumption for urban versus rural contexts (see Scott and Dawdy, this volume). Cuts of beef evidenced by this study appear to include chuck, the foreshank, ribs, the sirloin, the rump, and possible round. Cuts of pork evidenced by the faunal assemblage appear to include

Table 9.2. Unit and level summaries for butchering methods, Hermann-Grima House (16OR45)

Butchering Method	Unit 22, Level 8	Unit 24, Level 2B	Unit 24, Level 3
Sawn	25	7	
Hacked	10	2	
Cut	16	5	16
Cut/Hacked	4		
Sawn/Cut		1	
Total	55	15	16

the shoulder butt, the picnic shoulder, the rib belly, and the loin. These butchering units seem to represent the entire spectrum of expensive to inexpensive cuts of meat. At different times in the past, though, different cuts of meat would have been preferred by different social classes, and these preferences do not necessarily match what is preferred today.

In Table 9.3, I present an example of faunal remains that were recovered from the Hermann-Grima House. Nearly all the cut marks found on the ribs were perpendicular to the length of the bone, and the ribs had saw marks at the ends. This could indicate the use of a small instrument for cutting individual portions, or bites, of meat off the bone during a particular dining episode. The majority of marks present on long bones (n=29) and vertebra (n=17) were sawn or hacked; this would seem to indicate the marks of the butcher's trade. The cuts present on the distal end of a humerus of an *Ovis/Capra* appear to be a series of cut marks made in rapid succession, as if sawing. The cut marks present on the scapula fragments were not in any discernible pattern.

Table 9.3. Cut marks on faunal specimens, Hermann-Grima House (16OR45)

Worked/Cut Bones, All Units, Hermann-Grima House	N=	%
Mammalia	1	1.16
Mammalia, Large	50	58.14
Mammalia, Medium	21	24.42
Bos taurus (cow)	7	8.14
Sus scrofa (pig)	3	3.49
Ovis/Capra (sheep/goat)	4	4.65
Total	86	100.00

Ceramic Evidence

For the New World colonies of the Gulf Coast, the simpler wares of the *faience blanche* and *brun de Rouen* would have been the cheapest to import. Pieces that were multifunctional, like brown faience, would have been practical compromises for those early colonists who desired finer quality wares yet perhaps could not afford them. Only after the colonies were established and financially successful would finer wares of *faience blanche* and various regional factories be available to New World markets. This is not to say, however, that those individuals with the means did not bring with them or were unable to obtain these finer wares (Waselkov 1991; Yakubik 1990). These include faience pieces manufactured in Moustiers and Rouen, in addition to Chinese porcelains.

Observations of ceramic assemblages from archaeological sites across the Gulf Coast region have yielded patterns of both availability and preference. Vessel functions indicated by ceramic sherds suggest both table service and utilitarian wares; table service pieces of faience, creamware, pearlware, and porcelain, and utilitarian and multifunctional brown faience and coarse earthenwares have been recovered from eighteenth-century horizons throughout the region (Table 9.4) (Beavers and Lamb 1990, 1993a, 1993b; Birkedal and DeMarcay n.d.; Davis and Giardino 1983; Dawdy 1998, 2000; Hammersten 1990; Hardy 1998, 2002, 2004; Hardy et al. 2004; Lamb and Beavers 1983; Shenkel 1977; Waselkov 1991; Yakubik 1990; Yakubik et al. 1989). The wide variety of vessel forms, including platters, plates, mustard pots, jelly jars, salt cellars, teacups, bottle coolers, and a wide variety of bowls, is evidence for the presence of the new cuisine in the Gulf Coast colonies from the earliest settlement.

Many of the ceramics that have been archaeologically recovered from southern Louisiana and across the Gulf Coast reflect both southern and northern French cultural influences. Sherds excavated from Old Mobile to New Orleans demonstrate an affinity or possible points of origin in Provence, especially wares from Moustiers and Marseilles, as well as trade from around the Mediterranean, such as Albisola brown on black wares and Spanish wares (Figures 9.4, 9.5). Other sherds, though, are undeniably from Normandy, namely from Rouen and Saint-Cloud, as well as from Brittany (Figure 9.6). The multipurpose brown faience, with white tin enamel on the interior and manganese oxides on the exterior, also originates from this region. From 419 Decatur Street and the Hermann-Grima

Table 9.4. Comparisons of ceramic types from various sites mentioned in the text

Ceramic Type	Ship Island n	Ship Island %	Rodriguez Plantation n	Rodriguez Plantation %	419 Decatur St n	419 Decatur St %	Hermann-Grima House, 1996 n[a]	Hermann-Grima House, 1996 %	Old Mobile n	Old Mobile %
Lead-glazed Coarse Earthenwares (French)	198	19.5	7	3	85	3.3		5.91		15.82
Lead-glazed Coarse Earthenwares (Other)	0	-	1	.4	0	-				
Unglazed Coarse Earthenwares	125	12.3	3	1.3	0	-				
Other Coarse Earthenware	4	.4	0	-	22	.9				
Fine Lead-glazed Earthenware	0	-	0	-	0	-				
Refined Redware	0	-	3	1.3	6	.2				
Slip Decorated Coarse Earthenwares	0	-	0	-	1	.04				
Tin-glazed Earthenwares (Faience)	174	17.1	5	2.1	42	1.6		4.6		74.41
Tin-glazed Earthenwares	0	-	9	3.9	0	-				
English White Salt-glazed Stoneware	0	-	0	-	0	-				
Jackfield	0	-	1	.4	1	.04				
Olive Jar	0	-	0	-	17	.7				1.14
Creamware	0	-	50	21.5	710	27.8		47.44		
Pearlware	0	-	71	30.5	1450	56.8		36.66		
Whiteware	0	-	61	26.2	45	1.8				
Refined Earthenware	0	-	0	-	60	2.4				
Stoneware	9	.9	3	1.3	50	2.0		1.97		2.42
Refined Stoneware	0	-	0	-	40	1.6				
Porcelain	0	-	12	5.2	21	0.8				4.28
Soft Paste Porcelain	0	-	1	.4	0	-			0	
Aboriginal	507	49.9	0	-	2	0.07		0.39		1.93
Other	0	-	6	2.6	1	.04		1.18		

Notes: a. For the Hermann-Grima data, percentages were taken off of ceramic weight in grams, not individual sherd counts. See Hardy 1998 for specific numbers.

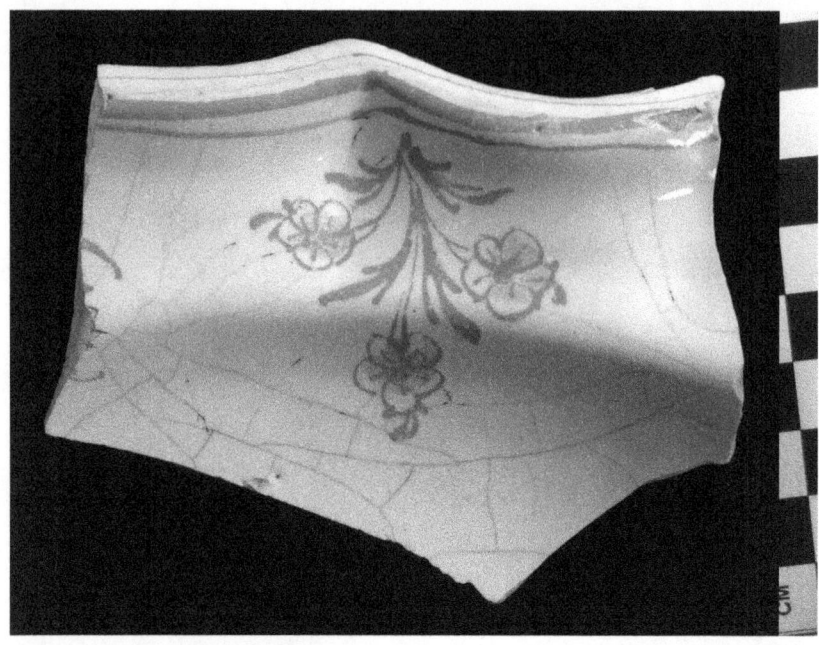

Figure 9.4. *Faience blanche*, Moustiers yellow on white plate rim with Moustier-style designs. Sample 280, FBL5, 1MB161. Rochon Plantation, Dog River. Image courtesy of Gregory Waselkov, University of South Alabama.

Figure 9.5. Albisola brown on black wares, ca. 1720–1740. French Warehouse site, Ship Island, Gulf Islands National Seashore.

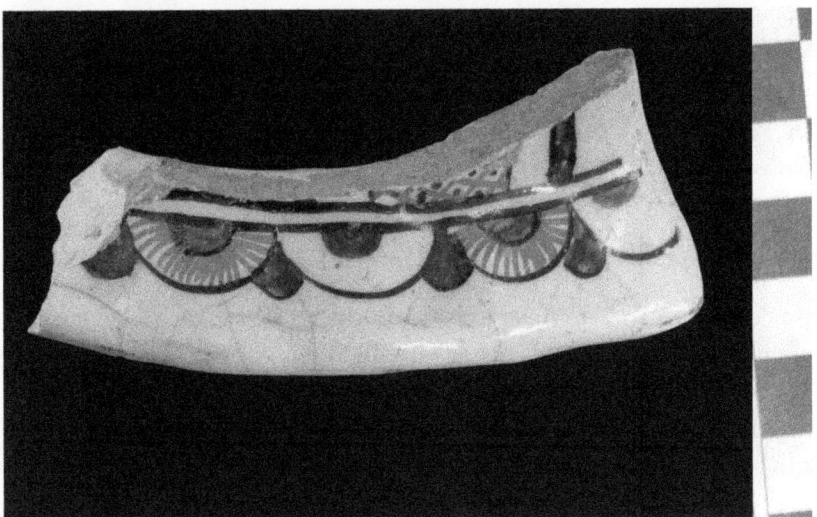

Figure 9.6. *Faience blanche*, Seine polychrome rim. Sample 58 FBL3, 1MB262. Fort Condé. Image courtesy of Gregory Waselkov, University of South Alabama.

House in New Orleans comes evidence that vessels from Rouen, Saintonge, Albisola, and other areas were available in the New Orleans market (Hardy 2002; Hardy et al. 2004). Faience that is probably attributable to Moustiers has been recovered from the British colonial settlement at Fort Fredericka National Monument on St. Simon's Island, Georgia, raising some interesting questions regarding the acquisition of tablewares and the prevalence of French goods among British settlers on the barrier islands of Georgia.

Coarse earthenwares, similar to those associated with the potteries of Saintonge, have also been recovered throughout the region, and would have also served multiple purposes—food preparation, storage, and even service. The presence of wares like olive jars, pieces from Albisola, and faience produced in Moustiers and Marseilles could also be indicative of southern French and Mediterranean maritime influences on the developing local cuisine.

Frequencies of lead-glazed coarse earthenwares apparently vary in accordance to relative dating of a site (Hardy 2002; Hardy et al. 2004). There is a tendency for greater amounts of coarse earthenwares resembling those produced in Saintonge, Charente, and Albisola in contexts dating to the first quarter to first half of the eighteenth century, with proportions of *faience blanche* increasing in the second and third quarters of the eighteenth century. Brown faience was also recovered in these early colonial contexts. By the 1780s, mass-produced wares like British creamwares, once available only through illicit trade, become dominant due to the relaxing of trade and import restrictions and the opening of formerly closed markets.

Comments on Creolization Theory

As European colonists traveled to the North American continent looking for new futures, fortunes, and adventures, they encountered a multitude of peoples who had already lived there for thousands of years. Slaves were also imported from Africa to undertake the strenuous manual agricultural labor that Europeans were unwilling or unable to do themselves. In French Louisiana, this ongoing interaction of many cultures allowed for the development of a creolized system of food production, preparation, and consumption, a kind of "alimentary trade," if you will.

The analogous relationship between linguistic change and cultural change has long been recognized. Ferguson (1992:xlii) and Joyner (1984) referred to the process of cultural borrowing, adaptation, and interpretation as "cultural grammar." Ferguson identified that the material culture of a people is analogous to the structural "lexicon" of a culture. How materials were utilized and the meanings they may have symbolized act as the "cultural grammar," the rules by which that culture abides, and these rules change according to locally available resources, environment, experience (both learned firsthand and taught from older generations), and other influences such as the cultural heritages of the people involved or their historical trajectories. As Mintz (1985:6) states: "When unfamiliar substances are taken up by new users, they enter into preexisting social and psychological contexts and acquire—or are given—contextual meanings by those who use them."

And this is where creolization comes into the picture. In the archaeological context, creolization has been defined as "a process involving multicultural interaction and exchange that produces new cultural forms" (Singleton 1999:5). Creolization is not necessarily a unidirectional or a voluntary means of culture change or transmission; it results from both hegemonic and physical pressures and exposure to a multitude of influences such as the physical environment, local historical experience, and the historical trajectories of both the dominant social group (superstrate) and of the subjugated group(s) (substrate). Creolization theory encompasses the dynamic and diachronic nature of social interaction by utilizing an amalgamation of symbols and materials from a variety of sources without necessarily assuming cultural superiority of one group over another. The creole language develops as the result of contact and a need to communicate, while at the same time serving (whether intentionally or unintentionally) as a marker of social identity and group belonging.

A three-step process of creolization has been proposed—reduction, configuration, and exchange—in which symbols are simplified, reorganized, and exchanged when exposed to new, foreign traits (Buisseret 2000; Scott and Dawdy, this volume). These symbols are passed from generation to generation, are taught communally, and are reinforced on the individual level by daily practice and experience dependent on unique circumstances. This is akin to Heath's (1978, 1984) and Gumperz and Wilson's (1971) notion of a simplification of languages to a "lowest common denominator" when cultures enter contact situations, clearing the way for the development of new forms of communication. The simplification of supposed common elements between two social groups, whether cultural or linguistic, should not be assumed to be true for all circumstances. In instances where simplification occurs, those elements that are common between the parties are those that are simplified. Thomason and Kaufman state (1988:32) that the amount of simplification is dependent upon the degree of substratum influence; a light or moderate degree of influence usually does not result in "lowest common denominator" reduction.

I do not want to enter the arena on the theoretical debate of terminology and meaning between creolization, hybridity, syncretism, and bricolage (Chaudenson 2003; Kapchan and Strong 1999; Palmie 2006; Stewart 1999; Thomas 1996); this is a discussion too expansive for this chapter. Creolization theory does not necessarily negate the existence of implied power relations between superstrate and substrate groups, nor should the controversial history of the term itself be ignored (Stewart 1999). The theoretical concept of "creole," removed from its historically defined implications, does act as a kind of medium of exchange, a proverbial "transfer of goods and capital," whether symbolic, aesthetic, or economic. In this light, creolization as a cultural process of change is dynamic, and is defined by unique historical and social trajectories.

Conclusion

As physical elements of cultural expression, the ceramics brought to the region by the colonists, and later those demanded and selected for purchase in markets, are indicative of both cultural preferences and market availability. Decorative elements on those ceramic wares selected for table service can be seen as being intentionally chosen not only for aesthetic value but also as a deliberate statement and demonstration of cultural affinity, and as efforts to create and maintain group and social identity in a new land. They can also provide insight into the relations between consumer, the market, and the manufacturer. A detailed study of bills of lading, insurance lists, and stock inventories of stores could provide a better understanding of these relations.

Many of the stylistic elements present on these eighteenth-century wares appear to indicate an affiliation with regions of southern France and the Mediterranean. The presence of Italian wares and vessels typical of Moustiers and Marseilles would appear to serve as evidence for consumer preference of southern French ceramic wares, or are indicators of market availability. The prevalence of southern French and Spanish culinary traditions and techniques also argues for a cross-Atlantic relationship, with strong influences from the Caribbean, Africa, and indigenous North Americans. At the same time, many other ceramic vessels appear to have northern French decorative elements, such as those from Rouen, Saint-Cloud, and Brittany, though the culinary traditions from these northern regions have not been widely observed in either historical recipe books or modern "Classic" Creole cuisine.

In conclusion, the investigation of French colonial foodways in southern Louisiana and along the Gulf Coast, or, more specifically, the style that is today considered Creole cooking, is a study of many systems of actions and ideas. The market, the kitchen, and the dining table all served as crossroads of social interaction, exchange, and communication via processes of food selection, acquisition, and preparation. Common elements in cooking methods were recognized, and new methods were learned and adopted. Both the cuisine and the market diversified. The blend of French sauces and cooking techniques with French and Spanish herbs and spices, and the use of fish and both African and North American vegetables, gourds, and fruits, began to develop into today's distinctive regional style.

Acknowledgments

I would like to thank the National Park Service–Southeast Archeological Center for allowing me to photograph and study the ceramic collections from the following parks: Gulf Islands National Seashore, Fort Fredericka National Monument, and Jean Lafitte National Historic Park and Preserve. Thanks are also in order to Gregory Waselkov, University of South Alabama, for supplying images and much needed advice. I would like to thank Glen Doran, William Parkinson, and Michael Uzendoski from Florida State University, and George Smith from the National Park Service–Southeast Archeological Center (ret.) for reading and making comments on drafts of this article. Finally, thanks to Richard Beavers, formerly of the New Orleans Regional Archaeology Program at the University of New Orleans, for all of his advice and support through the years, and access to the Hermann-Grima collections.

References Cited

Anderson, Jay Allen
1970   Scholarship on Contemporary American Folk Foodways. In *Ethnological Food Research in Europe and US*, edited by Nils-Arvid Bringéus and Günter Wiegelmann, 56–63. Reports from the First International Symposium for the Ethnological Food Research, Lund, Sweden.

Barton, Kenneth J.
1981   *Coarse Earthenwares from the Fortress of Louisbourg*. National Historic Parks and Sites Branch, Parks Canada, Ottawa.

Beavers, Richard C., and Teresia R. Lamb
1990   *Hermann-Grima House Wine Room Excavations, New Orleans, Louisiana*. Research Report No. 16. Archaeological and Cultural Research Program, University of New Orleans, New Orleans.
1993a   *Hermann-Grima Historic House New Orleans, Louisiana, Ironing Room and Mystery Building Archaeological Testing*. Research Report No. 18. Archaeological and Cultural Research Program, University of New Orleans, New Orleans.
1993b   *Report of Current Research*. Archaeological and Cultural Research Program, University of New Orleans, New Orleans.

Birkedal, Ted, and Gary B. DeMarcay
n.d.   Faunal Remains. In *The Search for the Lost Riverfront: Historical and Archeological Investigations at the Chalmette Battlefield, Jean Lafitte National Historical Park*. Vol. 4. National Park Service, Southeast Archeological Center, Tallahassee, Fla.

Blanchette, Jean-Francois
1981   *The Role of Artifacts in the Study of Foodways in New France, 1720–1760*. History and Archaeology No. 52. National Historic Parks and Sites Branch, Parks Canada, Ottawa.
Boone, Marylou
1998   *Terre et Feu: Four Centuries of French Ceramics from the Boone Collection*. University of Washington Press, Seattle.
Bourdieu, Pierre
1977   *Outline of a Theory of Practice*. Cambridge University Press, Cambridge.
Brown, Ian W.
1979   Early 18th Century French-Indian Culture Contact in the Yazoo Bluffs Region of the Lower Mississippi Valley. Ph.D. diss., Brown University.
Buisseret, David
2000   Introduction. In *Creolization in the Americas*, edited by David Buisseret and Steven G. Reinhardt, 3–17. Texas A&M University Press, College Station.
Caiger-Smith, Alan
1973   *Tin-glaze Pottery in Europe and the Islamic World: The Tradition of 1000 Years in Maiolica, Faience, and Delftware*. Faber & Faber, London.
Chaudenson, Robert
2003   Creolistics and Sociolinguistic Theory. *International Journal of the Sociology of Language* 160:123–146.
Clark, John G.
1970   *New Orleans, 1718–1812: An Economic History*. Louisiana State University Press, Baton Rouge.
Crété, Liliane
1978   *Daily Life in Louisiana, 1815–1830*. Translated by P. Gregory. Louisiana State University Press, Baton Rouge.
Davis, Dave D., and Marco J. Giardino
1983   *Archaeological Excavations at the Hermann-Grima House*. Center for Archaeology, Tulane University, New Orleans.
Dawdy, Shannon L.
1998   *Madame John's Legacy (16OR51) Revisited: A Closer Look at the Archaeology of Colonial New Orleans*. Greater New Orleans Archaeology Program, University of New Orleans, New Orleans.
2000   Understanding Cultural Change through the Vernacular: Creolization in Louisiana. *Historical Archaeology* 34(3): 107–123.
Douglas, Mary
1966   *Purity and Danger*. Routledge, London.
Du Pratz, M. Le Page
1972 [1774]   *The History of Louisiana, or of the Western Parts of Virginia and Carolina: Containing a Description of the countries that lie on both Sides of the River Mississippi: with an Account of the Settlements, Inhabitants, Soil, Climate, and Products* [first English translation]. Claitor's Publishing Division, Baton Rouge, La.

Ferguson, Leland
1992   *Uncommon Ground.* Smithsonian Institution Press, Washington, D.C.
Flandrin, Jean L.
1999a Dietary Choices and Culinary Technique, 1500–1800. In *Food: A Culinary History from Antiquity to the Present,* edited by Albert Sonnenfeld, 403–417. Penguin, New York.
1999b The Early Modern Period. In *Food: A Culinary History from Antiquity to the Present,* edited by Albert Sonnenfeld, 349–373. Penguin, New York.
1999c From Dietetics to Gastronomy: The Liberation of the Gourmet. In *Food: A Culinary History from Antiquity to the Present,* edited by Albert Sonnenfeld, 418–432. Penguin, New York.
Fleetwood, Jenni, and Marina Filipelli
2004   *The Caribbean, Central and South American Cookbook.* Anness, London.
Giacomotti, Jean
1963   *French Faience.* Universe Books, New York.
Giraud, Marcel
1987   *A History of French Louisiana.* Vol. 5, *The Company of the Indies, 1723–1731.* Translated by B. Pearce. Louisiana State University Press, Baton Rouge.
Gumperz, John J., and Robert Wilson
1971   Convergence and Creolization: A Case from the Indo-Aryan/Dravidian Border. In *Pidginization and Creolization of Languages,* edited by Dell H. Hymes, 151–167. Cambridge University Press, Cambridge.
Hammersten, Susan
1990   *Archaeological Investigations at the French Warehouse Site East Ship Island, Mississippi Gulf Islands National Seashore.* National Park Service, Southeast Archaeological Center, Tallahassee, Fla.
Hardy, Meredith D.
1998   A Question of Origin: Archaeological Evidence of 18th Century Spanish Trading Practices in the New Orleans Colony, Hermann-Grima House 16OR45. M.S. thesis, University of New Orleans.
2002   New Surfs, New Turfs: A Preliminary Model of 18th Century French Colonial Foodway and Trade Systems. Paper presented at the 35th annual meeting of the Society of Historical and Underwater Archaeology, January 8–12, Mobile, Ala.
2004   Living on the Edge: Early Expressions of Creole Culture on the French Colonial Gulf Coast. Paper presented at the 37th annual meeting of the Society of Historical and Underwater Archaeology, January 8–10, St. Louis.
Hardy, Meredith D., John E. Cornelison, Tammy D. Cooper, and Jeff Jones
2004   *Reconstruction of Building IV, the 419 Rue Decatur Site, Vieux Carré, New Orleans, Louisiana.* National Park Service, Southeast Archeological Center, Tallahassee, Fla.
Hearn, Lafcadio
1990 [1885]   *Lafcadio Hearn's Creole Cook Book.* Pelican, Gretna, La.

Heath, Jeffrey G.
1978   *Linguistic Diffusion in Arnhem Land.* Australian Institute for Aboriginal Studies, Canberra.
1984   Language Contact and Language Change. *Annual Review of Anthropology* 13:367–384.

Hilliard, Sam B.
1972   *Hog Meat and Hoecake: Food Supply in the Old South, 1840–1860.* Southern Illinois University Press, Carbondale.

Hodder, Ian
1995   *Reading the Past: Current Approaches to Interpretation in Archaeology.* 2nd ed. Cambridge University Press, Cambridge.

Holm, John
2000   *Introduction to Pidgins and Creoles.* Cambridge University Press, Cambridge.

Hyman, Philip, and Mary Hyman
1999   Printing in the Kitchen: French Cookbooks, 1480–1800. In *Food: A Culinary History from Antiquity to the Present*, edited by Albert Sonnenfeld, 394–402. Penguin, New York.

Joyner, Charles
1984   *Down by the Riverside: A South Carolina Slave Community.* University of Illinois Press, Urbana.

Kapchan, Deborah A., and Pauline T. Strong
1999   Theorizing the Hybrid. *Journal of American Folklore* 112(445): 239–253.

Lamb, Teresia R., and Richard C. Beavers
1983   *Archaeology of the Stableyard Complex, Hermann-Grima House, New Orleans, Louisiana.* Research Report No. 8. Archaeological and Cultural Research Program, University of New Orleans, New Orleans.

Lane, Arthur
1948   *French Faience.* Van Nostrand, New York.

Meigs, Anna
1996   Food as a Cultural Construction. In *Food and Culture: A Reader*, edited by C. Counihan and P. V. Esterik, 95–106. Routledge, New York.

Mintz, Sidney W.
1985   *Sweetness and Power: The Place of Sugar in Modern History.* Penguin Books, New York.

Mitchell, Patricia B.
1991   *French Cooking in Early America.* Mitchells, Chatham, Va.
1993   *Soul on Rice: African Influences on American Cooking.* Mitchells, Chatham, Va.
1994   *At the Table in Colonial America.* Mitchells, Chatham, Va.
1998   *Plantation Row: Slave Cabin Cooking.* Mitchells, Chatham, Va.
1999   *An Affair of the Heart: America's Romance with Louisiana Food.* Mitchells, Chatham, Va.

Palmié, Stephan
2006   Creolization and Its Discontents. *Annual Review of Anthropology* 35:433–456.

Pitte, Jean-Robert
2002 [1991]   *French Gastronomy: The History and Geography of a Passion*. Translated by J. Gladding. Columbia University Press, New York.

Rebora, Giovanni
1998   *Culture of the Fork: A Brief History of Food in Europe*. Translated by A. Sonnenfeld. Columbia University Press, New York.

Rice, Prudence
2006   *Pottery Analysis: A Sourcebook*. University of Chicago Press, Chicago.

Rosenberger, Bernard
1999   Arab Cuisine and Its Contribution to European Culture. In *Food: A Culinary History from Antiquity to the Present*, edited by Albert Sonnenfeld, 207–223. Penguin, New York.

Shenkel, J. Richard
1977   *Archaeological Investigations at the Hermann-Grima House*. Department of Anthropology and Geography, University of New Orleans, New Orleans.

Singleton, Theresa A.
1999   An Introduction to African-American Archaeology. In *"I, Too, Am America": Archaeological Studies of African-American Life*, edited by Theresa A. Singleton, 1–17. University Press of Virginia, Charlottesville.

Stewart, Charles
1999   Syncretism and Its Synonyms: Reflections on Cultural Mixture. *Diacritics* 29(3): 40–62.

Tannahill, Reay
1988   *Food in History*. Crown Trade, New York.

Thomas, Nicholas
1996   Cold Fusion. *American Anthropologist* 98(1): 9–16.

Thomason, Sarah G., and Terrence Kaufman
1988   *Language Contact, Creolization, and Genetic Linguistics*. University of California Press, Berkeley.

Times Picayune
2002 [1901]   *The Picayune's Creole Cook Book*. Dover, Mineola, N.Y.

Usner, Daniel H., Jr.,
1992   *Indians, Settlers, and Slaves in a Frontier Exchange Economy: The Lower Mississippi Valley before 1783*. University of North Carolina Press, Chapel Hill.

Waselkov, Gregory A.
1991   *Archaeology at the French Colonial Site of Old Mobile, Phase I: 1989–1991*. University of South Alabama Anthropological Monograph No. 1, Mobile.

Wheaton, Barbara Ketcham
1996   *Savoring the Past: The French Kitchen and Table from 1300 to 1789*. Scribner, New York.

Yakubik, Jill Karen
1990   Ceramic Use in Late Eighteenth-Century and Early Nineteenth-Century Southeastern Louisiana. Ph. D. diss., Tulane University.

Yakubik, Jill Karen, Herschel A. Franks, and Marco J. Giardino
1989   *Archaeological Investigations of Six Spanish Colonial Period Sites. Barataria Unit, Jean Lafitte National Historic Park and Preserve, Louisiana.* Southwest Cultural Resources Center Professional Papers No. 22. Division of Anthropology, National Park Service, Santa Fe, N.Mex.

10

La Vie Quotidienne

Historical Archaeological Approaches to the Plantation Era in Guadeloupe, French West Indies

KENNETH G. KELLY

The timeless aspects of the rural landscape of present-day Guadeloupe obscure a remarkable history. In fact, this landscape has been dramatically transformed from the countryside that would have been recognized 20, 60, 100, or 200 years ago. While today sugar fields continue to be cultivated, their yield no longer makes sugar, but instead rum, once a by-product of the sugar industry. Individuals tend the fields with enormous tractors and harvesters that look like devices from science fiction. Large areas of former sugar plantations are now cropped in bananas, and few coffee groves remain in the mountains. Superficially, it appears to be a rural agricultural landscape, but it is largely a suburban rural world, where villages are occupied by commuters in their own late-model cars who endure traffic jams on the way to and from their workplaces in the major towns.

As with the landscape, so, too, does the written history of Guadeloupe obscure a remarkable past. Slavery, and the diaspora of Africans that resulted from that institution, provides a principal thread that weaves through the warp and weft of nearly 400 years of French colonial ventures in the region. Yet this aspect of Guadeloupe's past, and the historical events that shaped it, is little known at all outside of the French West Indies, and little explored within them (among the exceptions are Dubois 2004; Debien 2000; Fallope 1992; Benôt and Dorigny 2003; Régent 2004; Adélaïde-Merlande 2002; Adélaïde-Merlande et al. 2002; Dorigny 2003—of these, only Dorigny 2003 and Dubois 2004 are in English). For many reasons, including the destruction of records during cataclysms of earth, wind, and fire, and a different culture of record keeping, some of the kinds of knowledge that have been accumulated over half a century of research on slavery in the British Caribbean have been slow to develop in the French West Indies (Delpuech 2001; Kelly 2004). But it is a region, and a cultural setting, that is well worth exploring so that we may learn something of the experiences of French Caribbean slavery, and how enslaved Africans interacted with the French colonial world to create the society and language that bears the name Kreyol (Creole) (Chaudenson and Mufwene 2001).

As we know, the histories of specific regions play a key role in the trajectories their cultures describe, so a bit of the history of Guadeloupe must be presented. From their colonization in the first half of the seventeenth century, Guadeloupe and its sister colonies have been associated with the production of the tropical commodities of indigo, cotton, tobacco, coffee, and primarily sugar, and for most of that time until 1848 they produced these crops using enslaved labor. During the eighteenth century, at the peak of the French colonial endeavor, nearly a third more Africans were enslaved on French Caribbean plantations than in the Anglophone Caribbean colonies. Their labor produced more sugar, rum, and molasses than the British possessions, and they also exceeded British coffee, indigo, and cotton production (Blackburn 1997). Furthermore, the French Revolution and its consequences set in motion several of the most remarkable events of the slavery period, including the only successful major uprising and overthrow of the slavery system in Saint-Domingue, and paradoxically, in Guadeloupe, the only large-scale emancipation of enslaved people in the Caribbean, followed at the end of the French Revolution by reenslavement less than a decade later (Bénot and Dorigny 2003; Saint-Ruf 2002; Régent 2004).

Guadeloupe and the French West Indies

Guadeloupe is the largest island of the Lesser Antilles, the arc of mostly volcanic islands that form the eastern boundary of the Caribbean Sea, stretching from Trinidad and Tobago in the south, and ending with the Virgin Islands just to the east of Puerto Rico. Guadeloupe is properly the name of an archipelago consisting of two large islands joined together by a mangrove swamp, the volcanic and mountainous Basse Terre, and the

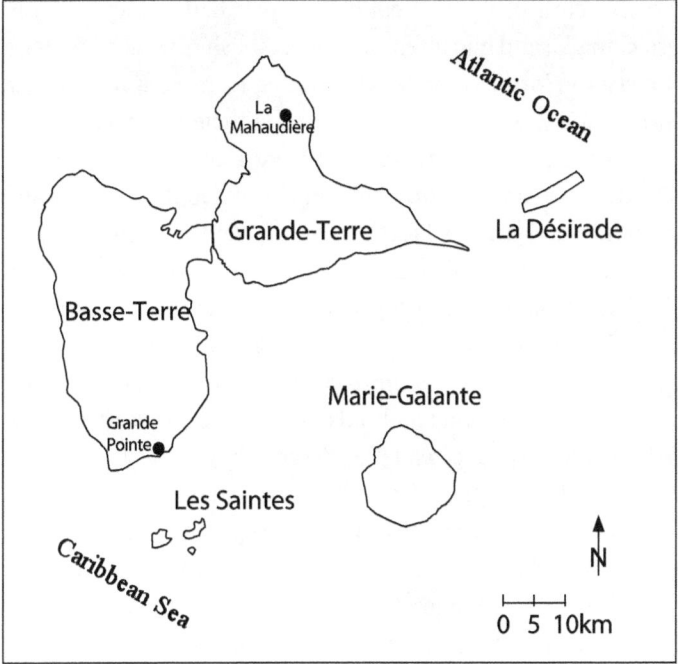

Figure 10.1. Map of Guadeloupe showing the locations of Habitations La Mahaudière and Grande Pointe.

low-lying limestone Grande Terre. Associated with these two islands are a series of smaller islands, including Marie Galante, which is geologically a version of Grande Terre at about one-third scale; la Désirade, an elevated dry plateau; les Saintes, a collection of small, dry, volcanic islands; and Petite Terre, a small coral atoll (Figure 10.1). Guadeloupe has been a French possession for most of its history, and since 1948 has been a *département* of France, administratively equal to all other *départements* of France.

Although Columbus briefly visited Guadeloupe on his second voyage to the West Indies, the Spanish never permanently settled the island, or, for that matter, any of the other Lesser Antilles, preferring to concentrate first on exploiting the wealth and dense population of Hispaniola, and later on the vastly greater wealth and possibilities presented by the conquest of mainland South and Central America (Delpuech 2001). As the sixteenth century progressed, English and French explorers first cut their teeth exploring the regions of North America that were less interesting to the Spanish, and thus safer options for incipient colonial ventures. By the end of the sixteenth century, French explorers had made claims to parts of eastern Canada, and had attempted to establish several forts along the southeast coast of North America. The French learned, however, that in the sixteenth century, Spain still maintained sufficient power to control the southeast coast, and the French forts were abandoned (Waselkov 1997). English attempts came slightly later in the sixteenth century, and were concentrated in present-day North Carolina, yet they, too, were unsuccessful. It was not until the first part of the seventeenth century that French and English colonial ventures were to prove viable, if not successful. By that time Spain was relatively less powerful and organized, while France, England, and Holland were more capable of fielding expeditions that could seize and retain colonial toeholds in North America, the Caribbean, and the South American coast (Blackburn 1997).

The first French colony in the West Indies was established in 1626 on St. Kitts, where French and English colonists partitioned the island and shared possession. This was less than ideal, and by 1632 there were fewer than 400 French colonists compared with over 6,000 English colonists (Nicolas 1996:48). In 1635, the former French colonists of St. Kitts chartered the Compagnie des Iles d'Amérique, and established settlements on Guadeloupe and Martinique. Although these settlements were established with three goals—military occupation, agricultural exploitation, and religious ministry and conversion of the native inhabitants—in practice they were agricultural ventures, as planters (called *habitants* on Guadeloupe and Martinique) began growing tobacco, indigo, and cotton. Labor was provided by the *habitants* themselves as well as by indentured servants, or *engagés*, who labored from sunup to sundown for a fixed term of years in exchange for transportation, food, and lodging, and the hope that when their indenture was up, they could claim a piece of land and become planters, too. Initially, Guadeloupe and Martinique were not very successful; due to aggressive policies, particularly in Guadeloupe, toward the native inhabitants of the islands, there was almost constant danger of raids or war with the Carib. Furthermore, the price of tobacco fell dramatically in the 1630s as colonies from Barbados to Virginia were producing excessive quantities. In the late 1630s and 1640s, *habitants* in Guadeloupe began to experiment with the cultivation of sugar, but with little success, as the secrets of processing it were poorly known (Butel 2002; Blackburn 1997). The Portuguese reconquest of northeast Brazil in 1654 changed that, as Dutch planters who had mastered sugar processing were expelled from Brazil and spread their knowledge throughout the Caribbean, revolutionizing the Caribbean colonies regardless of their European affiliation (Blackburn 1997:282; Stein 1988:41).

The principal aspects of this revolution were transformations of scale—scale of the wealth that could be accumulated by the planter, scale of the agricultural and industrial components of the plantation, and, most notably, scale of the labor required to produce sugar (Stein 1988:42). Whereas tobacco, cotton, and indigo could be profitably produced at the scale of the individual smallholder with one or two hands assisting, sugar required lots of people to work year-round clearing the land, growing and tending the crop, harvesting it, and immediately processing it into sugar.

Historical Archaeology in Guadeloupe

In spite of this dramatic history, and the centrality of slavery to it, the landscape of Guadeloupe reveals its secrets slowly. When traveling across the present-day and former sugar-producing districts, the vestiges of cane processing are visible in the ruins of windmills and water-mills. But the system is hard to see—the large and opulent houses of the planter class are mostly gone, victims first of the French Revolution and later of a degree of restraint not usually seen in the capitalist class. Also missing are the houses of the enslaved workers and the villages in which they lived. The image (Figure 10.2) of cane cutting from the distillery of Damoiseau exemplifies these silences—while harkening back to the cane fields where the courageous oxen pull the carts, the labor that cuts them is depicted, but not discussed. Of course, the distillery is selling rum, Caribbean sunshine in a bottle, and the history of slavery is not part of that message, just as the producers of other commodities such as coffee or cotton or tobacco do not seek to evoke similarly tainted histories. Nonetheless, the photograph is emblematic of these silences, as the gap between history and constructions that are more palatable is rarely bridged. Historical archaeology offers the potential to expose these contradictions.

Historical archaeology has only recently begun to be practiced in the French Caribbean, and it has followed a somewhat different trajectory from that described by the growth of North American historical archaeology. Instead of an initial focus on the dwellings of important colonial figures, or of significant sites, historical archaeology in the French West Indies began as an added-on aspect of what is essentially cultural resources

Figure 10.2. Photograph of a sign depicting cane field workers at the Damoiseau distillery, Guadeloupe.

management (CRM) compliance archaeology (Kelly 2008). Thus, for example, when bridges are widened, building sites are cleared, or historic sites are impacted, archaeological research is conducted and has tended to reveal posthole patterns and accumulate artifacts, but with little in the way of a framework of cultural or historical questions in light of which to interpret the results. Within the last few years, this has begun to change, as local people and cultural resource administrators have recognized the potential of historical archaeology to contribute in significant ways to a more complex history of the French Caribbean colonies (Delpuech 2001; Bégot 1991; Kelly 2004, 2008).

La Mahaudière and Grande Pointe

Several years ago I began a project in Guadeloupe to explore this gap between the standard histories of the island that tend to focus on military and political events and the possibility of developing an understanding of the more complicated aspects of slavery. This project would consider research questions such as the ways in which plantation slavery was expressed before and after the French Revolution; whether the revolutionary emancipation and reimposition of slavery contributed to changes in slavery; the similarities and differences between the better known British plantation system and that of the French; and the nature of life for enslaved people on the sugar plantations (*la vie quotidienne*). As historical archaeological research on the laboring sector of plantations was virtually unknown in Guadeloupe (Richard's [1998] work at La Grivelière, which included the laborers' village, is a notable exception), it was first necessary to develop a survey strategy to determine the archaeological potential of Guadeloupean plantations. Although documentary sources particular to Guadeloupean plantations are relatively scarce, the existence of a map covering all of Basse Terre and Grande Terre, completed in the 1760s, provided a departure point for plantation identification. Also useful is the presence of windmill ruins on much of Grande Terre, which permit the identification of the locations of the industrial complexes of sugar plantations. Using these data, a field survey was conducted of over 30 sugar plantation sites, and on at least 20, the slave village site could be identified (Kelly 2002). Following the identification of likely sites, a program of limited subsurface testing and mapping was initiated at two sites, Habitation Grande Pointe on Basse Terre, and Habitation La Mahaudière on Grande Terre. Both estates are located on public lands, enabling the results of work there to more easily reach a wider audience of residents and visitors on Guadeloupe. Other factors guiding the choice of the two sites included the degree of preservation, their size, the presence of the industrial complex, and the desire to sample one estate on each island. This initial testing phase was successful, resulting in detailed maps of each plantation complex clearly indicating the spatial organization of the village and the relationships between the village and the industrial complex, archaeological testing of a number of house sites yielding architectural data, and the recovery of material culture associated with occupations during and after the period of slavery (Kelly 2003a, 2003c).

Habitation La Mahaudière

In 2003, my team began the third phase of the project, extensive and intensive excavation of several house sites in the location of the eighteenth- and nineteenth-century laborers' village associated with Habitation La Mahaudière, the large northern Grande Terre sugar plantation. The slave village at La Mahaudière was located on the west-facing slope of a ridge running north from the industrial complex. Good-quality cane land surrounds this ridge on three sides, placing the village and the industrial complex in an ideal situation for access to the fields. Survey data collected in 2002 and supplemented in 2003 suggested that the village had been occupied throughout the slavery period, before and after the French Revolution (Kelly 2002, 2003a, 2003b). Differences in the layout of earthen platforms and masonry structural remains across the hillside appeared to be related to temporally distinct occupations, and our excavations were designed to explore this.

Nineteenth-century structures identified at La Mahaudière as well as at Grande Pointe were of standardized masonry construction, and appeared to be placed within regular alignment in the village areas. At La Mahaudière, there were at least three, and possibly more, parallel rows of houses along the slope of the hill (the lower portion of the village site has been adversely affected by recent clearing and charcoal burning). We began by excavating inside and just outside the visible foundations of three stone structures dating to the nineteenth century. Excavations of these structures, called Loci 18, 19, and 27, revealed relatively standardized dimensions (approximately 4 by 6 m), masonry foundations (possibly continuing to a height of about 80 cm as has been identified at La Grivelière by Richard [1998]), and floors initially constructed of earthen fill. However, two of these houses showed a later addition of a prepared floor of crushed and powdered limestone. Furthermore, the quality of foundation construction was not uniform. Some structures had well-constructed foundations of faced stones continuing all the way to bedrock (about 40 cm below present-day ground surface), whereas others had foundations of undressed stones that rested above the bedrock level. In addition to exterior differences, there were interior variations as well, such as the partition wall placed to bisect Locus 18 into two rooms. This partition was not original to the construction, but had been added at a later date in the nineteenth century, either before or during the addition of the limestone floor. Atop the surface of the prepared floor, in the northwest corner of the westernmost room, was an interior hearth. Interior hearths are an unexpected feature of Creole housing of the nineteenth century (Berthelot and Gaumé 2002:50), and we suspect that it may be associated with East Indian laborers who lived in the village after the end of slavery in 1848 (Kelly 2003b). Other artifacts recovered from the structure, such as a brass bell, also hint at the Asian origins of the later inhabitants of part of the village. These hints provide reminders that the Caribbean plantation world continued beyond the period of slavery, nor were Africans the only immigrants exploited (Armstrong and Hauser 2004; Kelly et al. 2011).

Excavations immediately outside these structures revealed other unexpected results. For one, it was clear that despite surface suggestions that the three structures were similar in construction, they were not. The wall of Locus 19 was much more ephemeral, and the building lacked the prepared floor found at Locus 18. Initial interpretations are that Locus 19 was not occupied as long or as recently as Locus 18. Excavation of Locus 27, by contrast, showed that it had been substantially modified, enlarging the original structure in both length and width. The earlier phase of masonry construction at Locus 27 was more substantial than that at Locus 19, and broadly similar to Locus 18, with well-built walls of dressed stone. The later remodeling phase incorporated a less substantial foundation and the placement of a prepared floor that overlay the lowest courses of the original wall. Further demonstrating the continued reuse and reinterpretation of space was a threshold added to the later structure after the foundation and wall were originally built.

In addition to the archaeological evidence of architectural transformations, another result of these excavations was the demonstration that the artifact-bearing deposits within and outside the houses extended all the way to the limestone bedrock, between 30 and 40 cm below the present-day surface of the sloping hillside. The density of artifacts in the soil speaks to a heavy use of the area outside and between the structures. This is not unexpected, given the pattern of extensive use of extramural spaces in African and African-Caribbean societies (Armstrong 1991).

Indeed, another prong to the research strategy was to excavate the area between Loci 18, 19, and 27 in an effort to identify any activity areas, features, or artifact concentrations that are indicative of particular behaviors one might expect to have taken place outside. While clear activity areas have been elusive, at least one hearth that predated the masonry structures has been found. This feature, which underlay the south foundation of Locus 27, was unfortunately over 50 percent destroyed by the builders' trench for the later masonry foundation. Nonetheless, it is possible that analysis of the ash removed from the remaining portion of the hearth may provide clues to dietary practices. Other features relating to the earlier eighteenth-century occupation of the site have also been found. In the exposure of nearly 200 m^2 a great number of features have been identified, including over 110 postholes as well as other features such as trash pits and unidentified linear features possibly associated with architecture. The vast majority of the features identified were postholes dug into the limestone bedrock. These postholes measure an average of 15 cm in diameter and between 10 and 30 cm in depth. Although postmolds were not usually preserved, in a number of the holes the stones used to stabilize the posts were present. One posthole retained a substantial chunk of the original post, which has been identified as *Amanoa caribea*, a species native to Guadeloupe and Dominica. The postholes have generally only been visible as contrasts with the surrounding bedrock, and could rarely be distinguished extending in the overlying soil, making it uncertain to which occupation layer they relate. However, they are remarkably free of artifacts, which, given the density of remains in the soil, suggests that the postholes date to some of the earlier occupations of the village area. When artifacts have been found in the postholes, they have dated to a narrow window at the end of the eighteenth century.

Thus, it is certain that these postholes predate the masonry foundations that remain visible on the site today, and therefore must predate the orderly arrangement of houses dating to the nineteenth century. Their predating the masonry ruins is clear in their juxtaposition below the prepared floor of Locus 27, below the foundation walls of Locus 19, and below the prepared floor, partition wall, and exterior wall of Locus 18. These postholes are the only definitive remains of housing associated with an earlier, pre-Revolution incarnation of the slave village at La Mahaudière, a presence that is otherwise entirely lost to the passage of time. Given their size, the postholes are associated with the construction of *kaz en gaulettes*, the local term for wattled and, occasionally, daubed houses (Berthelot and Gaumé 2002). *Kaz en gaulettes* is the architectural style attributed to slave villages by the early chroniclers and by the historian Debien, who compiled historical evidence on virtually all aspects of slave life during the eighteenth century (Debien 2000; Berthelot 1982). The maps of the posthole distribution unfortunately do not depict an unmistakable array of the rectilinear outlines that would clearly indicate the distribution of individual houses. Hints of their relationships are seen in the linear arrangements present in some of the excavated areas, and also in the pairing of some postholes, suggesting the replacement of earlier rotted posts. Instead, the apparently disordered arrangement of the postholes suggests that the area was heavily used, and probably had fences and other structures in the village as well as *kaz en gaulettes*. Gaps and variation in the density of postholes across the excavated portions of the site also suggest differences in the way the village site was used.

The transition from lightly built wattled structures to more durable masonry, board, or brick houses is not unique to Guadeloupe—indeed, this transition has been documented in many parts of the former slaveholding world. A number of these changes occurred in the early nineteenth century, as new ideas about hygiene, health, and management took hold, and as opposition to slavery became more vocal, provoking planters throughout the colonial world to make the conditions of slavery seem less horrific. In the West Indies, aspects of this architectural transformation have been documented in the former Danish Virgin islands, and in British possessions including Jamaica, the Bahamas, and elsewhere (Chapman 1991; Farnsworth 2001). Archaeological data from Guadeloupe now demonstrate that a similar materialization of new ideas took place in the French Caribbean possessions at about the same time. But were the causes the same? Did French slave housing change because of opposition to the institution, or were there other factors playing a role in this change? I suggest that the complexities and contradictions of slavery at the end of the ancien régime, during the Revolution, and into the Napoleonic era play as great a role in transforming French slavery.

The Role of Revolution

Recall that in 1794, in response to the discussions about the legitimacy of slavery in the new French Republic, and motivated in large part by the ongoing and seemingly unstoppable slave revolt in Saint-Domingue, France abolished slavery in its colonies (Dorigny 2003). This did not have the desired effect of nipping the incipient Haitian revolt in the bud, nor did it result in emancipation for the enslaved workers of Martinique, which at that time was occupied by the British, in part with planter collusion (Blackburn 1997:569). In Guadeloupe, slavery was ended, as the *esclaves* became *cultivateurs*, many of whom remained working on now nationalized sugar plantations (Dubois 2004; Régent 2004). La Mahaudière was one such nationalized plantation, or *Sucrerie Nationale*. As the workers on the plantations were reclassified away from the status of slave and in a new category of citizen, the workers embraced their new identity. Former slaves, although in many instances still working in the same tasks as under the ancien régime, styled themselves citizens and embraced the trappings of the Republic, including the tricolor. Some left the plantations and set themselves up on former estates that had been abandoned by their owners during the Revolution. Still others took advantage of the opportunities for advancement that lay with military service, as former slaves eagerly sought to uphold the Revolution in Guadeloupe against royalists and the British, and to export it to other islands. Although the social upheavals that occurred during this time period are poorly understood, it appears that even though daily life in terms of jobs, housing, and so forth changed little, the attitudes of people were transformed by their emancipation.

In 1802, that emancipation came to an end. Napoleon, in a bid to gather the support of the planter class in France, declared the revolutionary emancipation to be void, and began to restore the nationalized plantations to their owners. Along with the plantations, Napoleon restored the emancipated to their former status as slaves (Blackburn 1997:569). Again, this is where history only tells us what happened with the broadest of strokes. As slavery was reinstated, and laborers were compelled to return to their former state of bondage, there was widespread resistance. Although the French military led by General Richepance was ultimately successful in bringing slavery back, it was not before they had defeated an armed resistance led by Louis Delgrès that had fought a rearguard action across the island before their final martyrdom at Matouba on May 27, 1802 (Saint-Ruf 2002). Given the tricky problem of forcing slavery back on an emancipated population, and the potential for a resurgence of resistance, it appears that certain "negotiations" were entered into, and that conditions were placed on the nature of the new slavery. Again, historical sources are notably silent on this issue, but it appears that, among other things, night work in the sugar factories was eliminated, slave hospitals were required on large plantations, and greater protection of free days and access to markets was to be assured (Régent 2003:294). Certainly, apologists and defenders of slavery made extensive claims of this sort. It is just at this time that we see the new masonry structures appearing at La Mahaudière, and new villages being established on other plantations, such as Coquenda, where survey data has shown the relocation of the village at the beginning of the nineteenth century (Kelly 2002). Thus, while the improvement of the village at La Mahaudière may be explained with reference to the wider social processes hinted at above, it may also be that it shows us one aspect of the moment of the reestablishment of slavery. Among the changing conditions of slavery in Guadeloupe may have been material changes to the village environment of the plantation.

Other aspects of the daily life of village dwellers underwent changes at approximately the same time. Excavation data from La Mahaudière and survey data from 20 other village sites in Guadeloupe show us that in contrast to the materially impoverished eighteenth-century sites, where virtually no artifacts are present, nineteenth-century sites have a comparative wealth of material culture (Kelly 2002). Artifacts that are plentiful in the nineteenth century, particularly glass and ceramics, are virtually absent in the eighteenth century. While this may be due to the growing industrialization of production in the nineteenth century, that explanation alone simply does not suffice. In comparison, eighteenth-century British slave village sites have a considerable range of artifacts, including creamwares, pearlwares, white salt-glaze stonewares, slipwares, and so forth (Armstrong 1990), whereas the Guadeloupe sites have only limited amounts of *faïence brune* and what are believed to be locally produced earthenwares (Kelly et al. 2008). This changes dramatically at the beginning of the nineteenth century, as wider varieties of faience are found, as are more highly fired ceramics that approximate British pearlwares and whitewares. The abrupt nature of this transformation suggests again that we are not simply witnessing the gradual additive augmentation of material culture brought about by increasing industrial production, but that we are seeing another sort of change, a change in economic and social behavior that is being materialized in the ceramics. As with the transformation in housing, this may be another example of the adjustments to the institution of slavery that historical accounts of the reenslavement hint at, including greater access to market days, being captured in the refuse discarded by the enslaved residents of the villages. Detailed studies of the ceramics recovered from La Mahaudière have been completed by Heather Gibson (2007), in her exploration of just what role consumer abilities played in the character of the nineteenth-century artifact assemblage. Analysis of food remains recovered from the site may also speak to increased access to new sources of food, through marketing or increased opportunities to obtain such food on free days. The faunal remains have been recovered, but we await their analysis.

Conclusion: *La Vie Quotidienne*

The archaeological data from Habitations Grande Pointe and La Mahaudière in Guadeloupe provide a different view of a little known, but very important face of New World plantation slavery—that of the French colonies. These data suggest that although there were common trends in plantation slavery, there were also differences between the colonial regimes. As was the case in other parts of the West Indies, archaeology helps us to see some major transformations in the early nineteenth century. However, there is no way, and indeed it would be folly, to suggest that these data somehow show that slavery was "better" or less harsh in the French West Indies. Indeed, when data from nineteenth-century Guadeloupe are compared with data from slavery sites in the British or Danish West Indies, they show a great deal of convergence in terms of material culture. The comparison of eighteenth-century data, however, does not show convergence. Instead, what they suggest is that eighteenth-century slavery in French Caribbean possessions was that much more brutal and harsh. This observation must be considered in the light of the social context of eighteenth-century France, which was so deeply divided and unequal that it spawned a revolution that, at least for a while, attempted to strike privilege and class from society. A society as rigidly stratified as prerevolutionary France, in which the peasantry was essentially bound in feudal obligation (Weber 1976), could well produce a system of slavery that was particularly harsh. Hints of this are seen in some historical accounts, and will no doubt be revealed in bioarchaeological studies currently under way (Courtaud and Romon 2004). Historical archaeology of the villages themselves makes this abundantly clear as well.

References Cited

Adélaïde-Merlande, Jacques
2002   *Delgrès ou la Guadeloupe en 1802*. Karthala, Paris.
Adélaïde-Merlande, Jacques, Réné Bélénus, and Frédéric Régent, editors
2002   *La Rébellion de la Guadeloupe, 1801–1802*. Société d'histoire de la Guadeloupe, Gourbeyre, Guadeloupe.
Armstrong, Douglas V.
1990   *The Old Village and the Great House: An Archaeological and Historical Examination of Drax Hall Plantation, St. Ann's Bay, Jamaica*. University of Illinois Press, Urbana.
1991   The Afro-Jamaican House-Yard: An Archaeological and Ethnohistorical Perspective. *Florida Journal of Anthropology Special Publication* 7:51–63.
Armstrong, Douglas V., and Mark W. Hauser
2004   An East Indian Laborers' Household in Nineteenth-Century Jamaica: A Case for Understanding Cultural Diversity through Space, Chronology, and Material Analysis. *Historical Archaeology* 38(2): 9–21.
Bégot, Danielle
1991   Les Habitations-sucreries du littoral guadeloupéen et leur évolution. *Caribena* 1:149–190.
Bénot, Yves, and Marcel Dorigny, editors
2003   *Rétablissement de l'esclavage dans les colonies françaises*. Maisonneuve et Larose, Paris.
Berthelot, J.
1982   L'Habitat rural: la case guadeloupéenne. *Présence Africaine* 121–122 (1 & 2 Trimestres): 53–71.
Berthelot, J., and Martine Gaumé
2002   *Kaz Antiyé jan moun ka rété*. Editions Perspectives Créoles, Goyave, Guadeloupe.
Blackburn, Robin
1997   *The Making of New World Slavery: From the Baroque to the Modern, 1492–1800*. Verso, London.
Butel, Paul
2002   *Histoire des Antilles françaises, XVIIeme-XXeme siècle*. Perrin, Paris.

Chapman, William
1991   Slave Villages in the Danish West Indies: Changes of the Late Eighteenth and Early Nineteenth Centuries. In *Perspectives in Vernacular Architecture, IV*, edited by T. Carter and Bernard L. Herman, 108–120. University of Missouri Press, Columbia.

Chaudenson, Réné, and Salikoko S. Mufwene
2001   *Creolization of Language and Culture*. Routledge, London.

Courtaud, Patrice, and Thomas Romon
2004   Le Site d'Anse Sainte-Marguerite (Guadeloupe, Grande-Terre): présentation d'un cimetière d'époque coloniale. *Journal of Caribbean Archaeology* Special Publication No. 1: 58–67.

Debien, G.
2000   *Les Esclaves aux antilles françaises, XVIIe–XVIIIe siècles*. Société d'Histoire de la Guadeloupe, Gourbeyre, Guadeloupe.

Delpuech, André
2001   Historical Archaeology in the French West Indies: Recent Research in Guadeloupe. In *Island Lives: Historical Archaeologies of the Caribbean*, edited by Paul Farnsworth, 21–59. University of Alabama Press, Tuscaloosa.

Dorigny, Marcel, editor
2003   *The Abolitions of Slavery: From Léger Félicité Sonthonax to Victor Schoelcher, 1793, 1794, 1848*. Berghahn Books, New York.

Dubois, Laurent
2004   *A Colony of Citizens: Revolution and Slave Emancipation in the French Caribbean, 1789–1802*. University of North Carolina Press, Chapel Hill.

Fallope, Josette
1992   *Esclaves et citoyens: les noirs à la Guadeloupe au XIXeme siècle dans les processus de résistance et d'intégration*. Société d'Histoire de la Guadeloupe, Basse-Terre, Guadeloupe.

Farnsworth, Paul
2001   "Negroe Houses Built of Stone Besides Others Watl'd + Plaistered": The Creation of a Bahamian Tradition. In *Island Lives: Historical Archaeologies of the Caribbean*, edited by Paul Farnsworth, 234–271. University of Alabama Press, Tuscaloosa.

Gibson, Heather R.
2007   Daily Practice and Domestic Economies in Guadeloupe: An Archaeological and Historical Study. Ph.D. diss., Syracuse University.

Kelly, Kenneth G.
2002   African Diaspora Archaeology in Guadeloupe, French West Indies. *Antiquity* 76:333–334.
2003a   Anse-Bertrand: La Mahaudière. *Bilan Scientifique Guadeloupe 2002*: 13–15.
2003b   Anse-Bertrand: La Mahaudière. *Bilan Scientifique Guadeloupe 2003*: 12–16.
2003c   Trois-Rivières: Habitation Grande Pointe. *Bilan Scientifique Guadeloupe 2002*: 51–53.
2004   Historical Archaeology in the French Caribbean: An Introduction to a Special

Volume of the Journal of Caribbean Archaeology. *Journal of Caribbean Archaeology* Special Issue No. 1: 1–10.

2008 Creole Cultures of the Caribbean: Historical Archaeology in the French West Indies. In *The Archaeology of French Colonial and Post-Colonial Settlements*, edited by Elizabeth Scott. *International Journal of Historical Archaeology* Special Issue 12(4): 388-402.

Kelly, Kenneth G., Mark Hauser, Christophe Descantes, and Michael D. Glascock

2008 Compositional Analysis of French Colonial Ceramics: Implications for Understanding Trade and Exchange. *Journal of Caribbean Archaeology* Special Publication 2:85-107.

Kelly, Kenneth G., Mark Hauser, and Douglas V. Armstrong

2011 Identity and Opportunity in Post-Slavery Jamaica. In *Out of Many, One People: The Historical Archaeology of Colonial Jamaica*, edited by James A. Delle, Mark Hauser, and Douglas V. Armstrong, 243–57. University of Alabama Press, Tuscaloosa.

Nicholas, Armand

1996 *Histoire de la Martinique: des Arawaks à 1848. Tome 1*. L'Harmattan, Paris.

Régent, Frédéric

2004 *Esclavage, métissage, liberté: la révolution française en Guadeloupe, 1789–1802*. Bernard Grasset, Paris.

Richard, Gérard

1998 *L'Habitation caféière "La Grivelière" à Vieux Habitants, Guadeloupe*. Paper presented at the Congrès National des Sociétés Historiques et Scientifiques Antilles Guyane, Fort-de-France, Martinique.

Saint-Ruf, Germain

2002 *L'Epopée Delgrès: la Guadeloupe sous la révolution française*. L'Harmattan, Paris.

Stein, Robert L.

1988 *The French Sugar Business in the Eighteenth Century*. Louisiana State University Press, Baton Rouge.

Waselkov, Gregory A.

1997 *The Archaeology of French Colonial North America: English-French Edition*. Guides to Historical Archaeological Literature 5. Society for Historical Archaeology, Tucson, Az.

Weber, Eugen

1976 *Peasants into Frenchmen: The Modernization of Rural France, 1870–1914*. Stanford University Press, Stanford, Calif.

11

Archaeological Research at Habitation Loyola, French Guiana

ALLISON BAIN, RÉGINALD AUGER, AND YANNICK LE ROUX

> La Guyane est une colonie mal constituée, inutile, onéreuse à l'État autant que le serait à un particulier une terre dont les dépenses excéderaient les revenus.... [O]n y a prostitué l'argent, la terre et les hommes, on y a méconnu leur emploi. ... [T]ous les projets exécutés, exempté celui de l'introduction des bestiaux, ont eu le même caractère de déraison.
>
> Malouet 1802

> Guiana is a useless, poorly organized colony, a heavy charge on the State, just as it would be for any individual who owned a piece of land with larger expenses than income.... [T]here we were prostituted out for money, the land and men, we misunderstood their work.... [A]ll the projects carried out, except that of the introduction of cattle, had the same character of insanity (author's translation).

French Guiana (Guyane in French), neighboring both Brazil and Suriname, is a small parcel of land that is almost entirely made up of tropical forest. Formerly a French colony, Guyane became an overseas department of France (*départment d'outre-mer*) in 1946. It differs significantly from the islands of the Caribbean as its equatorial climate results in year-round high humidity and a long rainy season from December to June. Unlike the large plantation owners of Guadeloupe or Saint-Domingue (today Haiti), colonists in French Guiana were often *petits colons* (small farmers) harvesting the land with the help of a few slaves. These settlers and their slaves shared the colony with a resilient and, at times, aggressive Amerindian population, who after initial enslavement were freed by the king of France and protected by the Jesuit missionaries.

Excavation of colonial sites in French Guiana has only been undertaken since the 1980s, primarily the result of the efforts of Yannick Le Roux, Guy Mazière, and Marlène Mazière, who later formed the *Association pour la Protection du Patrimoine Archéologique et Architectural de la Guyane* (APPAAG) in 1992, with a mandate to excavate both colonial and prehistoric sites. Research on the colonial period is hampered by a lack of classification of many archival documents coupled with their poor state of preservation (Touchet 2004:17). Of the 200 or so known plantation sites, 38 are listed on the national register (*carte archéologique*), while only the Bergrave Pottery (1680), the Macaye (1720–1790), and the Poulain (1750–1790) plantations have been studied in some detail (Le Roux 1997:166–173). The excavation of the Jesuit plantation of Loyola, located just outside of Cayenne in Rémire, is the only long-term colonial archaeology research program in the department. Loyola was first registered as an archaeological site in 1987, and has been excavated annually since 1994. Two distinct loci, the Loyola and the Moulin à Vent (windmill) sites, make up the plantation (Figure 11.1), which was owned by the Society of Jesus and covered over 1,500 hectares at the time of the expulsion of the Jesuits from French Guiana in 1763.

Since 1997, archaeological research on these sites has proceeded as part of a research program organized by the *Direction régionale des affaires culturelles de la Guyane* (DRAC) and Université Laval of Quebec City, Canada. Canadian participation in the program has resulted in annual field reports, presentations at scientific meetings, two scientific articles (Auger and Le Roux 2001; Croteau 2004), and five master's theses (Bernier 2003; Chouinard 2001; Croteau 1999; Ene 2009; Girard 2008), and is the subject of a forthcoming doctoral dissertation at Université Laval. Another master's thesis was completed at the Université de Paris 1 (Sorbonne) in 2004 (Bigot 2004).

In this chapter, we discuss the results of our excavations at Loyola, contextualizing this discussion with a brief history of the settlement of French Guiana and the particular role of the Jesuits in this colonial venture (see also the recent volume by Le Roux et al. 2009 for a more detailed discussion). We hope to demonstrate how, in a marginalized colonial setting, the Jesuits ensured their success and importance in the local economy.

Settlement and Plantation Culture in French Guiana

The Treaty of Tordesilla (1494), between the Portuguese and the Spanish, left the colonization of South America west of Belem (in present-day Brazil) to the Spanish. However, Spain did not actively invest in the land

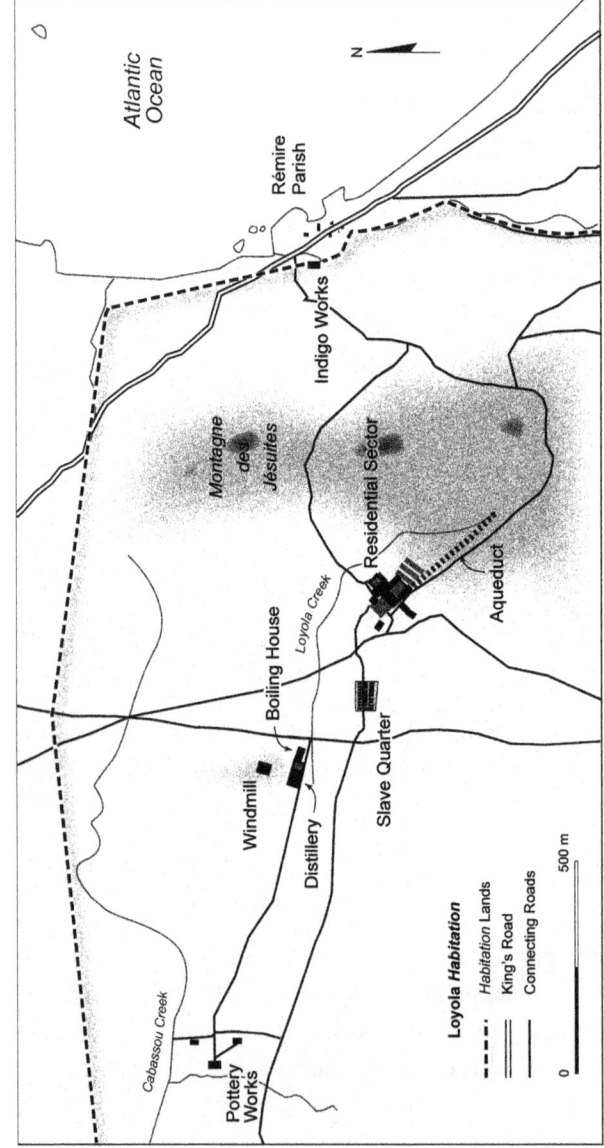

Figure 11.1. Map illustrating the layout of Habitation Loyola.

east of the Orinoco River, which was of little interest to them. This region, known as Guiana, was simultaneously explored and colonized by the Dutch, Portuguese, English, and French, who battled for control of the region (Mam-Lam-Fouck 1982:11).

Between 1604 and 1674, there were several attempts to settle French Guiana. The size of the expeditions varied from 20 to 1,000 people, with some settlements lasting only months while others endured a few years (Le Roux 1994:70). One of the largest attempts at settlement was in 1643 with over 400 soldiers and settlers, while 800 people were involved in a 1652 venture (Mam-Lam-Fouck 1996:25–26). Unlike the English or the Dutch campaigns, French noble officers and members of religious orders headed these missions, which must have appeared more like a crusade than a commercial enterprise (Le Roux 1994:72).

Large expeditions could be extremely problematic. The 1652 *Seigneurs associés* of 800 people under the leadership of Poncet de Brétigny set out for a rather disastrous stay in French Guiana. Members of the French noble classes, entrenched in the seigniorial model of the time, brought their allegiances abroad with them, resulting in mutinies, executions, and assassinations (Hurault 1989:34). Arriving in French Guiana poorly prepared, they promptly raided the crops of the local Galibi Amerindians, and then proceeded to kill over 30 of them. The French were later counterattacked, and by the time the remaining members of the expedition fled to Suriname, they had already buried 600 of their original members (Hurault 1989:34). Dutch occupation of the area from 1654 to 1663 also permitted the arrival of a small Jewish population fleeing Brazil in 1657. At that time, a Dutch venturer named Guérin Spranger established a sugar plantation in Rémire, with two communal mills and other installations (Mam-Lam-Fouck 1982:14).

The French *Compagnie des Indes occidentales* (1663) and the *Compagnie de la France equinoxiale* (1664) were founded to retake Cayenne from the Dutch, which resulted in the demise of the Jewish settlements, as the Jewish settlers were deported to Suriname, paving the way for the control of their lands by Jesuits in 1665 (Le Roux 1994:80). In 1664, Lefebvre de la Barre arrived with 1,200 colonists accompanied by Father Grillet, a Jesuit missionary.

Early colonists settled primarily on high ground (*terres hautes*), which had poor soils, and, over the course of a few years, they exhausted these of any nutrients as they grew sugarcane, roucou (*Bixa orellana* L. or annatto, a plant used in making red dye), indigo, tobacco, cotton, and cocoa, along with subsistence crops. Some did, however, learn to improve soil productivity by practicing slash-and-burn agriculture, a farming technique learned from the local Amerindian population (Mam-Lam-Fouck 1982:15). Lowland agriculture on the *terres basses*, exploited in a system of polders as seen in neighboring Suriname, was not employed until the late eighteenth century (Le Roux 1997:164). By settling on higher grounds, the colonists also profited from the *alizés*, or breezes, an important factor in keeping the persistent malaria-laden mosquito population away from their homes. Furthermore, the colonists also believed that the natural gases, or "miasmas," emitted from the marshy lowlands were deleterious to their health, reinforcing their settlement choice.

Another factor impeding the success of the early settlements in French Guiana was the colonists' lack of preparation; they were primarily marginalized individuals, vagabonds, and penniless nobles with little inclination to work. Before slavery was introduced to the colony, many of the colonists were soldier-colonists and indentured laborers, commonly called *les 36 mois* (thirty-six months), who were hired to work for an average of three years, at the end of which they would receive a parcel of land or a sum of money (Le Roux 1994:49; Mam-Lam-Fouck 1982:15). These feudal-type conditions, coupled with their lack of knowledge of tropical agriculture, were disastrous for the indentured laborers, given the tremendous workload and difficult working conditions (Le Roux 1994:49).

French Guiana appears to have been underpopulated by both colonists and slaves alike. During the seventeenth century, French Guiana maintained a small population of around 1,000 people, which only grew to around 14,000, including slaves, at the end of the eighteenth century (Le Roux 1994:22). For the same period, the late-eighteenth-century slave population on Saint-Domingue was almost 500,000, while the islands of Martinique and Guadeloupe each had over 80,000 slaves (Villiers and Duteil 1997:180). In fact, special trading arrangements were arranged with Suriname due to the paucity of slaves.

Trade winds made navigation to the area difficult, while the colonial capital, Cayenne, had a shallow port that required expert navigation. Historical sources indicate that ships larger than 300 tons were unable to enter the estuaries, and had to stay 5 leagues offshore, while small ships could only travel 15 or 20 leagues inland. These factors discouraged maritime traffic, which was erratic at best (Mam-Lam-Fouck 1982:48). For example, in 1668 the French port of Nantes sent over 30 ships to Martinique, and a dozen to both Guadeloupe and Saint-Domingue, with only one or two sent to Cayenne (Lemesle 1998:19).

Unlike colonies with absentee landowners living in the *métropole*, French Guianese plantation owners usually lived on their plantations (Le Roux 1994:63) and, on some of the smallest plantations, even participated in manual labor (Mam-Lam-Fouck 1982:58). In 1690, a small plantation growing primarily subsistence crops averaged only three or four slaves, while a third of the plantations some distance from Cayenne had no slaves at all (Le Roux 1994:56). Medium-sized plantations averaged around 40 slaves and grew cotton, cocoa, and annatto, crops considered less prestigious than sugarcane. Plantations that primarily raised livestock did not have the same demands for human labor, and therefore typically had fewer slaves (Le Roux 1994:56). The dozen or so large plantations with over 100 slaves were the minority.

French Guiana, with its small population and marginal economy, was essentially administered by the members of a single family of important plantation owners from 1664 to 1763. Governors La Barre, de Lezy, and d'Orvilliers were related either by birth or marriage. Their connections with other important families, such as the Macaye and Poulain families, resulted in French Guiana being governed on more of a clan-based structure with upper administrators representing mere figureheads rather than exercising any real power (Le Roux 1994:99).

The Jesuits in French Guiana

Early expeditions to the area brought a few Capuchin monks in 1635, while the first Jesuits arrived in 1664 (Le Roux 1994). The Jesuits quickly established their monopoly over the spiritual life of the colony, and soon owned several plantations supporting many missions and a school. Their plantations included Mont-Xavier in Kourou, Maripa and Saint-Régis in Roura, and Mont-Louis and Loyola in Rémire (Le Roux 1997:173). Some of their mission outposts were in the eastern region of the colony on land contested by both the French and Portuguese. These were small settlements of baptized Amerindians living under the protection and spiritual guidance of the Jesuits. Other Amerindians sought solace from poverty or needed protection from the Portuguese colonial authorities (Vissière and Vissière 1993:294). The Jesuits attempted to maintain peaceful relations with the Amerindians and ensured their enslavement was banned by

France. Furthermore, French colonists were barred access to huge tracts of lands set aside to both protect and assimilate local Amerindian populations (Le Roux 1994:96).

The Jesuits were flexible in adapting to the specificities of their flock, the Amerindians. They quickly learned to exploit the local tribunal structure, working with chiefs already in power, unless it was deemed these men needed to be replaced with more devout Jesuit-trained chiefs (Vissière and Vissière 1993:294). Letters from priests working in the missions speak at length of the difficult conditions, lack of a sufficient number of priests, and the importance of learning the Amerindians' languages. Their letters also detail the humility, poverty, and unfailing piety of these isolated men, traveling constantly in their mission work, often sick and malnourished (Vissière and Vissière 1993:293–295; see also Collomb 2006; and selected letters in Vissière and Vissière 1993).

The Habitation Loyola

Loyola, the largest *habitation*[1] in French Guiana, was founded in 1668 by Father Grillet when the Jesuits purchased part of their land from the viscount Quincy, Joseph-Fortuné Pinon (Le Roux and Bigot 2004:8). They received a second parcel of land taken from a Jewish plantation owned by Isaac Drague that same year. Though the second tract of land was a concession to the Jesuits, they traveled to Paramaribo, Suriname, to officially negotiate a price for these lands with the governor, Abraham Creysen (Le Roux 1994:128). By 1720, Loyola totaled 1,500 hectares (Le Roux 1997:173).

Loyola was first and foremost a profitable sugar plantation, thanks to the labor of an estimated 400 slaves, and its profits were an essential source of revenue needed to maintain many mission outposts. It also served as a place for both physical and spiritual convalescence for priests returning from missionary work in isolated parts of the colony. Important visitors to Loyola included colonial administrators and travelers, such as eighteenth-century naturalists visiting the region.

As the quality and quantity of sugar declined at the end of the 1740s, Loyola began to produce molasses and rum (Le Roux and Bigot 2004:8). Loyola's modest indigo production was a brief venture, and was soon replaced by cotton, which was eventually surpassed by coffee. Valuable coffee plants were initially smuggled in from Suriname, and by 1736 Loyola produced half of all coffee grown in the colony (Auger and Le Roux

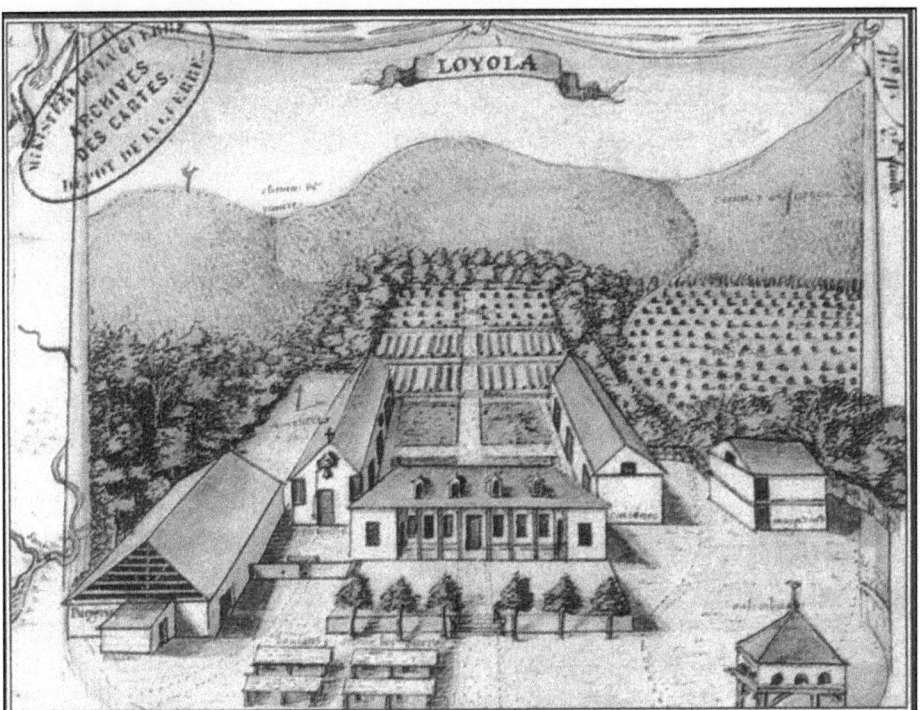

Figure 11.2. *Cartouche extrait de la carte du gouvernement de l'isle et terre ferme et colonie de Cayenne*, 1730. Service Historique de l'Armée de Terre (S.H.A.T.), Vincennes, 8 F 62.

2003:56). Around 1750, the sugarcane industry was abandoned at Loyola, and all the related equipment was sent to Saint-Régis Plantation (Le Roux and Bigot 2004:8).

The residential sector of the plantation complex (Figure 11.2) included the master's house (*maison de maître*) located at the center of the complex, in front of which there was a dove cote (*colombier*) symbolizing wealth. The master's house dominated the landscape overlooking both the cane fields and the ocean, and was oriented to benefit from the winds blowing from the northeast. Also identified in the residential sector of Loyola were the kitchen and hospital building and a small chapel with its adjacent cemetery. The 1730s watercolor (Figure 11.2) also shows a curing room for sugar as well as storage buildings and a terraced garden.

Situated on a paved terrace, the master's house was 80 by 56 *pieds français*, or 26 by 18 m, and was a seven-room structure, with verandas extending across the central portions of both the back and front of the building and stairs ascending to the garden from the back of the house. The building was organized around a central great room with four smaller rooms, each of which was 12 by 16 *pieds français*, or 4 by 5 m, exiting off to each side. The western half of the building was excavated and revealed traces of what may have been a dividing wall of the central room and the supports for stairs leading to the attic (Auger and Le Roux 2001:61). These vestiges are reminiscent of structures that can still be found in creole houses in French Guiana. All rooms excavated were paved in either bricks or tiles. Patterns on these floors were created using the different-colored tiles, which ranged from red to pale pink. Some of them still showed traces of wax. The western wall of the master's house appears to have contained vertical shutters with angled slats allowing constant ventilation, an ideal adaptation to the tropical climate.

Behind the master's house was a formal garden, which appears to have been landscaped in the French style, as well as two terraced levels, which are presumed to have contained a kitchen garden and perhaps a small nursery. Behind these terraces, a terra-cotta aqueduct brought water down the hillside to provision the residential sector as well as the nearby blacksmith shop (Le Roux and Auger 2002).

There was also a modest single nave chapel, Notre-Dame-de-Grace, a building measuring around 100 m^2, in this, the residential sector of the plantation. Located inside were the choir and sacristy, both of which were paved in earthenware tiles. As this was a private chapel, a small fenced yard in front of the chapel was reserved for the faithful to congregate while listening to the service. A space east of the chapel was reserved for the cemetery of baptized slaves, as was dictated by the 14th article of the *Code Noir*, a 1685 edict of Louis XIV, which was essentially a document that set out the guidelines for the management of slaves (Sala-Molins 2005). Due to the high acidity in these soils, no human remains have ever been recovered, although five burials have been identified. It appears that the individuals were interred without coffins and wrapped in shrouds with their heads facing east.

The kitchen and hospital building was a rectangular stone structure that had a roof partially covered in ceramic tiles. A stone wall divided it into two rooms, and excavations of the northern room indicate a hearth and a bread oven. The 1730 watercolor of Loyola indicates the use of the southern room of this complex as a hospital.

The curing room (*purgerie*) was a large structure with a partially paved stone floor where the molasses was separated from the crystallized sugar. It appears that the drying house (*étuve*) was also located in this building, which contained the remains of a 1.5-m-wide chimney. Other industrial buildings included a store and a smithy, which were built downwind from the master's house in the residential sector of the plantation. The excavation of the smithy revealed a platform to support bellows and several ingots, while many broken tools were recovered from a heap outside the smithy. Several forged metal agricultural tools such as hoes, scythes, and axes were submitted for neutron activation analysis and metallographic analyses to better understand the sources of Loyola's raw materials and to estimate the quality of tool production and repair (Chouinard 2001). Chouinard concluded that all tools examined were forged and repaired at Loyola, a reality likely dictated by the erratic maritime traffic with France. A fortuitous outcome of this research was the discovery that some of the metal ingots used to fabricate tools at Loyola were imported from New France's iron-producing Forges du Saint-Maurice in Québec (Chouinard 2001:66). It appears that the quality of the work of the blacksmiths at Loyola varied greatly; some of the blacksmiths were adequately skilled, yet lacked the cold water required to properly temper their tools (Chouinard 2001:106). Archival sources indicate that the Loyola blacksmiths probably produced and repaired tools for neighboring plantations, thus assuring a supplemental source of revenue (Le Roux 1997:173).

A 1764 map by the colonist Bruletout de Prefontaine reveals 14 slaves worked in the pottery works located next to the Cabassou creek, where they produced earthenware for daily domestic use as well as for sugar production. Loyola earthenware is of a pink to beige color, with a highly porous matrix. These products, some of which bear the Jesuit mark of IHS, were wheel-turned, resulting in smooth exterior bodies that appear to be the work of practiced potters. While the *poterie sucriere* (pottery used for sugar production) included drip jars, sugar molds, and molasses jars, dishes produced for domestic use were primarily terrines and deep plates.

Imported earthenwares identified at Loyola include Vallauris, Beauvaisis, Biot, Saintonge, and Albisola. Chinese porcelain was also found on site, but the most abundant ceramic type identified, other than the *poterie sucriere*, is faience. In Bernier's (2003) study of faience identified from the kitchen and its adjacent midden, she concluded that over 70 percent was, not surprisingly, of French origin. The primary types of faience were Rouen, Moustiers, and Delft, and were of a medium quality (Bernier 2003:34; Girard 2008). Due to the erratic provisioning of French Guiana in comparison with other colonies, the settlers may have not had access to the best of the French ceramic markets. Among the modest plantations of French Guiana, however, this rather mediocre faience may have represented the most luxurious faience in the colony (Bernier 2003:109; Girard 2008).

Our study of historic maps indicates that the slave quarters may have been located between the plantation's windmill and the residential complex (see Figure 11.1), though surveys have not been carried out yet to locate this area. Future investigations are planned to better document this sector of the plantation.

A couple of hundred meters to the north of the residential complex are the remains of a windmill and associated stone and shingled buildings, referred to as a *sucrerie* (boiling house) and a *vinaigrerie* (rum distillery) in a 1764 inventory of Jesuit possessions. The substantial remains of a 1730s windmill are one of two historic windmills in French Guiana, and it was classified as a historic monument in 1993. The walls are over 1 m thick, while the remains of the structure measure 4 m wide and 8 m high, constructed in a similar manner to other Antillean windmills (Flohic Éditions 1998:35–37). Excavations around the foundations suggest a single phase of construction (Auger et al. 2004:9). Two other buildings, both 20 m long by almost 9 m wide, are presumed to be storage or drying buildings associated with eighteenth-century coffee production at Loyola. At the moment, this seems to be the most plausible interpretation of their use; however, they are the only examples of this type of building recovered to date in French Guiana.

Remains of the *sucrerie* and the *vinaigrerie* mentioned in the Jesuit inventory were unearthed during the 2004–2006 excavations. Overlapping foundations of two buildings measuring 6 by 22 m have been partially excavated, and, according to Cazelles (2004, 2006), their construction is similar to that of the buildings of the residential sector of Loyola. Artifacts from the building believed to be the *vinagrerie* are primarily *poterie sucriere* and the remains of a large jar (*dame jeanne*), suggesting use during the first half of the eighteenth century. The second building, likely the *sucrerie*, was divided into three rooms, and contained an oven and a brick-lined canal (Cazelles 2008) (Figure 11.3).

Figure 11.3. Photograph of the brick-lined canal of the boiling house at Habitation Loyola.

A stone-lined well located just a few meters away provided water for cleaning out the *sucrerie*, as insects and ashes were a constant nuisance in sugar production. The well measures 1.5 m wide, descends to a depth of 6 m, and is filled by the water table with 2 to 3 m of water year-round. Our investigations indicate that the wooden shingles, beams, and bricks making up the superstructure around the well collapsed inward, and were left undisturbed at the bottom of the well until their excavation in 2003. The beams and shingles recovered were fashioned out of two species of tropical wood known locally as *wapa* (*Epeurua falcata* Aublet) and *maho noir* (*Eschweleria* sp.), and are rare examples of colonial wooden artifacts from this region. Next to the well is a small stone building measuring 5.5 by 3.5 m, which had a floor partially paved with bricks. Only the eastern end of this building has been excavated, and though its function eludes us, the building appears to be part of the eighteenth-century occupation of the site.

The Society of Jesus was dissolved by France in 1763, signaling the end of the reign of the Jesuits at Loyola, with the last members of the order leaving French Guiana in 1768 (Le Roux 1994:127). It appears that the residential sector of Loyola was abandoned at this time, and a new plantation, Beauregard, was founded 2 km to the south (Le Roux and Bigot 2004:9–10). During the excavations of the master's house at Loyola, it was noted that piles of construction materials such as bricks and floor tiles ready to be transported to their new location (Beauregard) were abandoned in situ (Auger and Le Roux 2001:62).

The Jesuit Economy and the End of Loyola

By the eighteenth century, all the French colonies were having financial difficulties, and French Guiana was no exception (Cardoso and Martinière 1981:406). With its small population, French Guianese agricultural output remained modest compared to other colonies in the Caribbean French colonial network dominated by Martinique, Guadeloupe, and Saint-Domingue. In 1740, 40,000 out of the 50,000 tons of sugar produced by the island colonies under French control came from Saint-Domingue (Villier and Duteil 1997:151). In contrast, in 1737 French Guiana had only 14 sugar-producing estates (Le Roux 1994:455). With a total population of only around 8,000 at the time, French Guiana continued to play a marginal role, if any, in the colonial economy. As a result, France began to neglect its commerce with Guiana in favor of more lucrative trade with prosperous Martinique and Saint-Domingue (Tarrade 1972:30; Viliers and Duteil 1997:151).

Since the second half of the seventeenth century, France exerted tight control over its colonies by means of the *Exclusif*, a series of protectionist measures established by Jean-Baptiste Colbert, finance minister under Louis XIV from 1665 to 1683. This prohibited the establishment of colonial industries already well developed in France, banned exchange with other nations that were in competition with France, obliged the use of products from the home country, and required that surplus commodities from the colonies be shipped to France. In the Caribbean basin, populated by England, Spain, and Holland as well as France, these must have been almost crippling trade restrictions for any of the capitalist-minded society of French Guiana. There were, however, exceptions to the *Exclusif*, as French Guiana was permitted to import slaves from Suriname and later traded with New England for certain products such as horses, salted fish, and other products that French merchants did not deliver to the colony (Cardoso and Martinière 1981:428–429). Even with these exceptions, the colonists in French Guiana were relatively isolated from France and serviced by few French vessels during the eighteenth century. It is then not surprising to see evidence of trade with other nations suggested at Loyola by the presence of a large number of Delft wares.

The primary role of the Jesuits in French Guiana may have been the conversion of Amerindians to Christianity, but they also played an important role in the colony's economy. According to the papal bull of Pope Gregory XIII in 1575, unlike other religious orders, the Society of Jesus was allowed to participate in commercial matters. This unique status granted them the freedom to run ranches, plantations, and other enterprises in the New World (Mörner 1965; Wright 2004). They circumvented or blatantly ignored certain laws and may have monopolized some aspects of the local economy in French Guiana (Le Roux 1994; Thibaudault 1995:178), becoming wealthy and influential landowners.

A telling example of the Jesuits' disregard for jurisprudence dates to the early eighteenth century. A 1703 ordinance, reintroduced again in 1721, banned religious orders from owning more land than could be worked by 100 slaves. It appears that the plantation at Loyola had much more land, almost six square miles in fact, and certainly had many times the prescribed number of slaves (Le Roux 1994:128). In 1744, the Jesuits were reminded again of this law by the governor, and were not allowed to take on any more land or holdings except with his express permission. It appears that this warning, like the previous one, was not respected (Le Roux 1994:128). As the Jesuits owned some of the most important plantations in the colony, they had a significant influence on local politics. One can imagine the difficult position of any colonist who dared to criticize the practices of these wealthy and influential landholders who also gave them the sacrament and heard their confession.

At the time of the Jesuit dissolution in 1763, an inventory of Loyola indicated they had four blacksmiths, while the 1764 map by Bruletout de Prefontaine refers to 14 slaves making pottery at the plantation. Both blacksmithing and the production of pottery provided the Jesuits with a stable source of revenue in addition to the profits of their agricultural production. Nonetheless, documents from this period deplore the paucity of revenues generated by the plantation. Despite unending complaints from the Jesuits, their sugar refinery was the most productive in the colony for a quarter century, and their coffee harvest equaled half of all the coffee produced in the colony.

The Jesuits had the financial means to experiment with various agricultural techniques. Their windmill was built in a location where the winds are not strong enough to actually turn its sails, and their venture into indigo production was short-lived, as was that of cotton. These forays would have ruined other colonists in French Guiana, but not the Jesuits, as they owned the only plantation with a sufficiently large and diversified economy to be able to sustain such losses. They had the profits from their pottery works and blacksmiths; they were herders; and they produced sugar and coffee. They consistently circumvented the law and were not subjected to, or simply chose to ignore, the restrictive economic measures imposed by France.

It is important not to vilify this particular group of French Guianese Jesuits for their riches and ingenuity. In the Americas, they were part of a vast network stretching from California southward, establishing missions, colleges, ranches, and plantations. They took advantage of the freedom granted to them to finance their work (see also Mörner 1965; Wright 2004). Without the constraints of other religious orders, or common citizens for that matter, they are a fascinating portrait of religious capitalists. They took individual oaths of poverty, but amassed significant collective wealth in present-day Mexico, Argentina, Bolivia, Paraguay, Brazil, and Peru (Bangert 1972; Chevalier 1965; Cushner 1980).

The official reason for Louis XV's dissolution of the Jesuit order in 1763 was both legal and economic (Thompson 1976). A telling example of the financial turmoil that brought their presence to an end is seen in the case of Antoine Lavallette, Father Superior of the French Antillean missions. A prosperous landholder who was found guilty of defrauding many creditors in the mismanagement of his extensive commercial enterprises, he contributed significantly to the bankruptcy of the French Jesuits (Wright 2004:183–184), ending their presence in the Caribbean basin and French Guiana after a century of relative prosperity.

Conclusion

As a colony, French Guiana's economic growth was limited by its difficult geographic position, fragile tropical soils, and a lack of sufficient slave labor. Small plantation owners were often indebted to slave traders, and were further hindered by disease and a highly regimented and restrictive economic structure in the control of a few families. The Jesuits, numbering around a dozen at any given time, were owners of several plantations, the most impressive being Loyola, which exploited a labor force of up to 400 slaves. The most important Jesuits lived in the master's house serviced by an aqueduct, had a private chapel and formal gardens, and dined on faience that was of a quality not enjoyed by most of the colony's inhabitants. They were a unique portrait of success in this marginalized colony representing a synergy of religious interests and economic prosperity.

Acknowledgments

The authors would like to thank Ken Kelly and Meredith Hardy for the invitation to participate in this volume. Nathalie Cazelles, who currently directs the fieldwork in French Guiana, and Gérald Migeon (DRAC-SRA) must be recognized for their dedication to the project. Field research was made possible through grants from the *Direction régionale de affaires culturelles de la Guyane* and its *Service régional de l'archéologie*, as well as from the *Fonds québécoise de la recherche sur la société et la culture*. And finally, we want to express our appreciation for the fine work of Andrée Heroux, who prepared Figure 11.1.

Note

1. In the French colonial context, a *habitation* encompasses a farming complex comprised of an ensemble of industrial buildings, the master's house, and a slaves' quarters. The English equivalent "plantation" is also used in this text.

References Cited

Auger, Réginald, and Yannick Le Roux
2001   Étude archéologique de l'habitation de Loyola à Rémire en Guyane française. *Archéologiques* 15:55–68.
2003   *Le Site du moulin à vent.* Rapport archéologique déposé au Service régional de l'archéologie de la Guyane, Cayenne.
Auger, Réginald, Allison Bain, Yannick Le Roux, Florence Artigalas, and Caroline Girard
2004   *Le Moulin à vent et le puits de l'Habitation Loyola à Rémire, Guyane Française.* Service régional d'archéologie de la Guyane, Cayenne.
Bangnert, William V.
1972   *A History of the Society of Jesus.* Institute of Jesuit Sources, St. Louis.
Bernier, Maggy
2003   Caractérisation typologique, microscopique et chimique des faïences du XVIIIe siècle du site Saint-Ignace de Loyola en Guyane française. *Des Cahiers d'archéologie du CELAT No. 14, Série archéométrie No. 4.* Québec.

Bigot, Viviane
2004 *L'Habitation Loyola après le départ des jésuites: une lecture de l'occupation du sol à partir des archives historiques (1763–1938)*. Mémoire de maîtrise, Université de Paris I, Sorbonne.

Cardoso, Ciro Flamarion, and Guy Martinière
1981 La Société et l'économie guyanaise au XVIIIe siècle. In *Historial Antillais*, Vol. 2, edited by Tony Djian, Jacques Sabatier, and Daniel Rouche, 405–454. Dajani Editions, Pointe-à-Pitre.

Cazelles, Nathalie
2004 *Le Site du moulin à vent: rapport scientifique de fouille*. Rapport archéologique déposé au Service régional de l'archéologie de la Guyane, Cayenne.
2006 *Le Site du moulin à vent: rappport scientifique de fouille*. Fouille programmé (97309008). Rapport archéologique déposé au Service régional de l'archéologie de la Guyane, Cayenne.
2008 *Rapport de fouille du site du moulin à vent*. Rapport archéologique déposé au Service régional de l'archéologie de la Guyane, Cayenne.

Chevalier, François
1965 The Formation of Jesuit Wealth. In *The Expulsion of the Jesuits from Latin America*, edited by Magnus Mörner, 94–103. Alfred A. Knopf, New York.

Chouinard, Alain
2001 *Archéologie et archéométallurgie de la forge et forgerons de l'habitation Loyola en Guyane*. Collection Des Cahiers d'archéologie du CELAT No. 11, Série archéométrie No. 2, Québec, Québec.

Collomb, Gérard
2006 *Les Indiens de la Sinnamary, journal du père Jean de la Mousse en Guyane (1684–1691)*. Éditions Chandeigne, Paris.

Croteau, Nathalie
1999 *Loyola, une habitation Guianaise sous l'ancien régime: programme de mise en valeur des vestiges archéologiques*. Mémoire présenté à la faculté des études supérieures de l'Université Laval pour l'obtention du grade de maître ès arts (M.A.). Université Laval, Québec.
2004 L'Habitation de Loyola: un rare exemple de prospérité en Guyane française. *Journal of Caribbean Archaeology*, Special Publication No. 1: 68–80.

Cushner, Nicholas P.
1980 *Lords of the Land: Sugar, Wine and Jesuit Estates of Coastal Peru, 1600–1767*. State University of New York Press, Albany.

Ene Raducu-Viorel
2009 *Le Moulin à vent dans le contexte archéologique de l'habitation Loyola en Guyane française*. Mémoire présenté à la faculté des études supérieures de l'Université Laval pour l'obtention du grade de maître ès arts (M.A.). Université Laval, Québec.

Flohic Éditions
1998 *Le Patrimoine des communes de la Guadeloupe*. Collection: Le Patrimoine des Communes de France, Flohic Éditions, Charenton-le-Pont.

Girard, Caroline
2008   *Aperçu de la vie dans le cadre de la maison de maître de l'Habitation Loyola en Guyane française (1668–1769).* Mémoire présenté à la faculté des études supérieures de l'Université Laval pour l'obtention du grade de maître ès arts (M.A.). Université Laval, Québec.

Hurault, Jean-Marcel
1989   *Français et indiens en guyane.* Guyane Presse Diffusion, Cayenne.

Lemesle, Raymond-Marin
1998   *Le Commerce colonial triangulaire: (XVIIIe–XIXe siècles).* Presses universitaires de France, Paris.

Le Roux, Yannick
1994   *L'Habitation Guianaise sous l'Ancien Régime: étude de la culture matérielle.* 3 vols. Thèse déposée à l'École des Hautes Études en Sciences Sociales, Paris.
1997   L'Archéologie de la période coloniale. In *Archéologie en Guyane,* edited by Marlène Mazière and Guy Mazière, 161–177. Ministère de la Culture, Cayenne.

Le Roux, Yannick, and Réginald Auger
2002   *Fouilles archéologiques à la source de l'habitation de Loyola.* Report submitted to Direction des affaires culturelles de la Guyane, Cayenne.

Le Roux, Yannick, R. Auger, and Nathalie Cazelles
2009   *Les Jésuites et l'esclavage: Loyola l'habitation des jésuites de Rémire en Guyane française.* Presses de l'Université du Québec, Québec.

Le Roux, Yannick, and Viviane Bigot
2004   Les données historiques sur le site du Moulin à vent. In *Le site du Moulin à vent: rapport scientifique de fouille,* edited by Nathalie Cazelles, 7–13. Rapport archéologique déposé au Service régional de l'archéologie de la Guyane, Cayenne.

Mam-Lam-Fouck, Serge
1982   *La Guyane française, de la colonisation à la départementalisation: la formation de la société créole Guianaise.* Désormeaux, Paris.
1996   *Histoire générale de la Guyane françiase, des débuts de la colonisation à l'aube de l'an 2000. Les grands problèmes Guianais: permanence et évolution.* Collection Espaces Guianais. Ibis Rouge Editions, Cayenne.

Mörner, Magnus
1965   *The Expulsion of the Jesuits from Latin America.* Alfred A. Knopf, New York.

Sala-Molins, Louis
2005   *Le Code noir, ou, le calvaire de Canaan.* Quadrige, Paris.

Tarrade, Jean
1972   *Le Commerce colonial de la France à la fin de l'ancien régime: l'evolution du régime de l'exclusif de 1763 à 1782.* 2 vols. Presses Universitaires de France, Paris.

Thibaudault, Pierre
1995   *Echec de la démesure en Guyane, autour de l'expédition de Kourou ou une tentative européene de réforme des conceptions coloniales sous Choiseul.* Imprimerie Pairault, Lezy, France.

Thompson, D. Gillian
1976   The Fate of the French Jesuits' Creditors under the Ancien Régime. *English Historical Review* 91(359): 255-277.
Touchet, Juien
2004   *Botanique et colonisation en Guyane française (1720–1848)*. Ibis Rouge Editions, Cayenne.
Villiers, Patrick, and Jean-Pierre Duteil
1997   *L'Europe, la mer et les colonies, XVIIe–XVIIIe siècle*. Hachette, Paris.
Vissière, Isabelle, and Jean-Louis Vissière
1993   *Peax-rouges et robes noires: lettres édifiantes et curieuses des jésuites français en amérique au XVIIIe siècle*. Collections Outre-mer. Éditions de la difference, Paris.
Wright, Jonathan
2004   *God's Soldiers: Adventure, Politics, Intrigue and Power: A History of the Jesuits*. Doubleday, New York.

12

Commentary

JOHN DE BRY

Archaeology is the scientific study of past human culture based on the analysis of remains that people left behind. Contrary to popular belief, however, archaeology does not always involve physical excavation of any given site. Cultural anthropology can also involve "archaeology of the mind," such as interpretation of oral tradition. The contributions to this book are all in the vein of investigating how *mentalité* can be seen in archaeology.

One of the questions raised is how can one evaluate cultural influences exerted by a minority population? French Huguenots played an important role in the shaping of the southeastern English colonies of North America as well as in the independence movement that was to follow, yet physical traces of their lives are scant and elusive. In her excellent chapter, Ellen Shlasko focuses on French Protestants of South Carolina, where physical evidence of their presence is found in the form of gravestones and commemorative monuments erected by their descendents. These monuments serve as cultural markers as well as reminders of Huguenot contributions to the shaping of a society erroneously perceived as purely Anglo-Saxon. But did the French leave a more definable trace of their presence and culture? Shlasko correctly suggests that historical archaeologists should scrutinize architectural remains of structures found on plantations, as such remains can yield valuable information on social status, group dynamics, and cultural background.

Comparative studies of architectural features, such as the *poteaux-en-terre*, or post-in-trench, construction technique, have shown that there is a remarkable similitude among French colonial sites in Mississippi, Missouri, and Illinois. I suggest that this comparative analysis should be extended to include French colonial sites in the West Indies, such as Martinique, Guadeloupe, St. Kitts, and Saint-Domingue (present-day Haiti), to name a few. By exercising such scrutiny in their investigations, archaeologists may be able to detect not only French building techniques and architectural influence but African techniques as well. Climatic conditions in the West Indies are not unlike those of parts of West Africa, and enslaved Africans working in French colonial plantations undoubtedly introduced innovative building techniques that were better suited and more efficient than those familiar to their French masters. It is also quasi-certain that French colonists did not adopt African building techniques as a whole but rather integrated some of the African elements within French architectural traditions. It should come as no surprise if this "mixture" is reflected in architectural remains of colonial dwellings found in the southeastern United States. Shlasko proposes that post-in-trench architecture is not a product of a social and economic situation unique to South Carolina, and that it is neither a wholly French nor African tradition. Comparative analysis of sites in the southeastern United States with sites in French colonial sites in the West Indies could help settle the debate on the origin of post-in-trench architecture once and for all.

This so-called archaeology of the mind is also reflected in Sara Rivers-Cofield's chapter. While the first revolt in Saint-Domingue took place in October 1790, ignited by mulattos from the northern part of the colony, followed by black slaves in August 1791 and by the mulattos of the south in August 1792, it was not until this last uprising that the French started to lose control of the entire colony, so we can assume that Jean Payen de Boisneuf and his family were some of the earliest French refugees from Saint-Domingue. Although the reasons and causes of the uprisings are many and more complex than just having been brought on by the French Revolution of 1789, the ultimate downfall for de Boisneuf and the Vincendière families and their colonist compatriots remained an ultimately common fate. It is clear that de Boisneuf was an affluent member of French colonial society and was able to bring with him a substantial sum of money that made it possible to purchase large parcels of land and establish the plantation of L'Hermitage, but more than kin and money, de Boisneuf also brought with him all the foul habits and prejudices of French slave owners.

The brutality of French colonists of Saint-Domingue toward their enslaved Africans is well known and documented by numerous travelers to the island, including the Jesuit missionary priest Jean-Baptiste Le Pers (Le Pers, in Charlesvois 1733) and Moreau de Saint-Méry (Moreau 1796), so it is no surprise that even in Maryland, at a time when slavery was lawful, the citizens of Fredrick County were shocked by the ill-treatment of slaves on L'Hermitage Plantation. The reason for de Boisneuf's unwillingness to return to France is clear; during the Reign of Terror (1792–1794) anyone with a "de" *particule* preceding his or her name stood a good chance to be sent to the guillotine, because such a *particule* suggests nobility, so it made good sense for de Boisneuf and his family to make the best of a bad situation and settle in Maryland. I am in agreement with Rivers-Cofield's assessment that the extreme brutality displayed by the de Boisneuf and the Vincendière families may have been aggravated by their anger and frustration for having lost their land and fortune to those they regarded as inferior. I surmise that some of this anger also had roots in the fact that these French Catholics were surrounded by German Protestants, and they felt isolated in what they perceived as a hostile society. This hypothesis is supported by the surviving sisters' actions; after selling off L'Hermitage and the slaves, Victoire and Adelaïde "expressed their cultural affiliation" by making large monetary contributions to the St. John Catholic Church in Frederick, perhaps an attempt as well to cleanse their parents' sins and redress their tarnished reputation.

Nevertheless, the French refugees' attempt to re-create their Saint-Domingue lifestyle is clearly reflected in their ill-treatment of their enslaved African laborers and servants. Living in virtual isolation, little is known of their day-to-day lives. How did these French émigrés dress? Did they have the same fine silver, crystal, and lace they were accustomed to in Saint-Domingue? What was their diet like? Did it differ from that of their German Protestant neighbors? And how did their slaves live? Were they allowed more freedom than in the colony? What type of meager possessions were they allowed to keep? Did they play ancestral music? Did they practice African-derived rituals, such as voodoo? It is hoped that an in-depth archaeological investigation of L'Hermitage slave village and other areas of the plantation will help answer many of the questions raised by Rivers-Cofield in her fascinating chapter.

So far we have discussed civilian colonists and settlers within ethnic, cultural, and religious contexts, but French presence in what is now the southeastern United States has not always been a peaceful affair. French ambitions in the region were spurred by Robert Cavelier, Sieur de

La Salle, the French explorer who first navigated the entire length of the Mississippi River in 1682 and claimed the vast Gulf region in the name of his sovereign, Louis XIV, naming it *la Louisiane*. He painted an idyllic picture of the area, a view that persisted even after the disastrous failure of his 1684–1687 expedition, which ended with his murder. It was not until 1699 that the colonization of Louisiana would be undertaken in earnest by Pierre Le Moyne, Sieur d'Iberville, regarded by many as the true founder of Louisiana (Villiers 1929), who, through his impetus, made the work of his brother, Jean-Baptiste Le Moyne, Sieur de Bienville, possible as first governor of the new colony (de Bry 2004). Louisiana never prospered, as did Saint-Domingue, for reasons clearly explained by Barbara Hester in her most informative essay. The elements that contributed to France's failure to fully control and capitalize on the region's resources and strategic location are many: inhospitable climate; unwilling and forced multinational colonists; hostile American Indian tribes; English and Spanish interference; and, principally, inadequate support from the *métropole*. Yet it was Jean-Baptiste Colbert's aim to increase agricultural production in the colony for the benefit of the population of the *métropole*, thus contributing to the subsistence of a larger number of men and women, and to contribute to increasing commerce with other nations (Furetière 1690).

Hester eloquently exposes the fact that French Louisiana clearly suffered from mismanagement and, oftentimes, neglect. Settlers, made up principally of French, transplanted Canadians, Germans, Flemings, and Swiss, as well as Swiss military regiments, included a large number of unskilled laborers. This is reflected in the many correspondences between Louisiana officials and Versailles asking for assistance in providing skilled labor and help in learning, among other things, how to cultivate tobacco: *"les habitants des Oumas et de la Pointe Coupée désirent qu'on leur apprenne à cultiver le tabac"* (Périer and La Chaise, New Orleans, November 2, 1727, Louisiane, Colonies C13 A 10, folio 184, Centre des Archives d'Outre-mer, Aix-en-Provence). While these requests seem to have been ignored, agricultural products were needed for the *métropole*, especially tobacco, which was essential to the survival and prosperity of France's colonies in most of the Americas due to the great demand for it in France and other parts of Europe (Labat 1998). Another example of the need for skilled colonists is seen in Iberville's choice of location for the establishment of the first colonial administrative center, Old Biloxi, which reflected poor judgment on his part, and contributed to the inability of

Crown officials and colonial administrators to manage and govern the colony effectively.

Diseases and famine (*disette*) claimed the lives of many, as did hostile action on the part of local tribes, further undermining any hope of prosperity. Hester points out that one of the main contributors to the disastrous state of the new colony was Ship Island (Ile aux Vaisseaux) when it was used as a staging point for newcomers to Louisiana, a sort of Ellis Island for thousands of unfortunate and often unsuspecting immigrants. Conditions on Ship Island were horrific, and scores died while awaiting transportation to Biloxi, Pascagoula, and other settlements on the mainland. For those who survived the ordeal on Ship Island, what awaited them in those settlements was not much better. As a result, many escaped to other parts of the colony or attempted to board ships bound for Saint-Domingue or France, while French and Swiss soldiers deserted their posts in search of food and better conditions away from the settlements, often influenced in their decision by Spanish and English "infiltrators" (*Désertion des Suisse du Nouveau Biloxi. Influence des Espagnols dans cette affaire*, Le Blond de La Tour to the Company, New Orleans, August 30, 1722, Louisiane, Colonies C13 A 6, folio 321, Centre des Archives d'Outre-mer, Aix-en-Provence). The new colonists were, for most part, unwilling to endure the hardships imposed by the harsh climatic conditions of the country and the lack of skilled labor, and asked the authorities that African slaves be brought in to lessen the burden (Le Blond de La Tour to the Company, New Orleans, August 30, 1722, Louisiane, Colonies C13 A 6, folio 321, Centre des Archives d'Outre-mer, Aix-en-Provence); the introduction of African slaves added to the ethnic and cultural mix already existing in the region.

To further aggravate the situation, there were proportionately few women in the new colony, prompting the director of the *Compagnie de la Louisiane* to write to Versailles, asking that women be sent to the new colony (Martin Diron d'Artaguiette, Commissary Officer, to the Minister, Fort Saint-Louis, February 12, 1710, Louisiane, Colonies C13 A 2, p. 531, Centre des Archives d'Outre-mer, Aix-en-Provence). This situation resulted in many settlers and soldiers taking American Indian women as brides or companions, something that profoundly displeased colonial authorities. In 1716, the Crown in Versailles issued orders forbidding marriages between Frenchmen and *sauvagesses* (Draft of a royal directive addressed to governor Lespinay, Versailles[?] 1716, Louisiane, Colonies

C13 A 4, p. 963, Centre des Archives d'Outre-mer, Aix-en-Provence). The nationality and ethnic diversity in the new colony of *la Louisiane* may account for the anomalous artifact forms encountered on Ship Island and Vieux Biloxi and support Hester's suggestion that they may reflect "expedient designs, cultural contact modifications, and illicit interregional trade networks." Hester raises interesting and complex questions regarding the ethnic and cultural landscape of French Louisiana, questions that can only be answered by meshing the archival record with the fragmentary archaeological remains. She is correct in assuming that the Moran site (22HR511) may provide some of those answers, but the complexity of the questions, combined with the disturbed mortuary context of the Moran site, may prove to be a daunting endeavor.

Hester's excellent essay provides us with an introduction to Marie Elaine Danforth's chapter on the Moran site, the oldest known French colonial cemetery in the southern United States. The Moran site is of particular significance inasmuch that burial practices seem to deviate significantly from known French Christian interment methods. One of the most surprising findings reported by Danforth is the possible presence of Amerindian skeletal remains among Europeans, something that was determined by evaluation of tooth and bone apatite carbon isotopes, but there is a distinct possibility that Africans and individuals of mixed ancestry were also buried at the Moran site; if this is the case, it would represent a blatant disregard for established rules and guidelines issued by French colonial authorities mandating that cemeteries be segregated (Colonies, Ile de France C4 58, *Plan du cimetière du Port Louis & des environs,* manuscript map by the Chevalier de la Martinière, November 20, 1782, Centre des Archives d'Outre-mer, Aix-en-Provence). Additionally, one of the questions raised by Danforth's work is why the Moran site does not seem to follow French Christian burial protocol; she observes that while most individuals were buried in the supine position with their lower arms and hands placed over the midsection of their body, their heads oriented toward the south, some are oriented to the north, others are slightly off true north–south, one individual had his arms extended to the side, and one was buried face down.

Could this simply reflect the somewhat chaotic situation created by the Law debacle? During this period of instability, it appears that French officials and administrators had little control over the population, and many laws and rules were systematically broken with obvious contempt.

However, Danforth does point out that such deviations in mortuary practices have been observed at other cemeteries, particularly at St. Peter's Cemetery in New Orleans (Owsley and Orser 1985–1986:95), and although the bodies there had been placed in coffins, unlike the majority of the Moran site burials, they were oriented parallel to St. Peter and Toulouse streets with heads in various orientations. The St. Peter's Cemetery burials are post-1722, but I would like to suggest that the paucity of artifacts associated with burials at both the Moran and St. Peter's sites reflects the calamitous state of the new colony, and the modest background of those interred there.

The ongoing osteological analysis of human remains from the Moran site is already yielding valuable data about the ethnicity of individuals buried there, their diet, and their state of health throughout their lives, and anticipated mitochondrial DNA analysis will most certainly contribute to our understanding of the evolution of this troubled French colony.

In her chapter, Ann M. Early discusses an important historical event that helped, in her own words, shape the economic and political landscape of France's North American centers for years. Early's contribution is particularly interesting because she looks at the second French-Chickasaw War from a different, fresh, and unbiased perspective, opening up vast possibilities for archaeological investigations.

It goes without saying that archival documents must be consulted before any fieldwork can be undertaken, but while Early makes mention of large known collections of archival documents, mostly in the United States and Canada, it should be emphasized that repositories potentially containing key documents to locating significant archaeological sites associated with the second French-Chickasaw War have yet to be explored. For instance, the vast Jesuit Archives known as *Collection Jésuite des Fontaines*, formerly housed at the Jesuit Cultural Center in Chantilly, was transferred to the Library of the City of Lyon, and is more accessible than previously; this particular repository contains many printed books and manuscripts pertaining to the Americas. The *Centre des Archives d'Outre-Mer* (the French Colonial Archives), in Aix-en-Provence, contains a wealth of documents pertaining to Louisiana; a few years ago I examined a large manuscript map drawn in 1733 by the military commander of Mobile (Crenay 1733). This particular hand-drawn and painted map covers a large portion of the Mississippi Delta region and contains valuable information on the location of Native American settlements, including

Natchez villages destroyed by the French, military forts and trading posts, missions and churches, and so forth. Although the map does not include the area where the second French-Chickasaw War's major battles took place, it provides a wonderful guide for identifying locations of potentially important archaeological sites. Such manuscript maps and charts are often neglected by archival researchers, yet they can be a key to successful surveys and excavation projects.

Analysis of faunal remains within the context of a settlement, be it rural or urban, can greatly contribute to our understanding of creolization, as eloquently exposed by Elizabeth M. Scott and Shannon L. Dawdy in their chapter. I find this contribution both fascinating and challenging, and, in my opinion, it provides an excellent explanation of the creolization process. Excavations at the Madame John's Legacy site (16OR51) and the St. Augustine site (16OR148) afford us a glimpse of French and Spanish colonial lifestyles and diets in early Louisiana. The fact that both sites contain architectural remains and intact underground features makes this study an ideal model for future research. Scott and Dawdy chose to focus on the early French colonial period (ca. 1718–1769) and the Spanish colonial period (ca. 1769–1803), but briefly made some interesting comparisons with the antebellum era. Both sites yielded a wealth of data resulting from the first in-depth analysis of faunal material from French colonial New Orleans.

From their research, it becomes clear that the first generation of foreign-born immigrants attempted to maintain a lifestyle closely matching the one they enjoyed in their home country, even if this lifestyle was difficult to sustain in a region vastly different from their places of origin, a phenomenon encountered to this day. In contrast, the ethnic acculturation phase is characterized by the second generation born in foreign lands being more practical than their forebears and less reluctant to adopt local customs, including diet. Economic position and class standing most certainly played important roles in influencing diet, although I am not sure I can fully agree that poorer colonists, as a whole, did not have the financial means to make the choices about food conducive to creolization. While this may be true of lower-class city dwellers, plantation owners and rural inhabitants had generally higher standings than in their land of origin and easier access to a variety of food stock often not available to them in the Old World. Conversely, a poorer foreign-born rural resident may not have had the financial means to maintain a wholly European lifestyle and had to supplement his or her diet by consuming foodstuff made available through trading with local tribes, thus accelerating the creolization process. Research in French and Spanish archival repositories suggests a lessening of class differences in the colonies. Although the Madame John's Legacy and the St. Augustine sites are now within the New Orleans city limits, they were once far apart; our perspective of distances changed in the industrialization era, so while Madame John's Legacy was located within a large city, by colonial standards of the time, the St. Augustine plantation was "in the country."

Thanks to the proximity of the Gulf and the Mississippi River "highway," a wide variety of meats from domestic animals, wild game, and seafood was available to the residents of New Orleans, and dietary choices could be made based on economic and class standings as well as ethnic preferences. It should be kept in mind that many French immigrants originated from Brittany and southwestern France, from such places as Nantes, La Rochelle, and Bordeaux, where seafood has been a larger part of sustenance for centuries. Furthermore, a substantial number of Spanish immigrants originated from Andalucía, in the southern part of the country, where pork has long been a major part of local diet as well as a delicacy, such as *Jamón serrano* (salt-cured ham); Scott and Dawdy correctly point to the fact that by the 1500s, eating pork in Spain had become a means of emphasizing that one was Catholic and not Muslim or Jewish (Sarasúa 2001).

Class and economic position differences are evident when comparing the French faunal remains assemblage of the Pascal-Martin household with that of the de Lorenzos. Traditionally, however, French colonists, and particularly plantation owners, lived better than their Spanish counterparts. Mary Hassal, an American traveler to Cape François in Saint-Domingue, found herself caught in the turmoil of the slave uprising in 1802 and sought refuge in Cuba, where her sister lived. Arriving aboard a British ship in Santiago, she stayed a few days at the house of a Spanish landowner. Writing to her uncle, General Aaron Burr, vice president of the United States, she expressed her surprise at the different lifestyle led by this wealthy Spaniard compared to the French colonists. Contrasting with her experiences in Saint-Domingue, where French colonists resided in beautiful houses; used the finest silver, crystal, laces, and furniture; and dined on fine cuisine and fine wines, this rich Spanish settler lived like a poor peasant (Hassel 1991). But I fully agree with Scott and Dawdy that, as a whole, the French and Spanish deposits reflect choices of foodstuff available at the markets of New Orleans rather than French or Spanish ethnic food preferences. British colonists and Anglo-American residents of the same region, just prior to and beyond the antebellum period (1803–1861), were less willing to incorporate wild species into their diet than were the French and Spanish. But is it not a fact that Anglo-Saxons have always been less adventurous in their culinary traditions?

The notion of finding diagnostic markers can be challenging, even controversial at times, which seems to be the case for colonoware, the much-debated low-fired earthenware that occurs within plantation contexts and colonial settlement sites across much of the eastern United States and the Antilles. The crucial question is: does colonoware reflect Native American or African ceramic ware traditions, or is it *just* another example of creolization? This problem is eloquently addressed by David Morgan and Kevin MacDonald, who chose to concentrate their research in Louisiana, where colonoware occurs on French, Spanish, and British colonial sites. Their decision to avoid classifying such wares as representing Native American and/or African traits is, in my opinion, a wise and prudent approach. I fully agree with their assessment that past research models have effectively rendered African potters invisible within archaeological contexts (Weisman 1992), to the point that one wonders if partiality, and even veiled and deeply rooted racism, may not have been a factor in previous research reporting. I do not mean to imply that some archaeologists have been purposely biased in their study of colonowares, but have simply followed a less than critical path based on traditional thinking. It seems to me that enslaved African contributions to colonial societies have been vastly ignored. This is a very complex puzzle as numerous similarities exist between Native American and African potters, and sorting these out is a daunting task. Ideas and tastes often develop along parallel lines throughout the world, and such similarities as found in African and Native American ceramic vessels are not uncommon. Although colonowares from Louisiana had not been, in the past, the subject of such scrutiny, this preliminary analysis raises more questions than it provides answers. What is clearly needed is a much broader research model that would encompass other geographical locations in the United States and beyond; comparative analysis of colonowares from French and Spanish colonial contexts in the Antilles may provide additional clues. Although preliminary examination of utilitarian vessels from Louisiana sites suggests a strong correspondence between early colonists and Native American potters, an African influence is not discounted. Morgan and MacDonald have opened the door for more critical analysis and interpretation of this much-debated cultural marker.

While ceramics can provide clues to ethnicities, what they were used for and what they contained can yield invaluable data about the people who used them, their customs, and their societies, and they can also help define adaptations and changes, something that Meredith Hardy addresses in her chapter. Once again we are dealing with the creolization process and all its intricacies. "Creole" indeed came to signify "native born," not only in Louisiana but also in other French colonies, in such places as Saint-Domingue, Martinique, Ile Bourbon (Réunion Island), and Madagascar, among others. Hardy points out that in addition to new creole behaviors and languages, a nouvelle cuisine emerged, resulting from the need to adapt to different environmental and agricultural conditions, social interactions, and exchanges between various ethnic groups. Indeed, artifacts associated with foodways can become valuable markers if they are studied within the context of culinary evolution rather than as isolated objects. Social status can be expressed by the type of foods consumed, how they are prepared, what spices are used, and how they are presented. Foods are cultural insignia that help define a people and separate classes.

As Hardy points out, during the 1650s through the 1700s France became the culinary, cultural, and artistic capital of Europe; the *cuisine bourgeoise*, however, was greatly influenced by Italian cooking under the reign of Italian-born queen consort Catherine de Médicis, wife of Henry II. After Henry died of injuries received during a jousting tournament in 1559, her three weak sons ascended to the throne—Francis II, who died in 1560, succeeded by his brother Charles IX, who died in 1574, and finally by the third brother, Henry III, that same year. During the reign of Charles IX, when she was appointed queen regent and granted sweeping powers, Catherine became most influential (Cloulas 1979). When she moved to France in 1533, she brought with her Florentine cooks who brought with them the secrets of Italian cooking, including peas and beans, artichokes, duck in orange (*canard à l'orange*), and *carabaccia* (onion soup). Pastry makers demonstrated their innovative genius with sorbets and ice creams, marmalades, fruits in syrup, pastry making, and pasta. Catherine, regarded by many as one of the most influential people in culinary history, also brought to the French table new protocol, such as the separation of salty and sweet dishes at a time when all over Europe sweets were still consumed together with meat and fish in the style of medieval times. Everyone in France was amazed by the Florentine elegance Catherine introduced: graceful table settings and dining, embroidery and handkerchiefs, light perfumes and fine lingerie, as well as luxurious silverware and glasses (Volpi 2003). However, we must not forget that European cuisine was dramatically altered by the introduction of new foodstuffs, including turkey, tomatoes, potatoes, maize, cacao, pimento, and so forth, following the European discovery of the New World.

The fact that many of the ceramic wares studied by Hardy display stylistic elements that indicate an affiliation with regions of southern France and the Mediterranean comes as no surprise; vast numbers of French colonists originated from Provence and the Charente region of southwestern France, with ships sailing from the port city of La Rochelle. It would be most interesting to conduct a comparative analysis of ceramic wares from Louisiana with those excavated from Canadian sites because many of the ships from La Rochelle brought settlers to Canada. This is a very well researched chapter with excellent background information and historical data. While Hardy addresses the creolization theory with prudence, she correctly points out that this process does not occur evenly across a geographical region, as creolization is a dynamic process that is governed by a multitude of socioeconomic factors as well as interaction between various ethnic groups, each with their own customs and traditions.

Little is known about the daily life of serfs in medieval Europe because the learned aristocratic class did not write about it; the same is true of the Maya, who wrote only about dynasty, religion, astronomy, and astrology, and ignored the "little" people. In the same fashion, we know very little about the daily life of slaves in the Americas. Thanks to historical archaeology, details of *la vie quotidienne* of enslaved Africans living and working on plantations are slowly emerging. Kenneth Kelly's investigations of Habitation La Mahaudière and Habitation Grande Pointe in Guadeloupe not only reveal little-known aspects of the daily life of slaves and indentured laborers but also show evidence of changes brought on by the French Revolution, the abolition and reintroduction of slavery—changes that had been invisible until now. Kelly's findings help paint a much different picture than the one painted by historians who, once again, failed to chronicle the lives of slaves and poor laborers. A few European travelers to the Americas recorded details of the everyday life and living conditions of African slaves. One such traveler was the Jesuit missionary Jean-Baptiste Le Pers, who spent several years in Saint-Domingue; his extensive manuscript notes were published in 1733 by the Jesuit priest Pierre-François-Xavier de Charlevois (Charlevois 1733). Le Pers described the harsh treatment of slaves by French plantation owners, who punished them by cutting noses, ears, even limbs, for various infractions we would today consider minor. It is hoped that Kelly's work will spur historians to rewrite the history of Guadeloupe to reflect eighteenth- and nineteenth-century realities.

French Guiana, or Guyane, was unique among French colonies in the Americas due to its tropical climate, vast jungle, and belligerent native Amerindian population. This distinctive setting made agricultural work particularly difficult, making it necessary for the colonists to adopt the slash-and-burn techniques used by local Amerindian tribes and forcing them to consume foods with poor nutritional values. Harsh climatic conditions and tropical diseases, such as malaria and dengue fever, took a heavy toll on the European population; writing to the secretary of state on February 19, 1677, Captain Desgranges, commanding the garrison at Cayenne, wrote:

> je vous supplie très humblement, Monseigneur, de considérer qu'avec si peu de force nous ne sommes point en estat de garder un fort dans lequel il avait 300 hommes qui ont esté pris dans un momant l'espée à la main . . . a cause du mauvais air et de la méchante nourriture. (Desgranges 1677)

> I humbly beg of you, My Lord, to consider that with so few forces we are not in a position to defend a fort in which 300 men were taken in an instant with sword in hand . . . because of the unhealthy air and the bad food. (Translation by the author)

All these factors combined to restrict the size and number of plantations as well as the number of owners and slaves. But the small number of slaves in French Guiana was also the result of economic factors that must be taken into consideration. In an official letter to the secretary of state dated January 28, 1688, the governor of Guyane, Pierre-Éléonor Marquis de Ferrolles, wrote:

> il a passé depuis quinze jours un vaisseau négrier des messieurs de la Compagnie du Sénégal qui n'ignorant pas la nécessité ou nous sommes de nègres pour n'en n'avoir pas fourny depuis longtemps, ont donné ordre à leurs commis de n'en pas laisser à moins de quatre cent frans [sic], et trois cent sept frans les moins bons payables contant [sic] en livres, nos habitants en ont offert jusqu'à trois cent frans ce qu'ils n'ont pas voulu accepter. (Ferrolles 1688)
>
> Fifteen days ago a slave ship belonging to the gentlemen of the Senegal Company came; they, knowing that we were in need of Negroes as we had not received any for quite some time, have given orders to their representatives not to sell any for less than four hundred francs, and three hundred and seven francs for those of lesser quality, all payable in cash in livres, our citizens offered up to three hundred francs, which they did not want to accept. (Translation by the author)

Clearly, plantation owners could not afford to buy slaves at the same price paid by French colonists in the Antilles. Let us keep in mind that Guiana was of strategic interest to the French and never seriously considered for economic potentials.

The unparalleled prosperity of Loyola Plantation was the direct result of the Jesuits' adaptability, management skills, and business acumen. Allison Bain, Réginald Auger, and Yannick Le Roux could not have picked a better site for their investigations. Loyola prospered for 100 years, resulting in a rich and diversified context as it successively produced sugar, indigo, cotton, and, finally, coffee; as a by-product of sugar, molasses and rum were also produced from the late 1740s onward, until the plantation was abandoned around 1768 when a new plantation was established 2 km to the south. While the Society of Jesus was dissolved by order of Louis XV on November 25, 1763, their properties were not seized until two years later, and the last Jesuit did not leave Loyola until 1768. The reason for this late departure was due to the fact that the Jesuit missionary who conducted mass services in the small church of Rémire, 1.5 km to the south of Loyola, was allowed to remain on the plantation until a (non-Jesuit) priest could be found to replace him. However, in April 1765 the plantation, buildings, domestic animals, and slaves officially became the property of the king (Turgot 1765). How did this transfer of ownership affect the living conditions of the enslaved Africans? It is probable that, not unlike the work at the Habitations La Mahaudière and Grande Pointe in Guadeloupe, ongoing excavations at Loyola will uncover evidence of changes and transformation brought about by continually changing living and working conditions on the plantation. Such findings will undoubtedly yield invaluable data on the way enslaved Africans lived alongside Jesuit missionaries who managed to prosper in this marginalized colony. Fourteen slaves were reported to have worked in the production of pottery. Did they produce wares under the strict supervision of the Jesuits, or were they allowed to introduce stylistic elements of their own? Careful analysis of ceramic shards in and around the pottery works of the property could reveal similarities with colonowares from North American plantation sites.

The authors of the chapters presented in this volume are helping in the development of definitive models of lifestyle that were so commonly recognized that no one thought to write them down (Fairbanks 1994). In the case of slaves, the omission was for the most part deliberate.

Conducting archaeology in geologically dynamic areas or urban settings can be physically challenging, such as is the case for the lower Mississippi Valley, Guadeloupe, and Guiana, where many archaeological and cultural markers are either invisible or have been eradicated altogether. The research presented in this volume points to the unique opportunity to study the processes of creolization through the systematic excavation and analysis of material culture throughout the southeastern United States, the Caribbean, and former French, English, and Spanish colonies in parts of South America. Creolization can be regarded as a complex cultural evolution driven by the need to accommodate one culture into another as dictated by sociogeographical conditions. Yet it is difficult to assign creolization a clear timeline because of frequent changes in social interaction among ethnic groups, that is, French slave owners, African slaves, and Native American tribes. Europeans' attitudes toward their enslaved Africans and Native tribes were often influenced by the prevailing polities within their own settlements, and driven by policies of expansionism of their home countries. If a local tribe with whom the French had traded and coexisted peacefully allied with the British, for instance, the French would seek an alliance with another tribe perceived as a traditional enemy of the former. In times of conflict, plantation owners who had routinely physically abused their slaves would soften their treatment and arm their servants for the defense of their properties.

Socioeconomic changes also altered the lifestyle of European settlers as they sought ways to improve their standard of living; for instance, on November 2, 1727, the residents of Pointe Coupee, a small but strategically important settlement on the west bank of the Mississippi near present-day Morganza, Louisiana, asked the French authorities in New Orleans to be taught how to cultivate tobacco, realizing the economic potentials for the small community. The archival record is, of course, very important, but often conflicting, so it is imperative to compare and evaluate each individual data set carefully. For example, it is widely believed, based on documents in various archival repositories, that the Tunica moved to the Pointe Coupee area in 1764 and established a village on the east bank of the Mississippi River "about two miles above the last plantation of Pointe Coupée" (Pittman 1764, in Brain 1988:42). Yet a manuscript map located in the French colonial archives in Aix-en-Provence, drawn by the Baron de Crenay in 1733, clearly depicts a Tunica village in approximately that same location 31 years earlier than reported by Pittman; the larger and bold lettering of the word "Tonica" emphasizes the importance the French placed on their presence. It is the duty of archaeologists to correct the inaccuracies reflected in the written record, something that can be best achieved through communication and exchange of research data. To this end, I would like to encourage my colleagues to learn other languages so they can read and appreciate research papers written by non-Anglophone archaeologists, something our colleagues outside English-speaking countries have done for many years (Nikolova et al. 2008). Failing to do so is to ignore valuable data published in languages other than English.

In closing, I want to emphasize the fact that archaeology is the confessor of history, and thus it is the job of archaeologists to correct mistakes of the past and get it right. I can only hope that the excellent chapters presented in this volume will serve to inspire others to dig deeper into the legacy left by French colonists in the southeastern United States, the Caribbean, and beyond.

References Cited

Brain, Jeffrey P.
1988 *Tunica Archaeology*. Peabody Museum of Archeology and Ethnology, Harvard University Press, Cambridge, Mass.

Cloulas, Ivan
1979 *Catherine de Médicis*. Librairie Arthème Fayard, Paris.

Charlevois, Pierre-François-Xavier
1733 *Histoire de l'isle Espagnole ou de S. Domingue. Escrite particulièrement sur des Mémoires Manuscrits du P. Jean-Baptiste Le Pers, Jésuite, Missionnaire, à Saint Domingue, & sur les Pièces Originales, qui se conservent au Dépôt de la Marine*. 4 vols. Par le P. Pierre-François-Xavier de Charlevois, de la Compagnie de Jésus. A Amsterdam chez François l'Honoré.

Crenay, baron de
1733 *Carte de partie de la Louisiane qui comprend le cour du Mississippy depuis son embouchure jusqu'aux Aerondak, et celui de la Mobile depuis la Baie jusqu'au Fort de Toulouse*. Par le Baron de Crenay, commandant la Mobile, 1733. Centre des Archives d'Outre-mer, Aix-en-Provence, Direction de Dépôt des Fortification des Colonies; III / 6 PFA / 1.

de Bry, John
2004 Aux origines de la Louisiane: l'archéologie des navires de Cavelier de La Salle (La Belle). In *Champlain ou les portes du Nouveau Monde; Cinq siècles d'échanges entre le Centre-Ouest français et l'Amérique du Nord*. Sous la direction de Mickaël Augeron et Dominique Guillemet, 95–96. Geste éditions, La Creche, France.

Desgranges, Captain
1677 Centre des Archives d'Outre-mer, Aix-en-Provence, C14 2. *Correspondance de Desgranges* (capitaine), F° 93, 19 février 1677.

Fairbanks, Charles H.
1994 [1977] Path to Prelude "What Is Past Is Prelude; Study the Past." In *Pioneers in Historical Archaeology: Breaking New Grounds*, edited by Stanley South, 216. Plenum Press, New York.

Ferrolles, Pierre-Éléonor Marquis de
1688 Centre des Archives d'Outre-mer, Aix-en-Provence, C14 2. *Correspondance de Ferrolles* (1688–1690), F° 20, 28 janvier 1688.

Furetière, Antoine, Abbé de Chalivoy
1690 *Dictionnaire universel contenant généralement tous les mots François tant vieux que modernes, & les termes de toutes les sciences & des arts*. Recueilli et compilé par Messire Antoine Furetière, Abbé de Chalivoy, de l'Académie Françoise, A Rotterdam.

Hassal, Mary
1971 *Secret History, Written by a Lady at Cape François*. Book for Libraries Press, Freeport, N.Y. Originally published 1808, *Secret History, or, The Horrors of St. Domingo*, printed by R. Carr, Bradford & Inskeep, Philadelphia.

Labat, Jean-Baptiste, Père
1998   *Voyages aux isles, chronique aventureuse des Caraïbes, 1693–1703*. Phébus, Libretto, Paris. Originally published 1722, *Nouveau Voyage aux isles Françoise de l'Amérique*, Paris.

Moreau de Saint-Méry, Médéric Louis Élie
1796   *Description topographique, physique, civile, politique et historique de la partie française de l'isle Saint-Domingue*. Philadelphia.

Nikolova, Lolita, Claire Smith, and Heather Burke
2008   Archeologists as People. Paper presented at the Sixth World Archaeological Congress, June 29–July 5, 2008, Dublin, Ireland.

Owsley, Douglas, and Charles E. Orser
1985–1986 *An Archaeological and Physical Anthropological Study of the First Cemetery in New Orleans, Louisiana*. Department of Geography and Anthropology, Louisiana State University, Baton Rouge.

Sarasúa, Carmen
2001   Upholding Status: The Diet of a Noble Family in Early Nineteenth-Century La Mancha. In *Food, Drink, and Identity*, edited by Peter Scholliers, 37–61. Berg, New York.

Turgot, Étienne-François, Marquis de Sanomons
1765   Centre des Archives d'Outre-mer, Aix-en-Provence, Sous-série C14 28, Correspondance à l'arrivée en provenance de la Guyane française. *Saisie des biens des Jésuites à Cayenne par Turgot* (Governor of Guiana), Fº 193, 29 mars; Fº 195, 6 mai; Fº 196, 3 avril 1765.

Villiers, Marc, de
1929   La Louisiane: histoire de son nom et de ses frontières successives, 1681–1819. *Journal de la Société des Américanistes* 21(1): 1-70.

Volpi, Anna Maria
2003   *The Timeless Art of Italian Cuisine*. Palatino, New York.

Weisman, Brent Richards
1992   *Excavations on the Franciscan Frontier: Archaeology at the Fig Springs Mission*. Ripley P. Bullen Series, Florida Museum of Natural History. University Press of Florida, Gainesville.

Contributors

Réginald Auger, Ph.D.
Professor, Département d'histoire
Les Laboratoires d'archéologie de l'Université Laval
Université Laval

Allison Bain, Ph.D.
Professor, Département d'histoire
Les Laboratoires d'archéologie de l'Université Laval
Université Laval

John de Bry, Ph.D.
Director, Center for Historical Archaeology
Indiatlantic, Fla.

Marie Elaine Danforth, Ph.D.
Professor, Department of Anthropology and Sociology
University of Southern Mississippi

Shannon Lee Dawdy, Ph.D.
Associate Professor, Anthropology and Social Sciences
University of Chicago

Ann M. Early, Ph.D.
State Archeologist
Arkansas Archeology Survey

Meredith D. Hardy, Ph.D.
Archeologist, National Park Service-Southeast Archeological Center
Tallahassee, Fla.

Barbara Thedy Hester
Graduate Student, Department of Anthropology & Sociology
University of Southern Mississippi
Hattiesburg, Miss.

Kenneth G. Kelly, Ph.D.
Professor, Department of Anthropology
University of South Carolina

Kevin C. MacDonald, Ph.D.
Reader, Institute of Archaeology
University College London

David W. Morgan, Ph.D.
Director, Southeast Archeological Center, National Park Service
Tallahassee, Fla.

Sara Rivers-Cofield
Curator of Federal Collections, Maryland Archaeological Conservation Laboratory
St. Leonard, Maryland

Yannick Le Roux
Lycée Félix-Éboué
Cayenne, French Guiana

Elizabeth M. Scott, Ph.D.
Associate Professor, Department of Sociology and Anthropology
Illinois State University

Ellen Shlasko, Ph.D.
President and Principal Investigator, Integrated Archaeological Services, Inc.

Index

Abenaki, 87, 89
Abolition, 13, 31, 236
Acadien, 4
Africa, 56, 141, 143, 153, 180, 182; and architecture, 8–9, 23, 25–26, 226
Africans, 117–26, 134, 156, 165
African Americans, 9, 11–12, 25, 117, 126, 153
African Caribbean, 198
African contribution to ceramics, 12, 136, 140, 142–44, 234–35
African Diaspora, 13, 245
African foods, 163, 167, 182
African Habitation Site, 49, 53
African identity, 7, 73–74, 153
Africanization, 118
African slaves, 3- 5, 11, 239; Arkansas, 89–90; Caribbean, 190, 197–98, 236–37; Louisiana, 109, 113–14, 128; Maryland, 227; Mississippi, 48, 53, 55–56, 229–30
Aix-en-Provence, 228–31, 240
Albisola, 172, 176, 179, 215
Ancestries, 20–22, 73–74, 121, 164, 230
Andalucía, 233
Annatto, 209, 211. *See also* Roucou
Architecture, 7–8, 23, 25–26, 121, 198, 226, 245
Archives, 67, 77, 82, 94, 228–31, 240
Arkansas, 11, 82, 85, 88, 90
Arkansas River, 85

Bahamas, 199
Baltimore, 32
Barbados, 192
Bear oil, 105, 125
Bienville, Jean-Baptiste Le Moyne, Sieur de, 49–50, 82, 85–91, 228
Biloxi, 10, 47–51, 53, 55–59, 65–66, 77–78, 229
Biloxi, New (Nouveau): archaeological site, 47, 49, 55; historic settlement, 51, 53, 57, 64–65, 72–74, 76–77, 229
Biloxi, Old (Vieux): archaeological site, 47, 49, 230; historic settlement, 51, 53, 55, 57, 228
Biloxi Bay, 10, 49, 51, 53–54, 57, 64
Biloxi ethnic group, 123, 134
Biloxi Village site, 133–35, 138, 140–41
Bioarchaeological, 10, 65, 73–74, 77, 203
Biomass, 100–101, 105, 107
Biot, 215
Boiling house, 216, 217
Boisneuf, Payan, 9, 29–39, 226–27
Bordeaux, 23
Brittany, 159, 176, 182, 233
Broutin, François, 82
Broutin, Ignace, 85
Burials, 56, 65–67, 69–70, 74, 77, 214, 231

Cacao, 162, 163, 168, 236
Caddo ethnic group, 120–25, 132–33, 135–36, 139, 142–43
Cajun, 4, 114
Canada, 1–6, 11, 49, 87–88, 94, 192, 207, 231, 236

Cane River, 122–23, 125, 127–29, 131–33, 135, 142, 144
Caribbean: archaeology of, 13, 29–30, 42, 190, 239; colonies in, 1–6, 190, 192–93, 206, 218; foods of, 153–54, 163, 182; plantations in, 9, 34, 35, 43, 197
Caribbean (British), 4, 13, 190
Caribbean (French), 6–7, 29, 44, 195, 199, 202, 220
Catholic(s), 39–40, 69, 73, 108, 159, 227, 233
Cayenne, 207, 209–11, 237
Ceramic(s), African, 119; archaeological, 41, 121–22, 176, 201–2; European, 128–29, 132–39, 154, 155, 168–72; food preparation/service and, 12, 160–61, 164, 182, 235; trade in, 153, 167, 215, 216, 236. *See also* Colonoware; Pottery
Chantilly, 231
Chapels, 213–14, 221
Charleston, 17–18, 20–22, 26
Chausseros de Léry, Joseph Gaspard, 82, 94
Chickasaw, 11, 81–93, 231–32
Chocolate, 158, 162
Choctaw, 82–84, 91–92, 121, 123–24, 134, 136, 139
Code Noir, 214
Coffee: beverage, 158, 168; crop, 4, 189–90, 193, 212, 216, 219–20, 238
Coincoin plantation, 127–29, 132, 134–36, 139–42
Coincoin, Marie Thérèse, 127, 129
Colbert, Jean-Baptiste, 47, 51–52, 218, 228
Colonoware, 7, 117–18, 234; Louisiana, 11–12, 119–20, 122–23, 126–31, 138–44, 234
Commoditization, 10, 47–49, 51–53, 56
Commodity, 51, 59, 125
Community: Huguenot, 26–27; intervention against slave cruelty, 38, 43; multiethnic, 92, 123, 240
Company of the Indies, 65, 98, 99

Company of the West, 55
Cotton, 133, 168, 190, 192–93, 210–12, 220, 238
Coustilhas, Jacques, 86, 90
Creole cuisine, 164–65, 182
Creole culture, 152–54, 235
Creole ethnicity in Louisiana, 90, 97–99, 105, 109, 113–14, 121–23, 133–35
Creole housing, 197, 214
Creole society, 11, 190
Creolization: in Louisiana, 97- 99, 107, 153, 232–33; process, 8, 11–12, 114, 140, 180–81, 235–39
Crozat, Antoine, 50–51, 123
Cuba, 32, 233
Cultural Resource Management (CRM), 10, 195
Curing room, 213–14

D'Artaguette, Pierre, 84
De Lanzos, Manuel, 98, 100–102, 105–10, 112–13
De Verges, Bernard, 85–86, 90
Diaspora, 8, 13, 189, 245
Diet: archaeological evidence, 74, 77, 173–74, 231; Creole, 97–99, 101, 105–8, 113–14, 163–64, 232–34; French, 159, 227, 232–33
Distillery, 193, 216
Domestic species, 107
Dumont (dit Montigny), Jean François Benjamin, 83, 94
Dutch Guyana, 4

English architecture, 8, 26
English Caribbean, 13, 191–92, 239
English colonies, 1–3, 5–6, 12, 119–20, 122, 126, 142, 209
English cuisine, 153
English identity, 20, 23, 164, 225
English traders, 84–85, 167, 228–29
Ethnic dietary preference, 114
Ethnicity, 11, 97, 126, 134, 140, 231

Faience: food consumption/ preparation, 154, 160, 168–72, 182; French Guiana, 215–16; Guadeloupe 201; Louisiana, 121, 128, 176, 179–80
Foodways, 7, 12, 99, 152–56, 162, 182, 235
Fort Assumption, 82, 87–88, 90–92
Fort Maurepas, 53, 64
Fort St. Francis, 82, 86–87, 90–93
Frederick County, Maryland, 29, 33–40, 227
French Chickasaw War, 11, 81, 83, 93, 231–32
French Guiana (Guyane), 4–6, 13, 206–7, 209–21, 237–39
French Revolution: consequences of, 5, 13, 190, 193, 226; refugees from, 30–31, 34–36, 227; slavery and, 195–96, 199–200, 236
French West Indies, 189–90, 193, 202. *See also* Caribbean

Georgetown, SC, 35, 40–41
Georgia, 3, 100, 114, 126, 179
Georgian World View, 5
Globalization, 47–48, 59
Grave goods, 77
Grave(s), 36, 69–70, 77
Grave stones, 20–21, 23, 225
Greater Antilles, 3
Great Lakes, 2, 11, 72, 85, 87–88
Guadeloupe: colony, 3–5, 210–11, 226; plantation slavery, 13, 189–96, 198–202, 206, 236–37, 239
Gulf Coast: colonization efforts, 1–6, 12; Louisiana, 83, 154, 163, 165, 173–74, 176, 182; Mississippi, 10, 59, 77

Habitation: Caribbean, 13, 195–96, 202, 236, 239; French Guiana, 206, 212, 239
Haiti, 29, 206, 226
Haitian revolution, 3, 6, 9, 200
Hispaniola, 3, 191
Historical archaeology, 2, 6, 13, 26, 193, 195, 203, 236

Housing, 197, 199–200
Huguenots, 6, 8–9, 15, 17–23, 26–27, 225

Iberville, Pierre LeMoyne, Sieur d', 49–51, 53, 57, 64, 83, 228
Identity: Creole, 164, 181–82; French, 11–12, 200; Huguenot, 20, 22–23; materialization of, 7–9, 93, 99, 118, 135, 138, 155–56; Native American, 121–22
Illinois: country, 6, 23, 49, 83–85, 93–94, 113; settlements, 88–90, 168, 225
Indentured labor, indentured servants, 76, 192, 210, 236
Indigo: crop, 3–4, 31, 43, 190, 192–93, 210; plantations, 34, 212, 220, 238
Inscriptions, 9, 27
Interment(s), 69–70, 230
Iroquois, 87, 91

Jamaica, 3, 118, 199, 245
Jefferson, Thomas, 31
Jesuit(s): archives, 231; in French Guiana, 206–7, 209, 211–12, 215–21, 238, 239; missionaries, 82, 86, 94, 227, 237; plantations, 13
Jews, 108, 209, 212, 233
Joe Clark site, 132, 135–36

Laberon, Pierre, 33
Lambre Point site, 132, 135–36, 139, 142
La Rochelle, 233, 236
La Tour, Le Blond de, 48, 53, 55, 57–59, 229
Law, John, 10, 48, 50–52, 56, 64
LeBlanc Concession, 65
Lesser Antilles, 1, 3, 190–91
L'Hermitage Plantation, 9, 29–30, 33–35, 37–40, 42–43, 226–27
Linear enamel hypoplasias, 76
Los Adaes site, 120, 121–23, 139, 174
Louis, Pierre, 33, 38
Louis XIV, 17, 47, 50, 168–69, 214, 218, 228

Louisiana: 88–90, 94, 97–98, 138–39; archaeological sites, 100, 107, 133–34, 176, 236; coast, 14, 165; colonoware, 122, 131, 143–44, 234–35; colony, 56, 64, 77, 101, 105, 113, 167–68, 228–29; cuisine, 114, 153–54, 156, 162–64, 182, 232; French, 47, 49–53, 57, 81–85, 120, 180, 230; Native American groups, 123–25, 141–42; plantations, 3, 119, 126; Spanish period, 4

Louisiane, 228–30

Low Country SC, 3, 17, 23, 25–26

Lowe, Esther Winder Polk, 39

Loyola, 13, 206–7, 211–19, 221, 238, 239

Lyon, 170, 231

Madame John's Legacy, 97–101, 105, 107–8, 112, 121, 232–33

Maison de maître. See Master's House

Maize (corn), 74, 77, 162, 164, 167–68, 236

Marseilles, 170–71, 176, 179, 182

Martinique: colony, 3–5, 192, 210–11, 218, 226, 235; French Revolution and, 200

Maryland, 6, 9, 29, 32–39, 43–44, 227

Master's House, 213–15, 221

Material culture: archaeology, 59, 121, 152, 196, 201–2; identity, 7, 92–93, 143, 156, 180, 239; studies, 2

Meat cuts, 109–10, 112

Mediterranean: ceramics of, 171–72, 176, 182, 236; cuisine of, 162, 179; stylistic influences of, 154, 157, 182

Melrose plantation, 129, 133–35

Mentalité, 5, 225

Mercantilism, 52

Métropole, 52, 59, 211, 228

Minimum number of individuals (MNI), 100

Missions, 93, 209, 211–12, 220

Missionaries: Arkansas, 84, 87, 89, 94; French Guiana, 206, 209, 212; Saint-Domingue, 227, 237–39

Mississippi: Gulf Coast, 10, 14; Sound 51, 53, 55, 57, 59; State of 64–65, 77, 81, 84

Mississippi Bubble, 55, 65

Mississippi River, 2, 55, 84–87, 89–90, 228, 240; transportation, 101, 168, 174, 233

Mississippi Valley, 83, 88, 239; archaeology, 23, 26, 90, 172, 225; French colonization, 1–2, 6, 10–11, 49, 64, 93, 113

Missouri, 7, 23, 225

Missouri ethnic group, 88

Missouri River, 168

Mobile Bay, 6; Old Mobile and, 154, 176; settlement of, 50–51, 53, 64, 231

Mobile River, 85–86

Molasses, 190, 212, 215, 238

Monocacy National Battlefield, 9, 29, 34, 36, 42–44

Montigny. See Dumont

Moran Site, 10, 47, 55, 57, 65–77, 230–31

Mortuary practices, 70, 231

Moustiers. See Faience

Mulatto(es), 31–32, 226

Muslims, 108, 233

Nantes, 211, 233; Edict of, 19–22

Natchez ethnic group, 83–84, 91, 121, 126, 136, 139, 162, 232

Natchez War, 83

Natchitoches, 12, 88–90, 123–27, 132–33, 136–39, 144

Native Americans: archaeological sites, 72, 92, 128, 139, 231; ceramics, 117–26, 132–36, 140–44, 234–35; cuisine, 153–54, 156, 162–63; ethnicity, 11, 56; identity, 66, 73–74, 114; interactions with Africans, 12; trade with, 101, 105, 167

Netherlands, 169

New Orleans: archaeological sites in, 97–98, 100–102, 121, 154, 176; colonial capital, 50, 57, 64, 87, 88; cuisine, 12, 105, 107, 109, 113–14, 232–34; St. Peter's Cemetery in, 10, 65, 70, 73, 231; as trade center, 3, 58, 174, 179; urban life, 11, 113–14, 168

Niemcewicz, Julian Ursyn, 35–37, 40

Normandy, 159, 169, 172, 176

Ohio River, 93, 168
Outre-mer, 206, 228–31

Pascagoula, 123, 229
Pascal-Marin, 99, 105, 107–8, 110, 113
Payen de Noyan, Gilles Augustin, 90
Plantation(s): 6–7; Caribbean, 9–10, 13, 29–31, 42, 236–37; economy, 3, 193; Louisiana, 97–103, 107, 109, 112, 120–22, 125–36, 140–41, 232–33, 240; Maryland, 29–30, 33–36, 39–40, 43–44, 226–27; South America, 4, 207, 209, 211–16, 218–21, 238–39; South Carolina, 17–18, 23, 25–26, 225; sugar 189–90, 195–97, 200–206; Virginia, 118, 234
Poitevent, Shuyler, 53–54
Potawatomi, 87, 91
Poteaux-en-terre (post-in-trench), 8, 23, 25–26, 225–26
Poterie sucriere, 215
Pottery, 12, 118, 121, 125, 128–29, 132–34. *See also* Ceramics; Colonoware
Pottery, African, 119, 125, 139–43
Pottery, Native American, 58, 66, 119, 121, 133–36, 139–43
Pottery workshop, 215, 219–20, 239
Protestants, 3, 8, 18–22, 36, 40, 225, 227
Prudhomme-Roquier site, 132, 135
Purgerie. *See* Curing room

Quapaw, 84–86, 90

Rebellions, 32
Refugees: from Haitian revolution, 3, 6–10, 26–38, 43, 226–27; from revocation of Edict of Nantes, 17, 19; Natchez, 84, 91
Rémire, 207, 209, 211, 238
Repositories, 14, 231, 233
Resistance, 10, 47–48, 53, 59, 125–26, 200–201
Rice, 3, 20, 52, 163–64, 167
Robleau site, 133–35, 137
Roquier site, 132–35

Roucou, 209. *See also* Annatto
Rouen. *See* Faience
Rum, 4, 189–90, 193, 212, 216, 238

St. Augustine Plantation, 97–99, 101–3, 107–9, 112, 232–33
St. Croix, 3
St. Croix Island, ME, 65, 76
Saint-Domingue: colony of, 3–4, 31, 206, 228, 233, 235; refugees from, 33, 39, 43, 226–27; slavery on, 35, 237; trade with, 210–11, 218
Saint-Domingue slave uprising, 5, 9–10, 29–32, 35, 190, 200, 226
St. Lawrence River, 1, 49, 83, 85
St. Maurice site, 132, 135
Saintonge, 54, 121, 129, 172, 179, 215
St. Peter's Cemetery (New Orleans), 10, 65, 70, 73, 76, 231
Santee River, 17, 26
Ship Island, 47, 49, 53, 55, 57, 154, 229, 230
Skeletons, 67
Slavery: basis for plantation economy, 3, 5, 7; French Guiana, 210; French Revolution and, 13, 31, 227; Guadeloupe, 189–90, 193, 195–97, 199–203, 236; Louisiana, 118, 124; Maryland, 37, 39
Slaves: French Guiana, 206, 210–12, 214–15, 218–19, 221; French Revolution and, 5, 200, 226–27; influences on cuisine, 153, 156, 167; Louisiana, 105; Maryland, 30–39, 43; military campaigns, 88, 90; plantations, 236–40; pottery production in Louisiana, 12, 117–18, 121–22, 124–29, 143; trade in, 56, 229; underrepresentation in historical accounts, 2
Slave village, 9, 40–43, 195–96, 199, 201, 227
South Carolina: colonowares in, 117, 119, 126; Huguenots in, 3, 6, 8–9, 17–34, 225–26

Index · 249

Spanish ceramics, 172, 176
Spanish colonial archaeology, 58, 105, 108–9, 112–14, 120–21
Spanish colonies, 1, 3–4, 64, 119, 191, 207, 228–29, 239
Spanish cuisine, 153–54, 156, 159–60, 162–65, 182, 233–34
Spanish period in Louisiana, 11–12, 97–98, 101, 134, 142, 232
Stable Isotope Analysis, 74
Stature, 74, 76
Sucrerie. See Boiling house
Sugar: colonies, 3–4; crop, 4; in foods, 158–59, 163; plantations, 13; plantations in French Guiana, 209, 211–13, 215, 217, 218–20, 238; plantations in Guadeloupe, 189–90, 192–93, 195–96, 200–201; plantations in Louisiana, 168; plantations in Saint-Domingue, 31, 34, 43
Suriname, 206, 209–10, 212, 218

Timber Hill site, 133–35, 140
Tobacco: crop, 3, 52, 210, 228, 240; Caribbean, 190, 192–93; Maryland, 34, 36
Trinidad and Tobago, 190
Tropical wood, 217

Vallauris, 215
Versailles, 228–29
Vinaigrerie. See Distillery
Vincendière, 9, 29, 32–35, 39–40, 43, 226–27
Virginia, 26, 29, 32, 118, 126, 192
Virgin Islands, 190, 199, 245
Vital Flores site, 133–35
Vitry, Pierre, 82–83, 86–87, 92, 94

War of Spanish Succession, 50, 168
Wells, 217
West Africa, 119, 226, 245
West African culinary traditions, 12, 154
West African people, 163
West African pottery traditions, 118–19, 138–39
Wild species, 100–102, 105, 112–14, 234
Windmill, 193, 195, 207, 216, 220
Wolf River, 87–88

Yucca House, 129, 133

Zimmerman Hill site, 133–35, 138, 140
Zooarchaeology, 100

Kenneth G. Kelly is professor and chair of anthropology at the University of South Carolina, where he teaches historical archaeology and African archaeology. Dr. Kelly's long-standing research focus has been on developing a transatlantic perspective on the archaeology of the African Diaspora and its impacts both in West Africa and the Caribbean. Professor Kelly directed archaeological research at the site of Savi, capital of a major slave trading state in Bénin from 1991 to 1999. Since 2001, he has returned to the Caribbean, having previously worked in Jamaica, and has directed long-term projects in Guadeloupe and Martinique that explore the nature of plantation slavery in the French colonial world. In 2013, he directed pioneering excavations of slave trading sites along the Rio Pongo in Guinea. He has published the results of his work in a variety of edited volumes and journals, including *American Anthropologist*, *World Archaeology*, the *Journal of Archaeological Method and Theory*, and *Ethnohistory*.

Meredith D. Hardy is an archaeologist with the National Park Service–Southeast Archeological Center. She has over fifteen years of archaeological and historic preservation experience throughout the southeastern United States and the Caribbean. Her research interests and expertise include prehistoric, colonial, and plantation archaeology; environmental archaeology; foodways; architecture; colonial urban planning; and the development of creole cultures. Much of her archaeological efforts with the National Park Service has focused on the U.S. Gulf Coast, New Orleans, and the U.S. Virgin Islands. She has conducted public outreach and education events across the Virgin Islands for schools, nonprofit organizations, the Virgin Islands National Guard, and a locally produced PBS television special, on topics such as archaeology, cultural resource and museum management, and cultural heritage and historic preservation.

RIPLEY P. BULLEN SERIES
Florida Museum of Natural History

Tacachale: Essays on the Indians of Florida and Southeastern Georgia during the Historic Period, edited by Jerald T. Milanich and Samuel Proctor (1978)
Aboriginal Subsistence Technology on the Southeastern Coastal Plain during the Late Prehistoric Period, by Lewis H. Larson (1980)
Cemochechobee: Archaeology of a Mississippian Ceremonial Center on the Chattahoochee River, by Frank T. Schnell, Vernon J. Knight Jr., and Gail S. Schnell (1981)
Fort Center: An Archaeological Site in the Lake Okeechobee Basin, by William H. Sears, with contributions by Elsie O'R. Sears and Karl T. Steinen (1982)
Perspectives on Gulf Coast Prehistory, edited by Dave D. Davis (1984)
Archaeology of Aboriginal Culture Change in the Interior Southeast: Depopulation during the Early Historic Period, by Marvin T. Smith (1987)
Apalachee: The Land between the Rivers, by John H. Hann (1988)
Key Marco's Buried Treasure: Archaeology and Adventure in the Nineteenth Century, by Marion Spjut Gilliland (1989)
First Encounters: Spanish Explorations in the Caribbean and the United States, 1492–1570, edited by Jerald T. Milanich and Susan Milbrath (1989)
Missions to the Calusa, edited and translated by John H. Hann, with an introduction by William H. Marquardt (1991)
Excavations on the Franciscan Frontier: Archaeology at the Fig Springs Mission, by Brent Richards Weisman (1992)
The People Who Discovered Columbus: The Prehistory of the Bahamas, by William F. Keegan (1992)
Hernando de Soto and the Indians of Florida, by Jerald T. Milanich and Charles Hudson (1993)
Foraging and Farming in the Eastern Woodlands, edited by C. Margaret Scarry (1993)
Puerto Real: The Archaeology of a Sixteenth-Century Spanish Town in Hispaniola, edited by Kathleen Deagan (1995)
Political Structure and Change in the Prehistoric Southeastern United States, edited by John F. Scarry (1996)
Bioarchaeology of Native Americans in the Spanish Borderlands, edited by Brenda J. Baker and Lisa Kealhofer (1996)
A History of the Timucua Indians and Missions, by John H. Hann (1996)
Archaeology of the Mid-Holocene Southeast, edited by Kenneth E. Sassaman and David G. Anderson (1996)
The Indigenous People of the Caribbean, edited by Samuel M. Wilson (1997; first paperback edition, 1999)
Hernando de Soto among the Apalachee: The Archaeology of the First Winter Encampment, by Charles R. Ewen and John H. Hann (1998)
The Timucuan Chiefdoms of Spanish Florida, by John E. Worth: vol. 1, *Assimilation*; vol. 2, *Resistance and Destruction* (1998)
Ancient Earthen Enclosures of the Eastern Woodlands, edited by Robert C. Mainfort Jr. and Lynne P. Sullivan (1998)
An Environmental History of Northeast Florida, by James J. Miller (1998)
Precolumbian Architecture in Eastern North America, by William N. Morgan (1999)

Archaeology of Colonial Pensacola, edited by Judith A. Bense (1999)
Grit-Tempered: Early Women Archaeologists in the Southeastern United States, edited by Nancy Marie White, Lynne P. Sullivan, and Rochelle A. Marrinan (1999)
Coosa: The Rise and Fall of a Southeastern Mississippian Chiefdom, by Marvin T. Smith (2000)
Religion, Power, and Politics in Colonial St. Augustine, by Robert L. Kapitzke (2001)
Bioarchaeology of Spanish Florida: The Impact of Colonialism, edited by Clark Spencer Larsen (2001)
Archaeological Studies of Gender in the Southeastern United States, edited by Jane M. Eastman and Christopher B. Rodning (2001)
The Archaeology of Traditions: Agency and History Before and After Columbus, edited by Timothy R. Pauketat (2001)
Foraging, Farming, and Coastal Biocultural Adaptation in Late Prehistoric North Carolina, by Dale L. Hutchinson (2002)
Windover: Multidisciplinary Investigations of an Early Archaic Florida Cemetery, edited by Glen H. Doran (2002)
Archaeology of the Everglades, by John W. Griffin (2002)
Pioneer in Space and Time: John Mann Goggin and the Development of Florida Archaeology, by Brent Richards Weisman (2002)
Indians of Central and South Florida, 1513–1763, by John H. Hann (2003)
Presidio Santa Maria de Galve: A Struggle for Survival in Colonial Spanish Pensacola, edited by Judith A. Bense (2003)
Bioarchaeology of the Florida Gulf Coast: Adaptation, Conflict, and Change, by Dale L. Hutchinson (2004)
The Myth of Syphilis: The Natural History of Treponematosis in North America, edited by Mary Lucas Powell and Della Collins Cook (2005)
The Florida Journals of Frank Hamilton Cushing, edited by Phyllis E. Kolianos and Brent R. Weisman (2005)
The Lost Florida Manuscript of Frank Hamilton Cushing, edited by Phyllis E. Kolianos and Brent R. Weisman (2005)
The Native American World Beyond Apalachee: West Florida and the Chattahoochee Valley, by John H. Hann (2006)
Tatham Mound and the Bioarchaeology of European Contact: Disease and Depopulation in Central Gulf Coast Florida, by Dale L. Hutchinson (2006)
Taino Indian Myth and Practice: The Arrival of the Stranger King, by William F. Keegan (2007)
An Archaeology of Black Markets: Local Ceramics and Economies in Eighteenth-Century Jamaica, by Mark W. Hauser (2008; first paperback edition, 2013)
Mississippian Mortuary Practices: Beyond Hierarchy and the Representationist Perspective, edited by Lynne P. Sullivan and Robert C. Mainfort Jr. (2010; first paperback edition, 2012)
Bioarchaeology of Ethnogenesis in the Colonial Southeast, by Christopher M. Stojanowski (2010; first paperback edition, 2013)
French Colonial Archaeology in the Southeast and Caribbean, edited by Kenneth G. Kelly and Meredith D. Hardy (2011; first paperback edition, 2015)
Late Prehistoric Florida: Archaeology at the Edge of the Mississippian World, edited by Keith Ashley and Nancy Marie White (2012)
Early and Middle Woodland Landscapes of the Southeast, edited by Alice P. Wright and Edward R. Henry (2013)

Trends and Traditions in Southeastern Zooarchaeology, edited by Tanya M. Peres (2014)
New Histories of Pre-Columbian Florida, edited by Neill J. Wallis and Asa R. Randall (2014)
Discovering Florida: First-Contact Narratives from Spanish Expeditions along the Lower Gulf Coast, edited and translated by John E. Worth (2014)
Constructing Histories: Archaic Freshwater Shell Mounds and Social Landscapes of the St. Johns River, Florida by Asa R. Randall (2015)
Colonial Interaction at El Chorro de Maíta, Cuba by Roberto Valcárcel Rojas (2016)

www.ingramcontent.com/pod-product-compliance
Lightning Source LLC
Chambersburg PA
CBHW031433160426
43195CB00010BB/713